Culturally Responsive Education

Culturally Responsive Education: Reflections from the Global South and North examines culturally responsive education's contribution to sustainable development and explores ways in which educational practitioners respond to cultures in and around educational contexts.

This book argues that cultural responsiveness in education is invaluable for sustainability in and through education, and explores methods with which to deepen understanding of the values and intercultural dialogue constantly present in education. Using a number of international and multidisciplinary studies, the authors offer a novel perspective on the consideration of diversity throughout education and provide a valuable contribution to the ongoing global and national debate surrounding the UN Sustainable Development Goal initiative.

With a focus on collaboration, this edited volume is vital reading for scholars, teachers and students of education, sociology and development studies as well as education professionals. The book will also be of interest to education policy makers and international and non-governmental organizations.

Elina Lehtomäki is Senior Researcher in the Faculty of Education, University of Jyväskylä, and Adjunct Professor (Docent) in Education Sciences at the University of Helsinki, Finland.

Hille Janhonen-Abruquah is a Lecturer in the Department of Teacher Education at the University of Helsinki, Finland.

George L. Kahangwa is a Lecturer in Educational Management and Policy Studies at the University of Dar es Salaam, Tanzania.

Routledge Studies in Culture and Sustainable Development

Series Editors:

Katriina Soini
University of Jyväskylä, Finland, and Natural Resources Institute Finland
Joost Dessein
Institute for Agricultural and Fisheries Research (ILVO) and Ghent University, Belgium

Culture as an aspect of sustainability is a relatively new phenomenon but is beginning to attract attention among scholars and policy makers. This series opens up a forum for debate about the role of culture in sustainable development, treating culture and sustainability as a meta-narrative that will bring together diverse disciplines. Key questions explored in this series will include: how should culture be applied in sustainability policies; what should be sustained in culture; what should culture sustain; and what is the relationship of culture to other dimensions of sustainability?

Books in the series will have a variety of geographical foci and reflect different disciplinary approaches (for example, geography, sociology, sustainability science, environmental and political sciences, anthropology, history, archaeology and planning). The series will be addressed in particular to postgraduate students and researchers from a wide cross-section of disciplines.

Culturally Responsive Education

Reflections from the Global South and North

Edited by
Elina Lehtomäki,
Hille Janhonen-Abruquah
and George L. Kahangwa

Routledge
Taylor & Francis Group

LONDON AND NEW YORK

First published 2017 by Routledge

2 Park Square, Milton Park, Abingdon, Oxfordshire OX14 4RN
52 Vanderbilt Avenue, New York, NY 10017

Routledge is an imprint of the Taylor & Francis Group, an informa business

First issued in paperback 2018

British Library Cataloguing in Publication Data
A catalogue record for this book is available from the British Library

Library of Congress Cataloging in Publication Data
Names: Lehtomäki, Elina.
Title: Culturally responsive education : reflections from the global South and North / edited by Elina Lehtomäki, Hille Janhonen-Abruquah and George L. Kahangwa.
Description: New York : Routledge, 2017. | Series: Routledge Studies in Culture and Sustainable Development
Identifiers: LCCN 2016050915 | ISBN 9781138706248 (hbk) | ISBN 9781315201900 (ebk)
Subjects: LCSH: Education–Developing countries. | Culturally relevant pedagogy–Developing countries. | North and south.
Classification: LCC LC2605 .C84 2017 | DDC 370.117091724–dc23
LC record available at https://lccn.loc.gov/2016050915

ISBN: 978-1-138-70624-8 (hbk)
ISBN: 978-0-367-15235-2 (pbk)

Typeset in Bembo
by Wearset Ltd, Boldon, Tyne and Wear

Contents

vi *Contents*

4 Culturally responsive qualitative research: issues and ethics 68
GUNILLA HOLM AND ELINA LEHTOMÄKI

PART II
Multidimensional and comprehensive approaches to learning 81

5 Incorporating cultural and linguistic diversity in Information and Communication Technology in education in Kenya 83
SUZANNE ADHIAMBO PUHAKKA

6 Relevance of schooling in Tanzania: educational leaders' perspectives on economically disadvantaged families 95
ANETH KOMBA

7 Culturally situated narratives: expanding insights and accountabilities 114
MONA SALEH ALSUDIS AND VENITHA PILLAY

PART III
Transforming, empowering and emancipatory experiences in learning 129

8 Reflections on North–South collaboration in music education 131
SANNA SALMINEN, PEKKA TOIVANEN,
JAANA VIRKKALA, SAMPO HANKAMA AND
JAANA VAHERMAA

9 Towards contextual understanding of gender: student teachers' views on home economics education and gender in Ghana and Finland 143
HILLE JANHONEN-ABRUQUAH,
HANNA POSTI-AHOKAS, HANNAH BENJABA EDJAH
AND MANASSEH EDISON KOMLA AMU

Contributors

Christine Adu-Yeboah is a senior lecturer at the Institute of Education, University of Cape Coast, Ghana. Her research interests are English language education, teacher education and gender in higher education. She has national and international research experience gained from working on the Africa–Asia Dialogue project hosted by the Hiroshima University in Japan; projects coordinated by the University of Sussex, UK, such as CREATE, Teacher Preparation in Africa (TPA) funded by William and Flora Hewlett Foundation and the Australian AID-sponsored Systematic Review on 'The impacts and cost effectiveness of strategies to improve performance of untrained and under-trained teachers in the classroom in developing countries'. Adu-Yeboah is also a visiting fellow of the Institute of Education, University of London. She is currently the Coordinator for the Centre for Educational Research, Evaluation and Development, College of Education Studies, University of Cape Coast, Ghana, and working on the DFID-funded project on teacher education (T-TEL, Ghana) and the research on 'Pedagogies for Critical Thinking'.

Mona Saleh Alsudis is an academic at the Ministry of Education in Saudi Arabia. She obtained her PhD from the University of Pretoria in South Africa.

Ruth Aluko is the Researcher and Instructional Design Supporter for the Unit for Distance Education, Faculty of Education, University of Pretoria, South Africa. Her areas of interest in Open Distance Learning (ODL) include quality assurance, access and social justice, student support and mobile learning. She is on the editorial board of *Africa Education Review*. Ruth extensively publishes in her field and has been involved in review of ODL departments and has facilitated workshops.

Joseph Ghartey Ampiah is the Vice Chancellor of University of Cape Coast, Ghana. He holds a PhD in Science Education and is Professor of Science Education and Provost of College of Education Studies. His interests are in research in education, especially at the primary and secondary school level, and teacher education. He led the DFID-funded CREATE project to research into educational access, transition and equity in Ghana from 2006–2011. He has worked on many international projects with researchers from Africa, Japan, the Netherlands, United Kingdom and the United States.

Manasseh Edison Komla Amu is an assistant lecturer at the Department of Vocational and Technical Education, College of Educational Studies, University of Cape Coast, Ghana. He has an MPhil degree in Home Economics (Family Management) and is currently a doctoral candidate. His research interests are vulnerability, personal finance, issues in home economics and home economics education. He has been working and teaching at the department since 2004 handling mainly undergraduate students. He teaches home economics-related courses at many other institutions across Ghana, prominent among these are the University of Education Winneba Distance Education programme and the Institute of Adult Education of University of Ghana.

Hannah Benjaba Edjah is an assistant lecturer at the Department of Vocational and Technical Education, College of Educational Studies, University of Cape Coast, Ghana. She is a doctoral candidate in curriculum and teaching. Her research interest lies in issues pertaining to home economics education and general human wellbeing. She handles courses such as curriculum studies, foundations of home economics and family studies, all at the undergraduate level. She has taught home economics-related courses at the University of Education Winneba Distance Education programme during its early inception and is now one of the chief examiners for the post-diploma in basic education sandwich programme run by the Institute of Education, University of Cape Coast.

Sampo Hankama is a music teacher at Jyväskylä's College of Music. During his teaching career he has been awarded by student organizations both in Sibelius Academy and the University of Jyväskylä. His teaching topics currently include pop/jazz music theory and practice, ear training and band workshops. Besides teaching, he is a wannabe musician and composer.

Gunilla Holm is Professor of Education at the Institute of Behavioural Sciences at the University of Helsinki and Director of the Nordic Centre of Excellence in Education 'Justice through Education'. Her research interests are focused on justice-related issues in education with particular focus on the intersections of race, ethnicity, class and gender. She is also interested in, and writes on, photography as a research method. In addition, she has an interest in the portrayal of schooling in popular culture as well as in youth culture. Prior to coming to the University of Helsinki she worked as Professor in Teacher Education (Sociology of Education) at Western Michigan University in the United States. At the University of Helsinki she is the co-founder of a new elementary teacher education programme with the profile multilingualism, diversity and social justice.

Hille Janhonen-Abruquah is a university lecturer at the Department of Teacher Education at Helsinki University, Finland, and member of two research groups at her department called 'E4D Education for Diversities' and 'Food, Culture and Learning'. Janhonen-Abruquah is currently a principal investigator for a research project called 'Home Economics Education and Diversities'. Within her teaching career from compulsory school to polytechnic and university teaching she has also been a home economics teacher at Mfantsiman Girls' Senior Secondary School, Ghana. She has been the Administrative Coordinator for the Culturally Responsive Education network.

Said K. Juma is an assistant lecturer in the School of Education, State University of Zanzibar, Tanzania. He is currently a doctoral candidate in the Faculty of Education, University of Jyväskylä, Finland. His research interests include inclusive education development, educational action research, teacher continuing professional development and guidance and counselling in educational settings. He obtained his bachelor's and master's degrees from University of Dar es Salaam, Tanzania.

George L. Kahangwa is a lecturer in educational management and policy studies at the University of Dar es Salaam, Tanzania, where he has been employed since 2007. He is also currently a director of the Centre for Educational Research and Professional Development at the University of Dar es Salaam. Dr Kahangwa holds a PhD (2013) in Education from the University of Bristol, UK, a Master of Arts in Education (2007) and a Bachelor of Arts in Education (2004) from the University of Dar es Salaam. He has researched and published on issues that influence education policy making and development. His work also touches on issues related to education quality, higher education and knowledge-based economy. Apart from lecturing and undertaking research, he has been involved in several consultancies that include development of policy and plans for education, policy reviews and facilitating in-service training for educators.

Aneth Komba is a senior lecturer in educational management, leadership and administration at the School of Education, University of Dar es Salaam, Tanzania. She holds a PhD in Education Administration and Policy Studies from the University of Bath, UK, a Master of Arts in Education and a Bachelor of Education (Science) from the University of Dar es Salaam. Before joining the academia in September 2004, Dr Komba worked as a secondary school teacher in which she taught chemistry and biology at ordinary- and advanced-level secondary schools. At the University of Dar es Salaam Dr Komba worked in various positions including Acting Head of Department of Educational Foundations Management and Lifelong Learning between May 2012 and July 2012. From July 2012 to date, Dr Komba has been working as Associate Dean of the School of Education. She teaches courses in school administration, organizational behaviour, human resource management in educational organizations, educational leadership, educational policies, and planning and qualitative research methodologies at both undergraduate and post-graduate level. Her main research areas of interest are in poverty and children's schooling, school leadership, education financing, equity and equality in education opportunities, education quality, qualitative research and action research methodologies, and she has many published articles in these areas.

Christopher Yaw Kwaah has defended a doctoral research in curriculum and teaching at the University of Cape Coast, Ghana. He is a research fellow at the Centre for Educational Research, Evaluation and Development at the same university. He has worked on a number of projects with researchers from other African countries as well as researchers from the UK and Japan. His research interests include teacher education, economics education and higher education.

Elina Lehtomäki is Senior Researcher at the Faculty of Education, University of Jyväskylä, Finland, and Adjunct Professor (Docent) in Education Sciences at the University of Helsinki in Finland. Her research interests cover the social meaning of education, equity and inclusion in and through education, international expertise in education, cross-cultural collaboration and internationalization in higher education. Her current research projects include global responsibility and equity in international student mobility in Nordic higher education. Lehtomäki has been the principal investigator of a four-year Academy of Finland research project, 'Educated Girls and Women: Socio-Cultural Meaning of Education in Tanzania'. She has a long-term experience of collaborating with colleagues in several African countries through universities, ministries, local non-governmental organizations, international organizations and UN agencies.

Abebe Yehualawork Malle is a doctoral candidate in the Department of Education at the University of Jyväskylä, Finland. He is an executive director of Help for Persons with Disabilities Organization (HPD-O) in Ethiopia. Malle has held a teaching position in a secondary school and at the University of Addis Ababa. During his career he has also acted as an international consultant on special needs education, especially in technical and vocational education and training (TVET).

Agnes Mohlakwana is a lecturer in the Department of Education Management and Policy Studies at the University of Pretoria, South Africa. She is responsible for the module on financial management to BEd Hons students. Her other teaching and research interests include school leadership, school improvement and teacher development. She is currently involved in the 'Culturally Responsive Education' and 'North East Normal University with China (NENU)' projects. She also supervises MEd and doctoral students.

William Nketsia is a doctoral candidate at the University of Jyväskylä, Finland. His research interests include inclusive education, teacher preparation for inclusive education and inclusive pedagogy. William has teaching experience in primary and secondary schools in Ghana and the United Kingdom, and at university level in Finland. He obtained his bachelor's degree at the University of Cape Coast, Ghana, and his master's at the University of Jyväskylä, Finland.

Päivi Palojoki holds a professorship in Home Economics Education at the Department of Teacher Education, University of Helsinki, Finland. She is also Adjunct Professor (Docentship) at the Åbo Akademi University. Her research interest is in the development of teacher education and learning, especially in the context of home economics education. She is head of the research group 'Food, Culture and Learning', which focuses on the relationship between knowledge and activities in various formal and non-formal learning environments. She has participated in various international projects and has been external evaluator in many countries in Scandinavia, Europe and Africa.

Venitha Pillay is a professor at the University of South Africa and an education consultant for a number of international development agencies. She is committed to building higher education and research capacity in Africa. Her publications on research methodologies examine challenges for doing qualitative research that is cognisant of local political and cultural contexts. She works with universities in Africa, Europe and the United States.

Raija Pirttimaa is teaching special education in the Department of Education at the University of Jyväskylä, Finland, and is an adjunct professor at the University of Helsinki. Her research focus is on the education of persons with disabilities. She is also interested in supported adult education and supported employment. Pirttimaa has been the academic leader of the African–Finnish Network for Inclusive Teacher Education with partner universities in Ethiopia, Kenya, Tanzania and Finland. She has also been a visiting professor in Ethiopia and supervises doctoral students from Ethiopia and Ghana.

Hanna Posti-Ahokas is a postdoctoral researcher at the Department of Teacher Education, University of Helsinki. Her current research on teacher education focuses on internationalization, pedagogical development and innovative approaches to education for diversities. Her experience in student voice research for education development contributes to an actor-centred development of education. She has vast educational work experience in various African countries.

Suzanne Adhiambo Puhakka is a post-doctoral researcher at the Department of Psychology, University of Jyväskylä, Finland. Her research interests include ICT in education, early childhood education, learning in multilingual environments, cognitive neuroscience, child clinical neuropsychology and higher education teaching and learning.

Sanna Salminen has graduated from the University of Jyväskylä in Finland, music education being her main subject. She works as a university teacher at the Department of Teacher Education. Salminen has gained international reputation as a choral conductor. She is known as well from making school music books (Soi 3–4 and 5–6/Sanoma pro).

Pekka Toivanen is Senior Lecturer in the Department of Music, University of Jyväskylä, Finland. His areas of interest in music as teacher, researcher and performer cover a wide variety, ranging from medieval music via progressive rock to various music cultures of the world. He has been involved with the NSS MECI project since its beginning 2007, prior to that also in the previous NS phase. Since 2011 he has been the project's academic coordinator.

Jaana Vahermaa studied at the University of Jyväskylä majoring in music education, and she graduated in 2014. She participated in NSS MECI Intensive Period 2012 (held in Pretoria) as an assistant teacher, and during the first half of 2013 she was a MECI project exchange student at the University of Pretoria. Her master's thesis focused on her own project to create a music curriculum for kindergarten teachers in Swaziland (the thesis was a nominee for the best UniPID master's thesis in 2014). Currently she works as music and classroom teacher in southern Finland.

Jaana Virkkala has graduated from the University of Jyväskylä in Finland, music education and education being her main subjects. She works as a lecturer of music at the Department of Teacher Education. Earlier she has worked as a music teacher at the Kaustinen Music High School, Jyväskylä Adult Education Centre and several music schools. Her interests cover music education and folk music.

Series introduction

Finding pathways to ecological, social and economic sustainability is the biggest global challenge of the twenty-first century and new approaches are urgently needed. Scholars and policy makers have recognized the contribution of culture in sustainability work. 'Cultural sustainability' is also being increasingly discussed in debates in various international, national and local arenas, and there are ample local actor-driven initiatives. Yet despite the growing attention, there have been very few attempts to consider culture in a more analytical and explicit way in scientific and political discourses of sustainability, probably as a consequence of the complex, normative and multidisciplinary character of both culture and sustainability. This difficulty should not, however, be any excuse for ignoring the cultural aspects in sustainability.

The series 'Routledge Studies in Culture and Sustainable Development' aims to analyse the diverse and multiple roles that culture plays in sustainability. It takes as one of its starting points the idea that culture serves as a 'meta-narrative' which will bring together ideas and standpoints from an extensive body of sustainability research currently scattered among different disciplines and thematic fields. Moreover, the series responds to the strengthening call for inter- and transdisciplinary approaches which is being heard in many quarters, but in few fields more strongly than that of sustainability, with its complex and systemic problems. By combining and confronting the various approaches, in both the sciences and the humanities and in dealing with social, cultural, environmental, political and aesthetic disciplines, the series offers a comprehensive contribution to the present-day sustainability sciences as well as related policies.

The books in the series take a broad approach to culture, giving space to all the possible understandings and forms of culture. Furthermore, culture is not only seen as an additional aspect of sustainability – as a 'fourth pillar' – but rather as a mediator, a cross-cutting transversal framework or even as a new set of guiding principles for sustainability research, policies and practices.

The essence of culture in, for and as sustainability is being explored through the series in various thematic contexts, representing a wide range of practices and processes (e.g. everyday life, livelihoods and lifestyles, landscape, artistic practices, aesthetic experiences, heritage, tourism). These contexts concern urban, peri-urban or rural contexts, and regions with different socio-economic trajectories. The perspectives of the books will stretch from local to global and will cover different temporal scales from past to present and future. These issues are valorized by theoretical or empirical analysis; their relationship to the ecological, social and economic dimensions of sustainability will be explored, when appropriate.

The idea for the series was derived from the European COST Action IS1007 'Investigating Cultural Sustainability', running between 2011 and 2015. This network was comprised of a group of around a hundred researchers from 26 European countries, representing many different disciplines. They brought together their expertise, knowledge and experience, and based on that they built up new inter- and transdisciplinary understandings and approaches that can enhance and enrich research into culture in sustainable development, and support the work of the practitioners in education, policy and beyond.

We are very pleased to have this volume devoted to education and learning, as they are cornerstones of sustainability: means to support the capacities of teachers and students to act in a responsible and reflective way in a rapidly changing world. The topic of the book, culturally responsible education, highlights the sensitivity of culture in pedagogy. Ideally, culturally responsible education takes the cultural context of an individual student as a starting point for the education. As the chapters of the book reveal, although this aim is a valuable principle for education, it is relatively complex in a globalized world, where people are mobile, connected and networked, and have multicultural identities. It seems that it is not appropriate to give any straightforward recipe for culturally responsible education, as the students are embedded in broader cultural contexts forcing us to interpret such education in a multidimensional way. Here a transcultural learning, which was one of the results of this project, can be a valuable vehicle forward.

Katriina Soini and Joost Dessein

Acknowledgements

For the constructive comments on the compilation of manuscripts and suggestions for improvements, we would like to thank the book proposal reviewers, especially Professor Emerita Sue L. T. McGregor. We extend our sincere thanks to the *Routledge Studies in Culture and Sustainable Development* series editors Dr Katriina Soini and Dr Joost Dessein for their guidance in preparing this book proposal. Thank you to the editorial board and team at Routledge.

We would like to acknowledge the reviewers of the chapter manuscripts:

Dr Hanna Alasuutari is currently working with the World Bank, Washington D.C.; Associate Professor Dr Carol Benson, Teachers' College, Columbia University, NY; Professor Meeri Hellstén, Department of Education, Stockholm University; Professor Sirkku Hellstén, Nordic Africa Institute, Uppsala University; Ms Lea Kuusilehto-Awale, Institute for Educational Leadership, University of Jyväskylä; Dr Josephine Moate, Teacher Education Department, University of Jyväskylä; Dr Mari-Anne Okkolin, Department of Education Sciences, University of Jyväskylä; Dr Matti Taajamo, Finnish Institute for Educational Research; Adjunct Professor Dr Mikko Vesisenaho, Department of Teacher Education, University of Jyväskylä; and several others who prefer to maintain their anonymity.

Thanks to the students and staff of all the partner universities including the administrative staff in Africa and Finland, and to the Centre for International Mobility in Finland that financed the greater part of the network activities. It was in the active networking that the seed ideas for this collection were planted.

Introduction

Culturally responsive education

From vision to practice

Hille Janhonen-Abruquah, Elina Lehtomäki and George L. Kahangwa

The key question addressed in this book is *how education responds to the cultural variation that is always present and relates to power issues in and around educational contexts.* The book argues that cultural responsiveness in education is invaluable for sustainability in and through education. Understanding *culture as sustainability* with multiple dimensions and layers (Soini & Dessein, 2016) offers educational researchers, teachers and leaders a novel perspective from which to explore the meaning of education. In turn, this book adds the dimension of education and learning to the *Routledge Studies in Culture and Sustainable Development.* It contributes to the ongoing global and national dialogues on how to successfully realize the UN sustainable development goal (SDG) 4 – quality education for all – which emphasizes equity and equality in access, participation and achievements in learning (UN, 2015). Culture and power are at the core of global and local efforts to ensure equity and equality in education and learning. The aim of SDG 4 is to create a foundation for the implementation of the other 16 SDGs (Sayed & Ahmed, 2015; UNESCO, 2015).

The idea for this edited volume emerged and was developed during a long-term collaboration between the authors and between their universities. From 2012 to 2016, three North–South–South networks named CRE, AFNITE and MECI functioned between Finland and various African countries. The mobility funding provided by the Centre for International Mobility, Finland and the Finnish Ministry for Foreign Affairs gave students, teachers and scholars opportunities to travel between the Global North and South and thus put theoretical thinking into practice. AFNITE stands for African–Finnish Network for Inclusive Teacher Education, and Chapters 5 and 10 are inspired by the collaboration. The MECI network – Music, Education and Cultural Identity – is discussed in Chapter 8. The culturally responsive education network (CRE) focused on how to foster cultural responsiveness in education, teacher training and in schools through a qualitative research approach. Chapters 1, 2, 3, 4, 6, 7, 9 and 11 were written within the CRE collaboration. CRE operates among the Cape Coast in Ghana, Dar es Salaam in Tanzania, Pretoria in South Africa and Jyvaskyla and Helsinki in Finland. The University of Helsinki coordinated the project.

The CRE network and this book have followed professor Geneva Gay's (2000, 2013) theoretical thinking that education is and needs to be relevant in its own context and cultures. Culturally responsive education recognizes the challenges of each educational setting but finds ways to respond to these challenges in a culturally acceptable, constructive and positive manner. The project and the book chapters test Gay's North American thinking in different contexts – that is, Northern European and African settings – to explore whether and, if so, how it could be applied.

The book aims to deepen understanding among teachers, teacher educators and researchers of the values, cultures and intercultural dialogue constantly present in education and contributing to or affecting learning. Our main argument is that SDG 4, quality education for all (United Nations, 2015) – with an emphasis on equity and equality in access, participation and achievements in learning – requires responsiveness to cultures in schools, teacher education and wider social contexts.

The authors report on how spaces are successfully created for culturally responsive education in schools, teacher education and higher education. The book calls for a greater responsiveness in education, including learning contents, environments and pedagogical solutions, particularly in teacher education. The authors are senior and junior scholars in education. All have participated in exchange projects and research collaborations between African and Finnish universities. Thus, culturally responsive education is not only a phenomenon under study but also a part of the authors' daily work.

The book is organized into three parts which discuss cultural responsiveness through its various dimensions: (1) a focus on validating education; (2) multidimensional and comprehensive approaches to learning; and (3) transforming, empowering and emancipatory experiences in learning. This introduction defines the concept of 'culturally responsive education' with a brief review of research on the topic and describes the idea of this compilation of peer-reviewed chapters (see Table I.1).

The chapters in the first part describe different challenges and viewpoints when trying to validate the educational setting or, in other words, make education more relevant for the learner. In the first chapter, the Ghanaian teachers' use of the mother tongue makes the curriculum more relevant by connecting the learning to the pupil's experience, environment and culture, even though this does not reflect the local language policy. The South African experience (Chapter 2) recognizes the importance of teaching seizing the opportunity to become dynamic in its approach to developing its workforce to meet the current challenges by open distance learning. The Tanzanian study (Chapter 3) aims to develop the knowledge-based economy in low-income countries in the Global South by adding a cultural strategy which is mindful of these countries' cultural context. The last chapter (Chapter 4) in this part opens up the various means and tools that are available for doing research with people and thus making the research more culturally relevant.

Table I.1 Chapters' connections to culturally responsive education

Authors	Country of focus	Main content of the chapter	Respondent/whose perspective? Whose point of view?	Connection to culturally responsive education
1 Joseph Ghartey Ampiah, Christopher Yaw Kwaah and Christine Adu–Yeboah	Ghana	Implementation of a local language policy in multilingual Ghanaian classrooms.	Primary school teachers	Teachers' use of the mother tongue makes the curriculum more relevant by connecting the learning to the pupils' experience, environment and culture.
2 Agnes Mohlakwana and Ruth Aluko	South Africa	Developing in-service teachers' professionalism through open distance learning.	Educational research, Researchers	Recognises the importance of teaching seizing the opportunity to be dynamic in its approach to developing its workforce to meet the current challenges.
3 George L. Kahangwa	Tanzania	Knowledge-based economy (KBE) as one of the key ideas for development has cultural aspects such as discourses, technology, ideology and people's mobility.	Educational research, Researchers, Author's view	To develop KBE in low income countries in the Global South needs a cultural strategy which is mindful of these countries' cultural context.
4 Gunilla Holm and Elina Lehtomäki	Cross-cultural	Use of various qualitative research methods in culturally diverse settings.	Researchers	Means and tools that are available for doing research with people.

continued

Table I.1 Continued

Authors	Country of focus	Main content of the chapter	Respondent/whose perspective? Whose point of view?	Connection to culturally responsive education
5 Suzanne Adhiambo Puhakka	Kenya	The use of information and communication technology in primary education.	Educational policy	Use of information and communication technology should support and encourage cultural diversity and preserve and promote the language, distinct identities and traditional knowledge of indigenous peoples, nations and tribes.
6 Aneth Komba	Tanzania	Relevance of primary and secondary schooling for economically disadvantaged parents.	Educational leaders	Families should not be taken as empty vessels to be filled with policy makers' knowledge but involved as a resource in order to build a comprehensive learning environment for the child.
7 Mona Saleh Alsudis and Venitha Pillay	South Africa, Saudi Arabia	To understand across cultures the role of women academics in Saudi Arabia, and how they fulfil their research obligations in a conservative Islamic culture.	Doctoral student	Culturally situated narrative writing.
8 Sanna Salminen, Pekka Toivanen, Jaana Virkkala, Sampo Hankama and Jaana Vahermaa	Kenya, Botswana, South Africa, Zimbabwe, Finland	Evaluating multicultural music pedagogy and academic activities during 'Music, Education and Cultural Identity' intensive courses at the universities.	University lecturers, university students	Seeing many different ways of acting. Understanding much more about cultural issues and how the background influences one's thinking. Realising how sensitive talking about different cultural groups can be and how important everyone's cultural heritage is.

9 Hille Janhonen-Abruquah, Hanna Posti-Ahokas, Hannah Benjaba Edjah and Manasseh Edison Komla Amu	Ghana, Finland	Investigating students' understanding of the prevalent gender roles and structures in home economics education.	Teacher students at the University	The course and the study process served as eye-openers and positioned students to implement more gender-aware approaches in their future careers as teachers and educators.
10 William Nketsia, Said K. Juma, Abebe Yehualawork Malle, Raija Pirttimaa and Elina Lehtomäki	Ethiopia, Kenya, Tanzania, Finland	Cross-cultural dialogues on inclusive education.	University lecturers, university students	Participants noticed differences in social, cultural, and political contexts of the participating countries but found that it is possible to discuss the concept of inclusion together. One cannot speak about inclusion without sharing information about one's own culture, educational system, and general society.
11 Christine Adu-Yeboah	Ghana	Mature women's motives for entering higher education and what facilitated this action.	Mature women's narrations as university students	The findings point to the cultural change going on in Ghana, where both educated and uneducated parents as well as husbands encourage girls and women to study. Nevertheless, the participants' motives were predominantly personal, status-driven and also economic–instrumental.

In the second part, the chapters describe situations in which attention is given to the learners' culture so that learning becomes more multidimensional and comprehensive. In the Kenyan study (Chapter 5) the use of information and communication technology tries to support and encourage cultural diversity and preserve and promote the language, distinct identities and traditional knowledge of indigenous peoples, nations and tribes. The Tanzanian research (Chapter 6) among school leaders aims to include the family's perspective in the child's learning process. Families should not be taken as an empty vacuum to be fed with policy makers' knowledge; involving families should be seen as a resource to build a comprehensive learning environment for the child. Chapter 7 provides another multidimensional setting for the reader. Through culturally situated narrative writing, academic Saudi women's conservative religious life is described for the South African reader.

A common feature of all the chapters in Part III is that the research or study process has somehow opened eyes to see something that was not earlier obvious. For mature women, entering the university was the eye-opener (Chapter 11). Seeing one's own study, teaching or research field practised in another but equally relevant way is described in Chapters 8 (music education), 9 (home economics education) and 10 (inclusive education) as transforming, empowering and emancipatory by the participants.

Importance of the book in culturally responsive education

This book on culturally responsive education is of paramount importance in various ways. First, it will serve as material that can be read by scholars and other people interested in understanding subjects such as culturally responsive education, intercultural education and multiculturalism. It captures a wide geographical area by bringing together experiences from the global North and South. Second, the book gives the partner universities in the North–South–South cooperation an opportunity to collectively share knowledge with the general public, inform policy makers and educate education stakeholders across a broad spectrum. Third, the book puts together chapters that are positive with regard to equity and justice in education with the need to respect and appreciate cultural diversity in society. The book therefore stands for the interests of the cultures that continue to be marginalized or excluded from education. As for its technical importance, the book serves as a tangible output of the North–South–South cooperation and gives an opportunity for the academics who are part of the cooperation to grow academically, to be accountable and to visibly deliver for the societies they serve.

This CRE book will most certainly be useful to universities in both the North and South: the texts it contains will serve as one of the references that academics and students whose research interests centre on culturally responsive education will use. Moreover, it will be an important reference for students pursuing courses related to intercultural and international education as well as education in a global society. For instance, the University of Dar es Salaam has established a course titled 'Educational policies and practices in a global society', in which there is a module and leaning units on intercultural education. In addition, the academics who are taking part in this cooperation can aim to run academic seminars on culturally responsive education. In such seminars, presentations can be made on CRE and the book can be introduced to potential readers.

The culturally responsive education network – a way forward

During the CRE project (2012–2016) almost 100 mobility activities took place. Sixteen students took part in long (3–5 months) exchanges, and 21 teachers participated in teacher exchanges lasting 1–2 weeks. Six network meetings were arranged, each of them with 5–10 participants. A one-week intensive course was organized in Ghana. Besides the Ghanaian participants, 5 South Africans, 6 Tanzanians and 15 Finns took part in the course.

The culturally responsive education network has been beneficial in numerous ways. For example, through the network, university academics and students from both the South and the North have paid attention to the need for and importance of culturally responsive education. The network has indeed provided an opportunity for scholars from the South and the North to team up and work together, not only in their routine endeavours of teaching and researching but through sharing ideas for improvement in education and the advancement of knowledge. Through the variety of elements in its programme, such as meetings and intensive courses, the network has provided invaluable experiences for the participants, the students in particular. The students had opportunities to interact, share ideas and experiences and gain an understanding of different perspectives on a variety of educational issues. The network has indeed been a practical example of ideals of international collaboration in addressing societal issues and universities' cooperation in education.

This cooperation was not without points of weakness, however. First, it appears to have had an imbalanced representation of the North and South. While the partner universities from the South were from three different countries, the North was represented by only one country. Second, the cooperation events that involved physical meetings were hosted in only two countries out of the four. Third, not much attention was paid to conducting collective research projects for the advancement of knowledge on CRE.

Based on its usefulness and importance, the North–South–South cooperation needs to be sustained. The cooperation also needs to have a stronger focus on undertaking research projects collectively. Moreover, the cooperation could be transformed into a permanent international centre of excellence for CRE and international education. The centre could perform tasks such as creating opportunities for academics from different countries to share knowledge, skills and experiences in their areas of interest; organising international conferences; granting scholarships in the CRE area; hosting journals; organising the publication of books; and running an international depository of educational research outputs. This cooperation could also be developed further by extending it to other countries in the North to widen the sharing of knowledge and expertise.

Culturally responsive education approach

The CRE network has loosely followed Geneva Gay's (2013) theoretical thinking. To put it very briefly, culturally responsive education (Gay, 2013) means that the education is relevant in its own context. CRE recognizes the challenges of each educational setting but is able to respond in a culturally acceptable and positive manner. Content-wise, the core focus of the CRE project has been on qualitative research methods in education that aim to *produce knowledge with* students, teachers and teacher educators in their learning and work contexts. The key question addressed in this compiled volume is how education, learning and teaching and teacher education benefit from qualitative research processes and findings.

The project has created the chance to test Gay's (2000) North American thinking in different contexts – that is, Northern European and African settings – and see if and how it could be applied. Her theoretical thinking has grown from the culturally mixed schools in North America. She claims that culturally responsive pedagogy (Gay, 2000, 2013) is approaching social justice through using the cultural characteristics, experiences, and perspectives of ethnically diverse students as a means of creating a more meaningful learning environment. Gay is also convinced that all teachers are able to work with students who are from culturally different backgrounds to their own. However, she cautions that this requires that one is able to identify internalized biases and to accommodate the rich variety of students' cultural experiences into one's teaching (Gay, 2000, 2013). Gay's thinking seems to draw a very distinct line between the so-called ethnically diverse students and the rest of the pupils. As global migration is accelerating, the line between so-called ethnically diverse and non-ethnically diverse students in classrooms becomes even less relevant. Everyone is diverse, not only in relation to ethnicity but also in relation to all other differences such as gender, abilities and social class. Everyone is unique. This means that for the teacher it is even harder to get to know her pupils/students. Gay advocates knowing the child's primary culture and supporting the child's cultural heritage. It might be difficult to put it into a simple sentence, but it might go something like this: *my mother speaks Finnish and English but I grew up in Ghana where my father is from. He speaks Ga and English. I speak English but am not British.* Vertovec (2007) adds into the intersection of language and place of origin other identity markers such as religion, occupation, gender and race and comes up with the term 'super-diversity'.

How do you apply Gay's approach in a lecture room of 150 students? How do you have student–lecturer interaction when the place is so large that from the front of the lecture room you cannot be heard at the far end, and, when students respond to the lecturer's questions, the other students cannot hear each other's answers? How do you create a learning community within a classroom that is so congested that tables cannot be moved, and students are unable to stand up and turn to their classmates? The teachers' creativity must really be put into practice before Gay's culturally responsive approach can be applied. Different variations of study groups, peer group learning and peer support groups should be researched further. The role of the lecturer should be looked into as well. How would it be possible to divide and share one lecture's workload? Maybe have teacher trainees supervising the study groups?

According to Gay, culturally responsive education addresses the learner in a comprehensive way through a multidimensional engagement in learning activities. As culturally responsive learning aims for change and freedom, it is both transformative and emancipatory. Gay emphasizes the validating dimension of teaching. Teaching has to be carried out according to and through the strength of the students. Building bridges of meaningfulness between home and school experiences as well as between academic abstractions and lived sociocultural realities is vital for learning. It teaches students to know and praise their own and each other's cultural heritages. It incorporates multicultural information, resources and materials in all the subjects and skills routinely taught in schools. Villegas and Lucas (2002) see culturally responsive education as a starting point to move away from fragmented and superficial treatment of diversity. In other words, culturally responsive education makes learning more appropriate.

Education is essentially transformative, that is, helping students to develop the knowledge, skills and values needed to become social critics who can make reflective decisions and implement their decisions in effective personal, social, political and economic action. As education aims towards emancipation, it guides students in understanding that no single version of 'truth' is total and permanent. It does not solely subscribe to mainstream ways of knowing.

Culturally responsive education aims first of all at academic success of all learners. It highlights the importance of maintaining contact with and competence in one's primary cultural heritage. For transformation in learning, it is necessary to learn how to critique, challenge and transform inequalities, injustices, oppressions, exploitations, power and privilege. In-school learning should be connected to out-of-school living. Culturally responsive education promotes educational equity and aims to create community among individuals from different cultural, social and ethnic backgrounds and to develop students' agency, efficacy and empowerment.

The CRE project started with the primary idea of engaging voices on the ground in educational development (Lehtomäki et al., 2014). The idea was and still is to have the 'target groups' for educational development taking part as subjects and to involve them in contexts where change is expected to happen. This aims at promoting ownership in educational development and brings deeper cultural and societal knowledge into the development process.

Culture as a stage

During the CRE North–South–South mobility project, scholars have had the chance to meet colleagues in different environments. It has been possible to meet them in their local home universities and then in new environments, as participants travelling between the Global North and South. During these visits, culture has started to look like a stage.

When one travels between North and South, at first glance everything looks very different, even exotic, but soon the similarities are seen. It is like a continuum where similarities are at one end and differences are at the other. At first the contrasts are vast. Hot – cold. Bright sun – dark days. Noisy – quiet. Masses of people – empty streets. Then, the differences begin to diminish and communalities and common ground are found. In this project, the common ground was school. In the day in a school participatory observation project carried out in four different countries and viewed by 27 observers, observations focused on the school environment, pupils' actions and the teachers' role. For instance, after the school visits to Ghanaian elementary schools, the first impressions were of how surprisingly similar the schools were, despite all the differences. The school learning itself looked very similar, at least in the North–South comparison. Getting to know the new environment is like negotiations between new and old, similarities and differences.

Chapters in this book also explore the ways in which cultural visits can be developed towards deeper learning experiences and thus improve the quality of outbound mobility. The mobility programme has not only helped members to appreciate cultural diversity but also encouraged them to adopt culturally responsive activities and strategies in teaching. Exchange visits have helped to identify good practices, which were then remodified and replicated in other contexts. The collaborative work within the network has encouraged continuation of the sharing of ideas on culturally responsive education and its use in developing education in specific contexts.

In these times of extremely rapid growth both in global migration and in mobile technology, it is perhaps appropriate to end by quoting the much-admired author Taiye Selasi (2014): "Don't ask where I am from, ask where I am local". May this book be one step towards creating learning communities where new and old locals can learn together and from each other.

References

Gay, G. (2000). *Culturally responsive teaching: Theory, research and practice.* New York: Teachers College Press.

Gay, G. (2013). Teaching to and through cultural diversity. *Curriculum Inquiry, 43,* 1, 48–70. Willey Periodicals.

Lehtomäki, E., Janhonen-Abruquah, H. T., Tuomi, M., Okkolin, M-A., Posti-Ahokas, H., & Palojoki, P. (2014). Research to engage voices on the ground in educational development. *International Journal of Educational Development, 35,* 37–43. doi: 10.1016/j.ijedudev.2013.01.003.

Sayed, Y., & Ahmed, R. (2015). Education quality, and teaching and learning in the post-2015 education agenda. *International Assignment of Educational Development, 40,* 330–338.

Selasi, T. (2014). Don't ask where I'm from, ask where I'm a local. TEDGlobal. Filmed October 2014. Retrieved from www.ted.com/about/our-organization.

Soini, K., & Dessein, J. (2016). Culture–sustainability relation: Towards a conceptual framework. *Sustainability, 8,* 2, 167. doi: 10.3390/su8020167.

UN (2015). *Sustainable Development Goals.* Retrieved from https://sustainabledevelop ment.un.org/.

UNESCO (2015). *World Education Forum 2015.* Retrieved from http://en.unesco. org/world-education-forum-2015.

United Nations (2015). *Transforming our world: The 2030 Agenda for Sustainable Develop-ment.* Resolution adopted by the General Assembly on 25 September 2015. Retrieved from www.un.org/ga/search/view_doc.asp?symbol=A/RES/70/1&Lang=E.

Vertovec, S. (2007). Super-diversity and its implications. *Ethnic and Racial Studies, 30,* 6, 1024–1054.

Villegas, A. M., & Lucas, T. (2002). Preparing culturally responsive teachers: Rethinking the curriculum. *Journal of Teacher Education, 53,* 20–32.

Part I

Focus on validating education

1 Implementing a language of instruction policy in diverse linguistic contexts in Ghana

Joseph Ghartey Ampiah, Christopher Yaw Kwaah and Christine Adu-Yeboah

The aim of the sixth education for all (EFA) goal is to improve all aspects of the quality of education and to ensure excellence for all students, especially in literacy, numeracy and essential life skills. In many countries, though, the focus on access often overshadows attention to quality (UNESCO, 2004). However, the 2000 Dakar Framework for Action stresses the quality of education as a prime determinant of whether EFA is achieved. At present, in addition to making schools accessible to children, governments, especially in low-income countries, have been committed to providing quality basic education (Ampiah, 2011). The government of Ghana, for instance, has demonstrated its commitment to quality universal basic education through various initiatives aimed at making basic-school pupils literate. These initiatives include creating new schools, upgrading teachers' qualifications, introducing capitation grants and providing free meals for schoolchildren. Learning achievement, which is one of the indicators of educational quality, though, has remained low at the basic-school level; for instance, many Ghanaian schoolchildren are not literate or numerate by third grade (Ministry of Education, 2014).

National standardized examinations, such as the National Education Assessment and School Education Assessment, have shown that basic-school pupils are "challenged by both English and mathematics" (Ministry of Education, 2014, p. 7). The national Early Grade Reading Assessment (EGRA), which assesses reading skills in 11 Ghanaian languages and the English language, and the Early Grade Mathematics Assessment (EGMA), which assesses the basic mathematics skills which need to be acquired in early grades, produced similar results. The 2014 EGRA results showed that: "by the end of P2 (*grade 2*), the majority of public school pupils [7–8 year olds] could not yet read with comprehension – neither in a Ghanaian language nor in English" (Ministry of Education, 2014, p. 11). Ghanaian primary-school students' inability to read and perform basic mathematics is evidence that schools are failing to give children meaningful access to education.

Webley (2006) argues that education is power and that the language which is the medium of instruction in schools is the key to accessing that power. English is the language of the global economy and development and the official language in Ghana. However, in accordance with Article 30 of the United Nations Convention on the Rights of the Child, which asserts that all children have the right to learn and use the language of their family (Webley, 2006), the government of Ghana has instituted a national language policy for basic education. According to this policy, in the first three years of primary education, the most dominant of the 11 written languages (there are more than 79 spoken) recognized and recommended by the Ministry of Education for use in schools is to be used as the medium of instruction, while the English language is studied as a subject. Starting at primary 4 level, English replaces the Ghanaian language as the medium of instruction, and the Ghanaian language is then treated as just another subject on the timetable.

The language of instruction policy in Ghana is geared towards facilitating communication between the teacher and the child as, the better the communication is, the higher the chances are that the child will retain the educational content. The policy is also aimed at promoting the use of the language understood by the child in the first few years of education and to improve the quality of education from a cultural perspective. Again, the focus of the policy is to achieve reading fluency and comprehension in the child's first language as a bridge to gaining literacy in English, thereby improving teaching and learning. This goal is informed by research in local and international contexts which suggests that pupils learn to read and write better and faster in a language they understand and speak well and that they can transfer the literacy skills acquired in that language to learning to read in a second language (Hartwell, 2010).

The Ghanaian language policy has been reinforced recently by the National Literacy Accelerated Programme (NALAP) policy, a bilingual bi-literacy programme for early primary school started in the third term (May 2010) of the 2009/2010 academic year. It is aimed at helping pupils learn to read in a Ghanaian language while they learn to speak English, with the major Ghanaian language of each school community used as the medium of instruction until the primary 4 level. During implementation in the classroom, it is recommended that, of the 90-minute literacy lesson, 80 minutes should be used to teach literacy in the local language and 10 minutes in English at the kindergarten (KG) 1 level, and 70 minutes and 20 minutes in KG 2. This changes to 60 and 30 minutes in primary 1, 50 and 40 minutes in primary 2 and 45 and 45 minutes in primary 3.

Language policy in Ghana has had a chequered history. Owu-Ewie (2006) reveals that the use of the local language in traditional education dates to the Castle Schools and the missionary era before the introduction of formal education. He traces the development of the current language policy and shows that, with the opening of formal schools and the use of English as the medium of instruction, indigenous languages were seen as inadequate teaching media, and bilingual education was then begun (Owu-Ewie, 2006). According to Owu-Ewie (2006), the first legislation on the use of Ghanaian languages as the medium of instruction at the lower primary level, soon taken over by English, is believed to have come into effect when the British colonial government took on the administration of education in 1925. Owu-Ewie (2006) also points out that, since Ghana gained independence in 1957, the use of Ghanaian languages as the medium of instruction has been very inconsistent. For example, between 1957 and 1966, no Ghanaian languages were used; from 1967 to 1969, they were allowed only in the first year of elementary education; and from 1970 to 2002, a Ghanaian language was used in the first three years of schooling. However, the 2007 new education reform brought about shifts in policy, stipulating that, where feasible, schools should use a Ghanaian language for the acquisition of literacy and as a medium of instruction in lower primary school (Ghana Education Service, 2007). This shift was apparently based on the 2002 announcement by the then minister of education that the English language should be the only medium of instruction in primary schools (Hartwell, 2010). The minister advanced the following reasons for this stance, among others:

- Especially in rural areas, teachers never spoke English in class and used only the Ghanaian language.
- Students could not speak and write well in English even after secondary school.
- Teaching materials in the Ghanaian languages were lacking.
- There was a shortage of Ghanaian language teachers specifically trained to teach content subjects in the Ghanaian language.

(Hartwell, 2010)

These factors notwithstanding, research evidence shows that the use of the English language as a medium of instruction has an influence on the patterns of classroom interaction and presents communication difficulties for both teachers and pupils (Brock-Utne, 2000). For instance, Brock-Utne (2000) reports on the difficulties both children and teachers in some African countries (e.g. Uganda, Swaziland, Zimbabwe, Botswana, Namibia, Senegal) have mastering school subjects due to the use of English as the language of instruction when they have not mastered that language.

When English was the language of instruction, the children were silent, shy and did not participate if they were not spoken to. But when the instructor changed to mother tongue as medium of instruction, the children's behaviour changed dramatically. The children who had not said a word previously were now eager to answer and their hands were constantly in the air, showing how much they wanted to answer the instructor's questions.

(Brock-Utne, 2000, p. 9)

When the local language is used as the medium of instruction, it leads to what Chick (1996, cited in Brock-Utne, 2000) calls 'safe talk' by teachers as it is less demanding of the English skills of teachers and pupils, especially in the chorusing of responses. Resorting to such forms of talk allows for participation without loss of face by either teachers or pupils, whether through language errors or a lack of understanding.

The advantages of using African languages, in addition to the former colonial language, as the medium of teaching and learning are reported in the literature. Rubagumya (1997) refers to research studies in several African countries that show that maintaining and encouraging the connection between the language of the home and the language of the school has positive effects on the learning process. The use of the mother tongue, especially in the early years of schooling, has also been found to make the curriculum more relevant by connecting learning to pupils' experiences, environment and culture, resulting in faster and better acquisition of knowledge (Dembele, 2003). The use of the mother tongue is also effective in helping children with acquisition of a second language (Hartwell, 2010).

Teachers are key in the use of the child's mother tongue in teaching and learning. Obanya (2004) proposes the three-dimensional (input–process–output) model of education quality to show that, among other factors, teachers are fully devoted to the promotion of education when given adequate education and professional preparation to become pedagogically skilled. Obanya (2004, p. 5) contends that an important element in increasing or decreasing quality that has not been sufficiently taken into account is the role of the language used for and in learning (in addition to the language from which one is learning). Similarly, Hartwell (2010) points out that one factor contributing to the Quality Teaching Practice Index is teachers' language competence. Teachers are fundamental to the implementation of language policies, and their experiences of language policy implementation are central in determining the risks of implementation failure, as they are responsible for day-to-day pedagogical decisions in the classroom (Fillmore, 2014). Teachers' ability to speak, read and write the language of instruction in the early grades and to connect with pupils in ways that make them comfortable actively engaging in lessons contributes to the success of language policies. This is even more so the case in multilingual contexts where some pupils' mother tongues might not be the dominant language.

Challenges and difficulties in learning tend to be common in multilingual classrooms. Especially when English is the official language, the policy of using the mother tongue in the early grades and switching to the English language exclusively in upper primary school is not fully respected, as both teachers and learners have problems communicating in that language and are forced to switch between the first and official language in the course of lessons (Fillmore, 2014; Ghimire, 2014; Obanya, 2004). In the linguistically heterogeneous context of Nepal, for example, Ghimire (2014) reports that teachers of early grades usually switch to the mother tongues (which might be the minority language) for pupils who cannot communicate in the school's formal language, depending on their language proficiency. In Ghana also, an implementation study of the NALAP programme found that teachers and, in some cases, pupils were not fluent or literate in the Ghanaian language selected for the school, and that, in the given circumstances, teachers attempted to teach in that unfamiliar language (Hartwell, 2010).

Given the linguistic heterogeneity of many Ghanaian schools and the role of the teacher in facilitating learning, it is important to know how teachers manage teaching and learning using their language skills and pedagogical approaches. This study, therefore, explores some issues surrounding the implementation of the language of instruction policy in Ghana. The chapter presents a critical view of the role of teachers in achieving implementation success and highlights challenges which are likely to undermine the effective implementation of the language of instruction policy in Ghana. The study was guided by the following questions:

1   What are basic-school teachers' ethnic and language backgrounds, and how different are these from the language of instruction they mostly use?
2   What are teachers' perceptions of their local language competence?
3   Do teachers feel that training has prepared them to use the local language in teaching in primary schools?
4   What do teachers see as challenges to the implementation of the language policy in their schools?

Method

This study is exploratory in nature and uses basic-school teachers to investigate the implementation of local language policy in multilingual cultural settings in Ghanaian classrooms. The study was restricted to basic-school teachers, including teachers in private schools. Private schools were included in the study as there is a general perception that they offer higher quality education to pupils. Teachers from both urban and rural schools were recruited for this study to reflect the different cultural contexts in rural and urban settings. In this exploratory study, primary data were gathered using a questionnaire. The items in the questionnaire were chosen to reflect the multilingual context of basic-school classrooms and teachers' training. The authors developed and validated the questionnaire through a pilot study involving basic-school teachers in the Cape Coast Metropolis. Teachers' responses were analysed using frequencies and percentages and grouped under the themes which formed the basis of the questionnaire. Open-ended items were grouped into broad themes and quantified into percentages.

Participants

Participants in this study were drawn from three study centres hosting an upgrading programme of the Institute of Education, University of Cape Coast, for basic-school teachers from all ten regions of Ghana. These teachers had diplomas in education and had been trained at universities and colleges of education. The Institute of Education at the University of Cape Coast organized this sandwich programme for in-service teachers to upgrade their knowledge and skills to bachelor's degree level. Questionnaires were administered to teachers who were at the study centres at the time of the researcher's visits.

The respondents to the questionnaire were 526 teachers from public and private schools. The majority of teachers had been trained at two universities (38 per cent) and colleges of education (62 per cent). The participants were 44 per cent male and 56 per cent female. Approximately 87 per cent were primary-school teachers, and 13 per cent taught kindergarten. About 35 per cent of the teachers were younger than 30 years old, 64 per cent were between 30 and 50, and only 1 per cent were older than 50. On average, teachers had 7 years of teaching experience as basic-school teachers (ranging from 3 to 30 years of experience).

Results and discussion

Teachers' language background and language of instruction

The basic-school teachers who participated in this study taught in eight of the ten regions of Ghana and belonged to four of the five major ethnic groups (Table 1.1).

Table 1.1 indicates that the respondents were from four of five major ethnic groups in Ghana. Most (75.5 per cent) were from the Akan ethnic

Table 1.1 Ethnic and language background of teachers (N = 526)

	N	%
Ethnic group		
Akan	400	76.1
Ewe	76	14.4
Mole–Dagbane	37	7.0
Ga–Dangme	13	2.5
Language		
Twi	232	44.1
Fante	145	27.6
Ewe	76	14.4
Dagbani	34	6.5
Ga	13	2.5
Nzema	12	2.3
Wassa	4	0.8
Builsa	3	0.6
Akuapem	3	0.6
Ahanta	2	0.4
Akyem	1	0.2
Sefwi	1	0.2

group, which is made up of multiple linguistic groups such as Twi, Fante, Akwapem, Akyem, Akwamu, Ahanta, Bono, Nzema, Kwahu and Sefwi. This is not surprising, as the Akan group makes up 52.7 per cent of the Ghanaian population (GSS, 2008). The respondents were from different language groups, as shown in Table 1.2, and taught in areas with diverse sociolinguistic backgrounds.

Table 1.2 shows that 68.1 per cent of the teachers in this study had parents who both spoke the same language, while 31.9 per cent had parents who spoke different languages. This is expected as, in Ghana, most people prefer to marry within their ethnic or language group. Thirty-six respondents had mothers whose language was Fante but whose fathers spoke other languages, such as Nzema, Wassa, Ahanta and Sefwi, which are listed as other in Table 1.2. This situation results in some people in a particular community speaking multiple local languages but not always with the same level of fluency.

The connection between mothers' language and teachers' first spoken language was explored. It found that most respondents (74.3 per cent) first learnt to speak their mothers' language. However, for the rest (25.7 per cent), their first spoken language was different from their mothers' language. For example, 25 respondents spoke Twi first, but their mothers' language was Sefwi. In addition, 16 spoke Fante first, but their mothers' language was Ahanta. Thus, when these respondents were children, their first language was not their mothers' language. This means that children do not necessarily speak their mothers' tongue as their first language. When respondents' first spoken Ghanaian language was compared to the Ghanaian language most commonly used in teaching, it was noted that 13.3 per cent of respondents used only the English language to teach, even though they could speak and teach in a Ghanaian language. The Ghanaian languages most frequently used in teaching were Fante, Twi, Ga and Nzema, while the Ghanaian languages first learnt were Akuapem, Bono, Dagbani, Ewe, Fante, Ga, Mamprusi, Nzema, Twi and other minor tongues. Of the 526 teachers in the study, 53.8 per cent spoke Twi or Fante and taught in that same language. The remaining 46.2 per cent taught in languages other than their first spoken language. This

Table 1.2 Local language background of teachers' parents

Mother's language	Father's language						Total
	Fante	Twi	Ewe	Ga	Dagbani	Other	
Fante	147	17	3	4	2	36	209
Twi	41	80	1	0	0	7	129
Ewe	0	1	56	0	0	0	57
Ga	0	6	0	7	0	1	14
Dagbani	0	0	0	0	27	11	38
Others	10	16	0	12	0	41	79
Total	198	120	60	23	29	96	526

group was made of teachers whose first language was Fante (5.9 per cent) but taught in English, Nzema and Twi and of initial Twi speakers (15.0 per cent) who taught in Fante and English. The remaining 25.3 per cent of respondents also taught in languages other than their first language. Teachers needed to do so to teach in the dominant language of the school locality, as directed by the Ghana Education Service. It is not surprising that half of the respondents did not use their first language to teach as approximately one third of the 526 teachers indicated that they could not read well, and nearly one half reported that they could write not well in their first language. In addition, of the 483 teachers who offered a course in Ghanaian languages at diploma level, 40.8 per cent did not offer their first language; 8.2 per cent of the sample did not offer a course at diploma level in any Ghanaian language.

Respondents were asked to indicate the Ghanaian language they most frequently used in teaching their classes. The results in Table 1.3 indicate that respondents used Ghanaian languages for instructional delivery in upper primary school, contrary to the language of instruction policy, which limits the use of Ghanaian languages to kindergarten and lower primary school. Some respondents in private schools also reported the use of Ghanaian language in upper primary school, although they were in the minority. Instead of using the English language to teach at the upper primary level, 51.3 per cent of respondents used Fante, and 32.1 per cent Twi. The English language was used by only 13.3 per cent. In addition, at the kindergarten level in both public and private schools, the English language instead of the local language was used in teaching. This is also a violation of the language of instruction policy.

Table 1.3 Ghanaian language most commonly used by teachers in teaching

Level of teacher	Subject	N	%
Kindergarten	English	24	35.3
	Fante	37	54.4
	Nzema	1	1.5
	Twi	6	8.8
	Total	68	100.0
Lower primary	English	12	6.4
	Fante	132	70.6
	Nzema	1	0.5
	Twi	42	22.5
	Total	187	100.0
Upper primary	English	36	13.3
	Fante	139	51.3
	Ga	9	3.3
	Twi	87	32.1
	Total	271	100.0

Teachers' most frequently spoken local language and language of instruction

Respondents were asked to indicate the local language they spoke most of the time and the local language they used in teaching. Of the 13 Ghanaian languages the respondents had first learnt to speak, the majority (85.7 per cent) indicated they used only 4 (Twi, Fante, Ga and Nzema) in teaching. Approximately 16.0 per cent of respondents indicated that the children in their classes did not speak the language used to teach them. The other respondents had the challenge of teaching in the language they did not speak most frequently. For instance, 37 reported that they spoke Ewe most often but used either Fante or Twi in their teaching, as seen in Table 1.4.

Seventy respondents did not use any local language to teach and preferred to use English. In addition, 76 respondents spoke Twi most frequently but used Fante as the language of instruction. Teachers having to use languages that they do not speak often poses a challenge to teaching. This problem often arises, as the posting of teachers to basic schools does not take into account the local language background of teachers and the dominant language spoken in the localities where schools are situated. Some teachers have to learn the local language of the school community to be able to communicate well with pupils. Others who cannot do so resort to teaching in English, contrary to the language policy. This situation brings into sharp focus teachers' competency in the local language used in teaching.

Teachers' perceptions of their local language competency

Among the factors contributing to quality teaching is teachers' language competence, which can be used to facilitate pupils' learning (Fillmore, 2014). Literacy in the local language among Ghanaians is reported to be generally low. According to the most recent Ghana Living Standards Survey report, approximately 16 per cent of people age five and older were literate in only English, 3 per cent in only Ghanaian languages, and 30 per cent in both English and Ghanaian languages (GSS, 2008). Respondents, therefore, were asked to

Table 1.4 Teachers' spoken local language and language of instruction

Spoken language	Language of instruction					Total
	Twi	*Fante*	*Ga*	*Nzema*	*None*	
Twi	117	79	0	0	33	229
Fante	1	211	0	0	34	246
Ewe	11	17	9	0	0	37
Nzema	3	1	0	2	0	6
Others	3	2	0	0	3	8
Total	135	310	9	2	70	526

indicate the local language they could speak fluently and could write well. The data show that the 526 teachers could fluently speak a total of 16 languages but studied only 8 of these languages at diploma level in college. The remaining Ghanaian languages were either not offered at training institutions or were not among the 11 approved Ghanaian languages of study. Respondents who studied Ghanaian languages indicated they could speak them fluently and write well in them. However, respondents who reported that they could fluently speak two or more local languages indicated they could not write well in all of them. Speaking multiple languages is normal in the Ghanaian context due to the heterogeneity of ethnic groups in most communities, especially in urban centres.

About a quarter of the respondents stated that they did not know of the NALAP programme and still taught using a combination of English and a Ghanaian language. Therefore, respondents were asked to indicate the proportion of English and Ghanaian languages they used in teaching; the results are shown in Table 1.5. A total of 499 responded to this item. Table 1.5 shows that 12.6 per cent used the English language almost exclusively in teaching at the lower primary level. This finding raises concerns about these teachers' competency in using the local language to teach. In addition, 43.5 per cent of respondents indicated that they split their teaching equally between a Ghanaian language and English, which is also not in line with the NALAP methodology. These findings show that some respondents did not adhere to the language of instruction policy as envisaged. Even though the NALAP was implemented to reinforce the language policy by introducing a bilingual bi-literacy programme in early primary school, these findings indicate that teachers who participated in this programme had not yet felt its impact, as their language of instruction practices did not reflect the NALAP methodology. Respondents who used English more than Ghanaian languages in teaching, however, indicated that they were more comfortable using English to teach subjects, such as information communication technology, mathematics, integrated science and natural science. A lower-primary-school teacher writes: "I find it more comfortable to use English to teach as for some of the subjects, it is difficult to find the local language equivalents of some concepts in subjects like science." This teacher's comment makes one question teachers' training in using local languages to teach. Especially when all the textbooks used by teachers and pupils are written in English, teachers

Table 1.5 Proportion of English and Ghanaian languages used in teaching (N = 499)

Language use	N	%
100% Ghanaian languages	20	4
100% English	63	12.6
90% Ghanaian languages and 10% English	47	9.4
80% Ghanaian languages and 20% English	153	30.7
50% Ghanaian languages and 50% English	216	43.3

have to find their own equivalent words in local languages, even if inappropriate, for concepts and words used in some subjects. The use of the English language then becomes imperative in cases when teachers cannot explain lessons to pupils in the local language.

Respondents were further asked about training they had received in using local languages to teach, as the NALAP programme also offers such training. Of the 526 teachers who participated in the study, less than half indicated they had been taught how to use a Ghanaian language to teach. Hence, a majority of respondents were not formally trained in teaching using the local language. This situation poses a challenge to teachers as they struggle to help pupils understand subject matter in the local language. This finding corroborates the conclusion drawn by Hartwell (2010) that basic schools lacked Ghanaian-language teachers specifically trained to teach the content of subjects in a Ghanaian language. Teachers were not literate in the local language and so could not teach reading and writing skills or curricular content in local languages (Benson, 2010). Participants' responses shown in Table 1.6 indicate that 70.9 per cent entered teacher training without having learnt any local language at the senior-high-school level. Of the 29.1 per cent of teachers who offered a Ghanaian language in a senior high school, the majority also offered the language at college or university level. Students, therefore, are handicapped when they attend institutions which do not offer some of the approved local languages. Such students are forced to study a different local language than the one they want to offer at the institution. Unsurprisingly, 40.3 per cent of participants indicated that they cannot teach any Ghanaian language in primary school.

Table 1.6 Teachers' training preparedness for using local languages to teach in primary school

Items	Yes		No		
	N	%	N	%	Total
Did you offer Ghanaian language at the senior high school level?	153	29.1	373	70.9	526
If yes, is it the same Ghanaian language you offered at a training college or university?	136	88.9	17	11.1	153
Have you been taught how to use Ghanaian languages to teach?	213	40.5	313	59.5	526
Have you been trained in the National Literacy Accelerated Programme approach to teaching?	188	35.7	338	64.3	526

Challenges to implementation of the language policy in primary schools

Respondents were asked to indicate the challenges they faced using a Ghanaian language to teach. The spectrum of responses from the 425 teachers who responded to this item is summarized in Table 1.7.

An inadequate supply of teaching and learning materials in local languages was identified by 26.6 per cent of respondents as a major challenge to using the local language to teach. One lower primary teacher writes: "Even though the NALAP idea is good for introducing our pupils to their local language, we lack textbooks and materials, such as posters, stickers, etc. in the local language." Another challenge was the use of one particular local language in teaching in multilingual classrooms. Table 1.7 shows that 16.9 per cent of respondents indicated that pupils' different local language backgrounds made it difficult to use one particular local language in teaching. Two teachers from different schools describe this situation:

> In the community where I teach, pupils are made up of different ethnic groups, and most of them don't understand Twi at all, which is the language of the locality.

> Some of the children are of northern origin, and the school is a Muslim school. Teaching using Fante, which is the language I can speak, is difficult for most of the children as it is only the Fantes who are able to understand me.

This finding about the challenges faced by teachers in implementing the language policy is consistent with the views of Obanya (2004), Fillmore (2014) and Ghimire (2014), who argue that there are linguistic challenges in multilingual classrooms where English is the official language and the policy is to use students' mother tongues to teach in early grades. This challenge arises as neither the teacher nor some children are proficient in the local language of

Table 1.7 Challenges to the implementation of the language policy in primary school (N = 425)

Challenges	N	%
Inadequate teaching and learning materials in local languages	113	26.6
Different local language backgrounds of pupils	72	16.9
Teachers' difficulty reading and writing the local language	50	11.8
Difficulty explaining some mathematics concepts in local languages	45	10.6
Parental pressure for children to speak English	42	9.9
Lack of teacher training in local languages	28	6.6
Lack of Ghanaian-language textbooks	27	6.4
Difficulty explaining some concepts in local languages	19	4.5
Other	29	6.8

instruction. It is, therefore, unsurprising that more than 50 per cent of respondents indicated that they preferred to use the English language to teach. Ampiah (2008) finds that the main method of teaching in basic schools was the chalk-and-talk method, followed by the question-and-answer, demonstration and lecture methods, in that order. These methods require using languages which can be understood by all pupils in the class and are extremely important for the delivery of quality education.

One interesting challenge worth mentioning is parental pressure for children to speak the English language in early grades. Most parents in Ghana want their children to speak English, as it is the official language and the language of the global economy and development. Some respondents (9.9 per cent) indicated that they faced the challenge of resistance from parents when they used the local language to teach, as parents put pressure on teachers to encourage children to speak English. One teacher writes: "The parents of pupils put pressure on me not to use the local language in teaching as this prevent their children from speaking the English language."

Children seem to become so familiar with the use of the local language as it is used in teaching every subject that they hear less and less of the English language. Less exposure to the English language makes children tend to put less emphasis on learning to speak it. In the words of one of the teachers: "Pupils feel comfortable and bold [speaking] in class with the use of the local language and so do not want to learn how to speak and use the English language."

The use of the mother tongue in teaching in primary school remains a contentious issue in Ghana, as research supports the use of the mother tongue in teaching early grades to enhance pupils' learning achievement. However, a section of the Ghanaian public believes that children should start learning to speak English in the early grades, as it is the language of instruction throughout most of children's education.

Finally, when respondents were asked which language they prefer to use in teaching, the results show that, of the 503 teachers who responded to this item, approximately 45 per cent preferred to use the English language. The reasons given for the choice of the English language were difficulty pronouncing and writing the local language, which created comfort using the English language to teach, and the goal for pupils to acquire another language and be fluent speaking it. The 42 per cent of teachers who wanted to use only a local language to teach were of the view that pupils who speak that language understand lessons better, that pupils cannot speak English very well and that the NALAP programme stipulates the use of the child's first language. Participants who prefer teaching in a combination of a Ghanaian language and the English language (13.7 per cent) gave such reasons as that, when the English language is used, the teacher must say certain terms in the Ghanaian language for pupils to understand them and that some classrooms are multilingual, with children from different ethnic groups.

Conclusion

The language of instruction policy in Ghana is geared towards facilitating communication between the teacher and the child. However, many teachers experienced communication challenges with children in their classes due to such factors as the children's or teachers' lack of understanding of the language of the community, a lack of textbooks written in local languages to facilitate learning in local languages and the marginalization of some children in multilingual classrooms. Teachers, therefore, used their preferred systems of communication, which were not supported by the language of instruction policy or NALAP methodology. Given this state of affairs, the language of communication between teachers and the children perhaps should be dictated by the situation on the ground. By modifying the policy to support practising what is locally feasible, teachers will become policy reformers in the school context. The lack of compatibility of the language policy with the local context will then be minimized.

A number of studies on language policy have been conducted in countries where most people can speak one common local language. The findings from such studies are difficult to apply in countries such as Ghana, where classrooms are multilingual and the teacher might have difficulty speaking the language of the children. The lack of training for a majority of teachers on how to teach using a Ghanaian language, as seen in this study, is likely to make these teachers ineffective at connecting with pupils in ways that make them comfortable to actively engage in lessons. There should be some consideration at the policy level to address teachers' lack of proficiency in Ghanaian languages by making the study of a Ghanaian language compulsory in senior high school.

Also, the culture of some pupils was not promoted by teaching in local languages which were not their own. The implication is that, if the teacher cannot speak a local language which pupils understand, these pupils do not automatically share a set of understandings with the teacher, making it difficult to promote linkages between their home and school cultures (Benson, 2010). Thus, the practice of adopting the dominant language of the community might not be culturally sensitive to the language of some children, especially given the findings of this study that show that not all children speak or understand the dominant local language.

The organization of the language of instruction policy requires a number of adjustments to how the Ghana Education Service has implemented the policy so far. Support must be given to teachers through the provision of textbooks in local languages, opportunities to becoming literate in at least one local language, pedagogical training to promote bilingual education and consideration of teachers' backgrounds during school placement. This support is necessary for the language policy to function effectively.

References

Ampiah, J. G. (2008). An investigation of provision of quality basic education in Ghana: A case study of selected schools in the Central Region. *Journal of International Cooperation in Education, 11*(3), 19–37.

Ampiah, J. G. (2011). *Quality basic education in Ghana: Prescription, practice and problems* (Africa-Asia University Dialogue for Educational Development. Report of the International Experience Sharing Seminar (1). CICE Series 4). CICE, Hiroshima University.

Benson, C. (2010). Do we expect too much of bilingual teachers? Bilingual teaching in developing countries. *International Journal of Bilingual Education and Bilingualism, 7* (2–3), 204–221. doi:10.1080/13670050408667809.

Brock-Utne, B. (2000). *Whose education for all? The recolonization of the African mind?* New York: Falmer Press.

Dembélé, M. (2003). Teacher education in Sub-Saharan Africa: Learning from within and from without to improve policy and practice. Background paper commissioned by ADEA in the framework of the *Challenge of Learning Study*. Paris: ADEA.

Fillmore, N. (2014). *Mother tongue-based multilingual education policy and implementation in Mindanao, Philippines*. (Unpublished master's thesis). Deakin University.

Ghana Education Service (2007). *Ghana education sector review*. Accra, Ghana: Ministry of Education.

Ghana Statistical Service (2008). *Ghana living standards survey: Report of the fifth round*. Accra, Ghana: Ghana Statistical Service.

Ghimire, L. (2014). *Language policy of mother tongue-based education in Nepal*. (Unpublished doctoral dissertation). Tribhuvan University.

Hartwell, A. (2010). *National literacy acceleration program: Implementation study*. EQUALL: USAID.

Ministry of Education Ghana Education Service National Education Assessment Unit (2014). *Ghana 2013 early grade reading assessment and early grade mathematics assessment: Report of findings*. Accra, Ghana: MOE/GES.

Obanya, P. (2004). *Learning in, with, and from the first language*. Cape Town, South Africa: PRAESA.

Owu-Ewie, C. (2006). The language policy of education in Ghana: A critical look at the English-only language policy of education. In J. Mugane (Ed.), *Selected proceedings of the 35th annual conference on African linguistics* (76–85). Somerville, MA: Cascadilla Proceedings Project.

Rubagumya, C. M. (1997). Disconnecting education: Language as a determinant of quality of education in Tanzania. *Journal of Linguistics and Language in Education, 3*, 81–95.

UNESCO. (2004). *Education for all: The quality imperative*. Paris: UNESCO.

Webley, K. (2006). Mother tongue first: Children's right to learn in their own languages. *Id21 Insights Education, 5*, 1–2.

2 Teacher professional development through open distance learning

Introducing a new learning culture

Agnes Mohlakwana and Ruth Aluko

Introduction

The past decade has seen the recognition of the term 'teacher development'. It has emerged to include ways in which people understand "teachers' working lives" (Evans, 2002, p. 123). This notion is also referred to as professional development, as teachers are professionals. Teachers' professional development has to do with helping them to gain more experience with regard to their own systematic work. The Organization for Economic Cooperation and Development (2009) explains the term 'professional development' to mean activities that develop an individual's skills, knowledge, expertise and other characteristics as a teacher. Teacher development has moved beyond simple in-service workshops and expanded into a more robust system of continuing education (Quattlebaum, 2012). Today, there is a common understanding that a nation's educational level is linked to the development of the country's teaching force. Open distance learning (ODL) refers to flexible teaching and learning that is accessible to multitudes of people in various modes (Malaysian Qualifications Agency, 2010). This is a way of learning that is open to flexible approaches, accommodates learning in a teacher's own space, is accessible and can utilise various resources. ODL is not new to the South African education system, but rather has been used in the country for more than a century. However, South Africa appears to be late in tapping into ODL's many benefits, which include the development of individuals' pedagogic knowledge, maintaining their sense of purpose and improving their quality of teaching, due to the country's past. South Africa's past is fraught with separate developments in all spheres of life – some of which include politics, education and social concerns.

Scholars have described the education system in South Africa as one of "parallel development" (Barnard, quoted by Booyse, le Roux, Seroto, & Wolhuter, 2011). Teacher development during that period catered to different racial groups in different institutions over time and using differentiated standards. Education during the apartheid era was based on a racially segregated system of education that was unequal, and separate developments meant divisive education provision in schools. There was a "White–Black dichotomy"

(Behr, 1988), with Blacks, Coloureds, Indians and Whites (the terms used then) kept apart. Around 1910, when the idea of training white teachers in the Cape Colony was introduced, it was clear that any form of training and development was meant for a specific racial group. Other teacher development initiatives during the apartheid era took place in various teacher-training institutions across the country. These were ethnically based (Chisholm, 2004).

Wolhuter (2006) summarises education developments during apartheid up to the democratic era. When South Africa's four colonies, the Cape Colony, the Orange Free State, the Transvaal and Natal, were amalgamated in 1910, the responsibility for white education was to be handled by the four provincial governments. Between 1910 and 1994, teacher training took place in teachers' colleges. Later on, universities became involved in the training of teachers, too. In 1948, when the National Party took control of the government, rigorous segregation policies were introduced; these promoted what was called apartheid. These policies supported racial segregation and ethnic groupings, enabling each grouping to take charge of its own schooling system. These ethnic groupings were called the 'homeland system'. Homeland leaders realised the importance of building more teacher training colleges by the early 1990s. Sayed, in Chisholm (2004), defines this fragmentation of teacher training programmes as the "life spaces" of individual trainees. As a result of the above, teacher training colleges produced teachers according to race and ethnicity, with differentiated pathways and postings, fragmented systems within systems, and of less desirable quality (Sayed, in Chisholm, 2004). By 1994, every homeland had its own university where teacher training was included.

The political transition from apartheid to a democratic government in 1994 was a significant shift that impacted the skills of the South African workforce (Chisholm, 2004). School curricula had to be transformed from the Bantu Education curriculum, which was designed to socialise black people to servitude, to one that empowered all members of society, irrespective of race (Nakabugo & Sieborger, 2001; Onwu & Sehoole, 2011). This was a major shift in what teachers were trained at colleges to do. In addition to this political change, other changes had a direct impact on education. These include the impact of technology, new understandings about knowledge, teaching and learning, and diverse student populations. Given South Africa's historical background, it would take centuries to train teachers only through the conventional mode of education, because of their unpreparedness to teach in a democratic environment. Thus, like many countries around the world with similar backgrounds, South Africa has come to recognise the value that ODL can add to education in general. One of the most important reasons for opting for distance education in developing countries is to produce a corps of well-qualified educators (Ravhudzulo, 2003).

The teaching profession has benefitted greatly from ODL. According to UNESCO (2001), this mode of delivery has been used to teach, support and develop teachers for many years. This includes providing a route to the initial qualification of a significant number of teachers, both new entrants to the teaching field and experienced yet formally unqualified teachers. Learning culture is a process of acquiring information, interpreting it to the extent that its meaning is fully understood and, later, transforming the information into knowledge (Skerlavaj, Stemberger, Skrinjar, & Dimovski, 2007). If teachers are to meet the demands of society in the twenty-first century, they must unlearn old skills and learn new ones. Professional development is a key strategy available to schools and school systems for improving teaching quality (Wei, Darling-Hammond, & Adamson, 2010).

We are living in a school economy in which everyone seeks one form of training or another in order to improve his or her skills and employment prospects (McFarlane, 2011). For virtually all employees, the future consists of uncertainties and anxieties and requires the ability to cope with the unpredictable nature of the world of work (Brown & Scase, 1997).

In the next sections, we discuss the historical background of teacher development in South Africa, and teachers' professional development through ODL in view of the advent of the ever-changing and new learning culture pervading the society. We have done his through the lenses of Senge's concepts of 'learning cultures' and 'learning organisations'. Both terms are used interchangeably in this chapter.

Historical background of teacher development in South Africa

All educational systems are unique (Behr, 1988), and South Africa is no exception. When governors in Cape Town thwarted the initial concept of 'importing' teachers from Holland, De Mist (a Cape Town governor), introduced the establishment of training institutions for elementary (primary) schools. According to Behr (1988, p. 153), of the first cohort of 350 students trained between 1842 and 1859, only 12 were trained as teachers, "but not one of them entered the teaching profession". It is not surprising that, today, South Africa experiences a reluctance from learners preparing for post-school vocation (matriculants) to join the teaching profession. Green, Parker, Deacon and Hall (2011) highlighted a very bleak picture regarding the numbers of Foundation Phase (primary school teachers) student teachers enrolled at various universities in the country. In 2001, there were 13,000 students enrolled in teacher education programmes across the country. In 2007, there were 33,546 student teachers enrolled for different teacher training programmes. This constitutes 18 to 25 per cent of all new teachers per year. South Africa will soon need to respond to the effect AIDS has had on the teaching corps. It emerged that around 30,000 new teachers were needed by 2011 (Welch, 2002).

The pupil-teacher system, which was regarded as a cheap form of teaching, was introduced in the nineteenth century, with an expectation that pupils would be mentored and supervised to offer limited teaching services. Teacher certificates were a requirement in the later years. The training of non-white teachers started in 1817, when missionaries taught a Namaqua boy to read and write. The training of women teachers started much later, in 1894. Unfortunately, it coincided with the Anglo-Boer war, which brought this training to an end. Later, teacher education became theoretical and reflective (Behr, 1988). The financing of education was unequal and problematic. There was an expectation that South African citizens had to share teacher resources to teach subjects that were scarce (Behr, 1988). Communities had to fund their own education facilities from their own pockets, if costs exceeded the norm.

South Africa's racial division under apartheid and the preferential training of white teachers are known facts (Sayed, in Chisholm 2004). The racial geography determined the physical location of teacher training institutions, which placed the training of black teachers under severe strain (Sayed, in Chisholm, 2004). In 1960, South Africa adopted a homeland policy that separated teacher-training programmes even more, denying them 'independence' over taking control of the quality of their training programmes.

With the end of apartheid, a White Paper for Education was published aiming at introducing South Africa into a globalised environment (Adler & Reed, 2002). This resulted in the introduction of Curriculum 2005 (C2005) for Grades 1 to 9 in 1996 and 1997 (Nakabugo & Sieborger, 2001). Curriculum 2005, which has undergone some changes since being issued, clearly shows that teachers needed a lot of support to master the new approach to teaching. This was a nightmare not only for teachers, who had just emerged from the apartheid approach or 'old' system of teaching and learning, but also for departmental officials and subject advisors. Under the previous apartheid system, rote learning and teacher-centred approaches to teaching and learning dominated. This was in stark contrast to the 'new' learner-centred approach to teaching. It was critical that there was a shift from low-order to high-order knowledge acquisition. That meant there was a need for in-service training programmes, some of which were handled through distance learning (Adler & Reed, 2002). Teachers needed to embrace the new educational vision of critical thinking in South Africa. At this stage, teachers had to be trained and developed in this new learner-centred approach of teaching and learning. A paradigm shift was, to a large extent, an imminent necessity, particularly on the part of teachers enrolled through distance learning. Part of the changes experienced in the country's educational landscape was the closing down of teacher education colleges, leaving teacher training to institutions of higher learning. Religious colleges such as Lovedale, Zonneblom, Adam's College and St Peter's were closed down. The complexities of this learner-centred approach highlighted the essence of focusing on the broad aims of transforming institutions of higher learning in South Africa. Thus, new qualifications, new curricula and new policies were introduced (Adler & Reed, 2002).

Towards this end, the Council on Higher Education in South Africa (Council on Higher Education, 2007) developed the national policy framework for teacher education and development. Its aim is to ensure that:

- teachers are properly equipped to undertake their essential and demanding tasks;
- teachers are able to continually enhance their professional competence and performance appropriately; and
- there is a community of competent teachers dedicated to providing education of high quality, with high levels of performance and ethical and professional standards of conduct.

The Council considers teacher education as comprising two complementary sub-systems: the initial professional education of teachers and continuing professional teacher development.

Nonetheless, some of the challenges confronting teacher education in South Africa include: disparity between teacher demand and supply; quality of teachers; inadequate funding and inadequate resources for continuous professional development; and teachers teaching out of their areas of specialisation (Onwu & Sehoole, 2011). Efforts are being made to alleviate these challenges, and the changes in the philosophical approach of education no longer being teacher-centred and instead learner-centred in South Africa has meant a new conception of the role and identity of the teacher that requires continuing professional development (Onwu & Sehoole, 2011; Welch & Gultig, 2002). When learning programmes and materials are being developed, learners should be put first, with the aim of building on the knowledge and experiences they already have (Brodie, Lelliot, & Davies, 2002). These challenges are prevalent in African countries.

Teacher professional development through open distance learning

Open distance learning, both in developed and developing countries, has become a tool for human capital development using continuing professional teacher development (Pitsoe & Maila, 2012).

Professional development among teachers

According to the *Glossary of Education Reform* (2013), the term 'professional development' may be used in reference to a wide variety of specialised training, formal education or advanced professional learning intended to help administrators, teachers and other educators improve their professional knowledge. Evidence shows that professional development has an impact on teachers' beliefs and behaviours, which invariably affects students' performance (Villegas-Reimers, 2003). Teacher professional development includes workshops, short courses, mentoring, professional reading and classroom visits (Taylor, Yates, Meyer, & Kinsella, 2011). Classroom visits are meant to improve classroom practices, appraise teachers' practices, provide them with feedback and assure the quality of the work done in the classrooms.

Research among teachers has consistently shown that the top three topics for further professional development are the content of the subject taught and student discipline and management, teaching students with special needs and the use of technology in instruction (Coe, Aloisi, Higgins, & Major, 2014; Department of Education, 2008; Wei et al., 2010). Teachers need competence in the subjects they teach, for example mathematics. With the abolishment of corporal punishment, teachers also require new ways of dealing with learner discipline. Learners with special needs are now often included in the mainstream teaching environment, which may prove challenging for a teacher who has not been trained to teach such a learner.

Teachers' needs and preferences vary across school levels and contexts, and teacher development is linked to the quality of education teachers have to provide; therefore, teachers need to attend workshops that are often conducted by district officials as experts. They could also attend short courses provided by non-governmental organisations. Teachers need skills, knowledge, competencies and "to develop them continuously" (Scheerens, 2010, p. 12). With the above in mind, mentoring is another important aspect for developing teachers' skills. Though there is no singular definition for the term 'mentoring', most definitions suggest a hierarchical relationship in which the mentor is more experienced than the mentee, or the mentor has or can provide knowledge and skills that the mentee wants or needs (Ambrosetti & Dekkers, 2010). Mentoring provides valuable professional development for both new and veteran teachers (Holloway, 2001). Teachers are therefore regarded as lifelong learners. In addition to this, programmes that develop teachers must be coherently organised to enhance quality. In order for teachers to extend their borders of knowledge, they need to commit themselves to reflective practice by conducting research and gaining more knowledge through systematic engagement in continuous professional development (Scheerens, 2010). When a reflective practitioner's cognitive ability is developed, external support is necessary (Ling, 2003). Teachers have to learn to interact with their peers by exchanging ideas.

However, effective professional learning – which enables teachers to work regularly together to improve their practice and implement strategies to meet the needs of their students – must be a key ingredient in any effort to bolster student achievement (Wei et al., 2010). Though a lot has been achieved in South Africa since the advent of democracy, such as the introduction of programmes such as the Advanced Certificate in Education (ACE), much more remains to be done in the field of technology (Antonie, 2010). Antonie suggests that years, perhaps decades, of concerted and sustained effort will be required to confront the numerous challenges facing teacher education and development. The common-sense notion that has been affirmed by research is that professional development that is short, episodic and disconnected from practice has little impact, and well-designed professional development can improve teaching practice and student achievement (Wei, Darling-Hammond, Andree, Richardson, & Orphanos, 2009). Therefore according to

Wei et al. (2009), in order for professional development to be of "high quality", it ought to be focused on specific curriculum content, and on the pedagogies needed to teach that content effectively. South Africa has experienced challenges in the journey of teacher development. Welch (2002) has identified some of the challenges as follows: the supply and demand of qualified teachers; low numbers of young people entering the teaching profession; policy changes that have made it difficult for institutions of higher learning to adapt easily; and general concerns about the quality of trained teachers.

In contrast, the status of continuous professional development in European countries and regions differs from what happens in the South African context. In countries such as Luxembourg, Poland, Portugal, Slovenia and Spain (Scheerens, 2010), continuous professional development is optional, but career advancement and salary increases are based upon it. Teachers who decide to undertake professional development obtain leave of absence to continue with their studies. South Africa's scenario does not necessarily provide leave of absence from normal duties. A relevant example in South Africa is the ACE qualification, for which training was provided on Saturdays.

Teachers' professional development needs are diverse. Initial teachers, in this context, novices or those with one to three years of experience, will require classroom management strategies, whereas a teacher with more than ten years of teaching expertise will have to learn new concepts and theories about teaching and learning (Scheerens, 2010). There is also a difference in need based on whether a teacher comes from a rural or urban area (Scheerens, 2010). According to Scheerens, for instance, teachers from urban areas have a greater need to increase their knowledge with computer-assisted instruction using multimedia, which are more prevalent in their context than in the rural areas (Scheerens, 2010). Research conducted among science teachers in South Africa (Johnson, Hodges, & Monk, 2010) revealed that the teachers' work environment determines the teaching strategies needed.

Open distance learning to the rescue

Open distance learning appears to be the only option for adults worldwide to further their education so as to improve professionally. According to Jakobs-dottir, Mckeown and Hoven (2010), students are increasingly enrolling in ODL programmes, not just to overcome needs (or distance), but for the convenience – to fit studying in with their work, family or lifestyle commitments. In ODL, key aspects of education, such as access and multiple modes, are introduced. ODL makes it possible for teachers to gain access to education opportunities, with the aim of reskilling. More and more people are incorporating technology into their learning. As a result, an increasing number of institutions are transforming in this regard. There are a number of commonly used terms for ODL. Some of these are: adult education, independent study, learner-centred education and technology-based and mediated education. The essence of the above definition centres on the accessibility of learning. Though there is no single definition of the term, most definitions pay attention to the following characteristics: the separation of teachers and learners; institutional accreditation; the use of mixed-media courseware; two-way communication; the possibility of face-to-face meetings from tutorials; and the use of industrialised processes (Commonwealth of Learning, 2000).

Examples abound of countries all over the world (India, Mongolia, China, South Africa and Nigeria) that have used ODL to provide a route to initial qualifications for significant numbers of teachers, both new entrants to teaching and experienced unqualified teachers; to raise the skills, deepen the understanding and extend the knowledge of teachers; to empower teachers to understand and cope with programmes of curriculum reform that aim to change either the content or the process of education; and for teachers' career development (UNESCO, 2001). In South Africa, one of the ways of meeting the massive demand for training un- and under-qualified teachers, particularly at the intermediate and senior phases, has been the use of distance education schemes (Onwu & Sehoole, 2011).

Two main factors have led to an explosion of interest in distance learning: the growing need for continual skills upgrading and retraining and the technological advances that have made it possible to teach more and more subjects at a distance (UNESCO, 2002). Thus, ODL became a new way in which teachers could play 'catch up' with some of the developments in the transformed education system. Teachers enrolled for various qualifications with institutions of higher learning, with the intention of developing knowledge in their teaching specialties. The downside to this is that teachers experienced a need to improve their qualifications by acquiring diplomas and certificates, sometimes at the expense of learner performance (Adler & Reed, 2002).

The advantages of ODL are economic in nature. One of the advantages is that school buildings are not required, as it is virtual. It is always possible for teachers of students in ODL to accommodate as many students as necessary, including numbers that would exceed what a normal classroom could accommodate. Another advantage, argues Perraton (2000), is that, due to ODL's flexibility, teachers can study at their own time and in their own spaces. Teachers benefit from these programmes, as they allow them to work and to up-skill themselves at the same time. There are also advantages of access, quality, quantity and resources. Bearing in mind what transpired in South Africa's past, ODL is of great benefit to South African teachers.

What changes are taking place in twenty-first-century education in South Africa?

In view of globalisation, South Africa, like many African countries, has not been spared the changes taking place in twenty-first-century education. In this section, we focus on three key game-changers that are forcing stakeholders to rethink the idea of education and associated terms. These are, first, technology; second, new understandings of knowledge, teaching and learning; and, third, diverse student populations.

Technology

Rapid development in technology has prompted drastic changes in the way colleges and other institutions approach their teaching. The rapid development and ubiquity of ICT is resetting the boundaries of educational possibilities (Bolstad et al., 2012). It is a mode of learning that is difficult to ignore. Bates (2006, p. 93) argues that technological advancement is "learner-centred" and offers "better quality interaction". However, for this approach, Bates observes that there appears to be a continuous "widening gap in access between the rich and the poor" leading to "cultural imperialism". South Africa's marginalised majority of citizens are entangled in a web of poverty, giving them little room to improve their lives. According to Rodriques (2005), technologies have become relevant and accessible, so there is no way teacher development can be left behind. Teachers have to be given an opportunity to develop their technological skills (Rodriques, 2005). According to the Horizon Report (2013),[1] one of the major challenges with regard to professional development in the area of technology is the lack of adequate, on-going professional development for teachers who are required to integrate new technologies into their classrooms yet who are unprepared or unable to understand these new technologies. The second challenge, according to the report, is resistance to change (Horizon Report, 2013). Resistance to technology comes in many forms, but one of the key resistance challenges identified in the report is "comfort with the status quo". According to the researchers, teachers and school leaders often see technological experimentation as being outside the scope of their job descriptions. Regardless of the challenges, educational thinking has, for the most part, moved on from the idea that simply introducing new ICT tools and infrastructure into schools will trigger beneficial and meaningful educational changes (Bolstad et al., 2012).

While most people welcome the use of technology to advance their studies, most times distance students in Africa experience numerous barriers. Distance students need a computer, ICT connectivity and electricity. South Africa's rural masses often suffer from a lack of basic amenities including water, sanitation, electricity and other important infrastructure such as housing. While these barriers cannot be regarded as an excuse for the lack of technological skills, an added advantage is the opportunities created for all those who are prepared to venture into the unknown. Students need to be challenged to develop their professional skills, which is one of the best ways to survive in the twenty-first century.

New understandings about knowledge, teaching and learning

In contrast to the traditional past, where a learner's job was to absorb and assimilate compartmentalised knowledge that is assumed to be stored for later use during the learner's life, twenty-first-century knowledge involves *creating* and *using* new knowledge to solve problems and find solutions to challenges, as they arise and on a 'just-in-time' basis (Bolstad et al., 2012). In the view of Thomas and Brown (2011), the kind of learning that will define the twenty-first century does not take place in a classroom; rather, it is happening everywhere. Thus, Bolstad et al. (2012) advise that disciplinary knowledge should be seen, not as an end in itself, but as a *context* within which students' learning capacity can be developed. This necessitates the compelling changed roles of both teachers and students. Scholars (Bolstad et al., 2012; Thomas & Brown, 2011) who hold this view have asserted that this does not mean the teacher will lose his place, but it is about structuring roles and relationships in ways that draw on the strengths and knowledge of each, in order to best support learning. Scheerens (2010) is aware of the complexity in the environment in which teachers work. Teachers are not only expected to maintain the highest quality of education through knowledge acquisition and skills but they must also develop them continuously.

Diverse student populations

In view of the diverse student populations of the twenty-first century, considering issues of diversity should be an inherent part of course conceptualisation (Villegas & Lucas, 2002). Despite the steadily increasing numbers of culturally and linguistically diverse student populations in schools, not all teacher education programs (TEPs) readily embrace multicultural education or culturally responsive teacher education pedagogy (Gay, 2000). There appears to be reluctance among teacher education institutions to acknowledge the need for culturally competent teachers in the classroom and the responsibility of TEPs to properly prepare these teachers (Kea, Campbell-Whatley, & Richards, 2006). According to the same authors, this must be coupled with a willingness to truly value and celebrate diversity in programming and practices. Presently fuelled by globalisation, the issues of equity, diversity and inclusivity are particularly relevant to South Africa in view of its past. However, Bolstad and colleagues (2012) have advised that diversity needs to be recognised as a strength for a future-oriented learning system, something to be fostered actively, and not seen as a weakness that lowers the system's performance. This is because diversity encompasses *everyone's* variations and differences, including their cultures and backgrounds.

Introducing a new learning culture

One of the main goals in education today in South Africa is to restore the culture of learning and teaching in schools, with the net result of improving examination results in the matriculation (school leaving) examination and the general standard of education (Heystek & Lethoko, 2001). The term 'learning organisation' is a business term that was introduced and popularised by Senge in 1990, and it refers to organisations with a learning culture (Association of Schools of Public Health (ASPH) Foundation, 2012). This implies the organisation has values, systems and practices that support and encourage both individuals and the organisation to increase knowledge, competence and performance levels on an on-going basis (Blackwood, 2014; Senge, 1990). This, according to Blackwood (2014), promotes continuous improvement and supports the achievement of business goals, innovation and the ability to deal with change. Though all organisations have a learning culture, whether consciously or unconsciously created, the real question is whether an organisation has a transformative learning culture that makes it more successful and able to thrive (Britt, 2015). When schools make an effort to improve performance, change becomes inevitable. Teachers ought to embrace this change and become learning communities; they must create a culture of learning at their schools. One way of achieving this goal is to be interconnected, and for their schools to be seen to be 'moving'. Thomas and Brown (2011) have advocated that, in place of seeing culture as an existing, stable entity that changes and evolves over long periods of time, it should rather be seen as one that responds to its surroundings organically; it not only adapts, it also integrates change into its process as one of its environmental variables. Therefore, they note, the new culture of learning actually comprises two elements:

• the ability to learn alone and the motivation to learn from others, which leads to the emergence of new learning; and
• the use of imagination and play, which are the fuel that will sustain learning.

Senge (1990, 2006) identified five interrelated disciplines of a learning culture: systems thinking, personal mastery, mental models, shared vision and team learning. The authors of this chapter have applied these to teachers' professional development.

Systems thinking

According to the ASPH Foundation (2012), the term 'systems thinking' shows the interrelationship between parts as an incentive and as a vehicle to integrate across perceived organisational boundaries. A scientific rule states: "in order to understand any complex system, you break it up into pieces" (Capra, 1985, p. 475). The lack of systems thinking produces a mental model based mostly on what one can physically see, which tends to give a shallow understanding of the way a system works (Harich, 2014). For teachers to be relevant in the twenty-first century, they need, for instance, to develop and imbibe the six characteristics of a systems thinker. According to Rodriguez (2013), these are the need to:

- recognise the existing parts within a system and multiple systems within a larger system interacting and affecting each other;
- recognise all parts must exist in order for the system to run effectively;
- know parts within the system are arranged specifically to carry out their purpose;
- recognise that feedback is the driving factor affecting the system;
- recognise the system for predicting how events will play out; and
- inform one's opportunity to manipulate and intentionally manage the system's outcome.

All of the above needs are relevant to teachers, given the fact that each learner comes from diverse contexts and is influenced by such contexts. Further, according to Rodriguez (2013), for successful teaching and learning to take place, the teacher needs to realise the that there is an interplay between the three systems within teaching: the learning brain, which refers to the system of the learner; the teaching brain, which is the system of the teacher; and the system of teaching–learning interaction. Teachers make use of systems thinking on a day-to-day basis, particularly when explaining complex meanings or aspects to their students. This enhances understanding of the issues at hand. For teachers, it is always best to establish building blocks for learning in such a manner. A recent work by Goleman and Senge (2014) provides educators with a rationale for incorporating three core skill sets in the classroom – understanding the self, the other, and the larger systems within which we operate – and shows why these competencies are needed to help students navigate a fast-paced world of increasing distraction and growing inter-connectedness. Possession of these traits was needed by both teachers and learners.

Personal mastery

Personal mastery is the discipline of continually clarifying and deepening personal vision, focusing energies, patience and a realistic view of the world around us (ASPH Foundation, 2012). "Personal mastery is the capability to grow and learn on a personal level" (Garcia-Morales, Llorens-Montes, & Verdu-Jover, 2007, p. 547). According to Bolstad et al. (2012), people with a high level of personal mastery live in a continual learning mode. It is a life-long discipline that fosters new knowledge and builds acute awareness of personal ignorance, incompetence and areas for growth. For instance, learning in an information age will require continual personal mastery of new skills and competencies as job descriptions expand, change and shift (Costa & Kallick, 1995). A few inherent traits of people with personal mastery are a strong sense of purpose – a calling; an accurate view of current reality and the ability to identify changes quickly; and a strong intellectual curiosity for the new (Bolstad et al., 2012). With regard to all of these, teachers see teaching as a calling, wherein they have to make an effort to be passionate about their work; teachers should regard change as an opportunity to think systematically; and they are expected to be futuristic, strategic and expert planners.

In addition to the above, as teachers move from the continuum of a novice to an expert, there is the need to provide appropriate structures that facilitate novices' ability to learn what they do not know and experts' ability to become the novices' mentors (Costa & Kallick, 1995). Apart from educational attainment, foundational knowledge, skills and practical literacies (e.g., reading, maths, civic, scientific and technology education), broader competencies include critical reading and problem solving, communication and collaboration, creativity and self-sufficiency (Jerald, 2009). A teacher's reading skills need enhancement in order for learners to master the skill as well. We are living in a knowledge society, where personal mastery, described as personal and professional development, plays a major role. Organisational learning and innovation create an enabling environment for people to 'exploit' and 'apply' new knowledge in ways that will increase their performance (Garcia-Morales et al., 2007). South African education is in a constant state of evolution, where efforts are made to enable teachers to 'renew' their knowledge to produce excellence. Teachers are enabled to be at their best. As stated earlier, this role is played significantly well by ODL. In this regard, teachers are expected to link theory with practice by performing expertly in their own workplaces.

Mental models

Mental models are personal, internal representations of external reality that people use to interact with the world around them (Jones, Ross, Lynam, Perez, & Leitch, 2011). According to Jones and colleagues, individuals construct mental models based on their unique life experiences, perceptions and understandings of the world. Mental models are also known as mindsets (Hammonds, 2006) and are used to reason and make decisions; they can also be the basis of individual behaviours (Jones et al., 2011). However, scholars have long warned that mental models are typically incomplete, disorganised, naïve or based on deeply ingrained assumptions or generalisations (Howe, Tolmie, Anderson, & Mackenzie, 1992; Senge, 1990). In addition, holding an inappropriate mental model can lead to ineffective learning, or worse, no learning at all (Jih & Reeves, 1992). According to the ASPH Foundation (2012), organisations need to create a fundamental shift of mindset among their people that will create a stronger focus on adaptive learning and generative learning to continue to expand and build capability.

Though theoretical evidence continues to mount within the fields of psychology and cognitive science that people do, indeed, use mental models to reason and make predictions about the world around them (Jones et al., 2011), there is insubstantial research concerning the use of mental models in teaching and learning (Henderson, Putt, & Coombs, 2002). For instance, teachers' mental models regarding students with learning disabilities, children in poverty, immigrants and from diverse populations need to be challenged (Aguilar, 2015). This is necessary if teachers are to be relevant in the twenty-first century, and it can be addressed through teachers' professional development programmes.

In South Africa, though corporal punishment has been forbidden in schools since 1997, there is ample evidence that some teachers and school principals still find it difficult to do without it (news24, SAHRC).

Shared vision

Senge (2006) believes that the capacity to hold a shared image of the future we seek is a vitally important leadership responsibility and strength, second only to the ability to engage those around us in our vision. The most successful visions are collective – built on the individual visions of employees at all levels of an organisation, which in this case refers to the school. Visions are spread through reinforcing conversations – dialogue. Clarity builds enthusiasm, which leads to commitment, which rubs off on others.

Shared vision is also known as knowledge sharing, and it is beneficial to the entire organisation. Teachers today are faced with diversity in their classrooms (Darling-Hammond, in Runhaar & Sanders, 2015). Vision can be shared if it is linked to diversity. The global world expects teachers to teach for equity, which is what teachers have to learn by being interconnected with the world. With the gap between the rich and the poor in South Africa getting wider, producing teachers who will fit into the scholarship of diversity is a slow process. This will be achieved within the context of transformation. Teachers are expected to participate in discourses that will unveil various ways in which they will engage with the curriculum in order to reflect social cohesion. This role can be played expertly by teachers' participation in robust debates within the teachers' unions, which can be powerful tools in teacher development. For instance, in South Africa, teachers' unions have been encouraged to move from the level of militancy, dating back to the apartheid era, to the level of enhancing teacher professionalism (Heystek & Lethoko, 2001). Steps for achieving the latter include making members aware of different codes of conduct and the organisation of workshops where the aims and goals of education are shared (Heystek & Lethoko, 2011; South African Council of Educators, 2011). In that way, policies have to be relevant to these processes.

Team learning

Team learning is the process of aligning and developing members of a team to achieve the desired results, even when those results are not perceived as achievable. It accumulates individual learning to identify and share critical new learning for organisational advantage. Blackwood (2014) suggests the importance of creating a sustainable learning culture in every organisation.

She suggests that the first thing to embark on is conducting a self-audit, contextually referred to as an "evaluation". This will enable the teacher to identify the gaps for change. Teachers need time for both formal and informal learning, and they need to be allowed to make mistakes by identifying key learnings that can be shared in a team. This is regarded as part of a learning strategy that will, in the process, lead to accountability. One of the best ways of succeeding is to be a life-long learner, which involves having a wide repertoire of cognitive learning strategies, being metacognitive about learning and oneself as a learner, being motivated to learn and being able to manage one's feelings and available resources effectively (De la Harpe & Radloff, 2000). In this way, teachers develop a consistent alignment with the organisational values and behaviour around learning.

Britt (2015) discusses steps that are beneficial to professional development; these include the cultivation of leadership and emotional intelligence, which are among the key 'human skills'. Some of the skills to be learnt are: leadership, self-control, empathy, communication, conflict resolution and cultural competence. Classroom leadership is no longer confined only to the four walls of a building. With traditional classroom leadership behind us, teaching has become innovative with the introduction of technology. The concept of the 'flipped classroom' is used widely, with lessons being recorded online and the teacher's presence in the classroom being facilitative (Kovach, 2014). In that way, teaching and learning may take place anytime, anywhere. Teachers are also expected to resolve conflicts in school without violating learners' human rights. An organisation that respects all people's human rights is one that encourages harmony and the development of an environment conducive for learning and working. Teachers have to communicate with learners in a way that will encourage respect and embrace dignity at all times. Organisations need teachers with a 'growth mindset' who are creative and innovative, and who are prepared to work in teams. Such teachers will be motivated and willing to take risks. With mindsets of this nature, teachers are empowered to keep pace with technological developments.

De Kadt (2010) has found a lack of regulation surrounding teacher professional development disturbing. Despite the time teachers dedicate to educating their students, many fear there are too few quality training opportunities for staff. There are also very few rules dictating how much time schools should dedicate to developing staff members' skills (De Kadt, 2010). However, regardless of where training is taking place, career development programmes are only effective if they are research-based and easy for teachers to apply in their classroom (De Kadt, 2010). In addition to this, teacher-training institutions also need to have inclusive learning programmes that enable teachers to identify learners with special needs at the early stages of their learning.

In New Zealand, at least four strategies have been used to support educational ICT developments: providing enabling tools and infrastructure; providing inspiring ideas and opportunities to connect ideas; enhancing capability;

and supporting innovation (Bolstad et al., 2012). In South Africa, schools are divided into clusters to bolster teacher knowledge and develop the computer and teaching skills of those who will benefit from them. These clusters assist teachers to work collaboratively with their peers from neighbouring schools on matters affecting learner performance. Teachers are able to prepare common test papers and compare performance. In this way, teachers are able to share expert knowledge by working in teams. Even though teachers need strong pedagogical knowledge, they also need to be able to collaborate with other people who can provide specific kinds of expertise, knowledge or access to learning opportunities in community contexts (Bolstad et al., 2012).

Conclusion

The level of the development of a country's teaching workforce is akin to its educational level. Many countries have found the ODL delivery mode to be a useful tool for developing and supporting teachers, due to its ability to allow teachers to stay on the job while being supported and pursuing professional development. Despite the value of ODL, it is only recently that South Africa has started reaping its benefits, due to its dismal national history, which led to a gravely low quality of teachers among underprivileged groups. South Africa, therefore, needs to retrain its teaching workforce to meet the demands of the twenty-first century. These include emerging technology, new understandings about knowledge, teaching and learning and diverse student populations. In this chapter, we have applied Senge's five interrelated disciplines of a learning organisation to the professional development of teachers. Though a business term, we believe the field of teaching needs a dynamic approach that will encourage continuous improvement in order to deal with the ever-evolving changes in the twenty-first century. South Africa has not been left behind in these changes, and the ODL delivery mode affords the country the opportunity to enhance its teachers' professional development.

Note

1 The Horizon 2013 Report was put together by the New Media Consortium – a professional learning forum for educators, by educators – and EDUCAUSE Learning Initiative – a community of higher education institutions and organisations committed to the advancement of learning through the innovative application of technology.

References

Adler, J., & Reed, Y. (2002). (Eds). *Challenges of teacher development: An investigation of take-up in South Africa*. Pretoria: Van Schaik Publishers.

Aguilar, E. (2015). *Shifting mental models in educators*. www.edutopia.org/blog/shifting-mental-models-educators-elena-aguilar.

Ambrosetti, A., & Dekkers, J. (2010). The interconnectedness of the roles of mentors and mentees in pre-service teacher education mentoring relationships. *Australian Journal of Teacher Education, 35*(6). http://dx.doi.org/10.14221/ajte.2010v35n6.3.

Antonie, F. (2010). Educating the educators: Challenges facing teacher education and development in South Africa. *Focus, 59*, November 2010, 38–43.

Association of Schools of Public Health (ASPH) Foundation. (2012). *Culture of learning organizations.* Retrieved from www.ashpfoundation.org/…/Transformational Change11021211.html.

Bates, A. W. (2006). The impact of technological change on open and distance learning. *Distance Education, 18*(1), 93–109. doi: 10.1080/0158791970180108.

Behr, A. L. (1988). *Education in South Africa: Origins, issues and trends: 1652–1988.* Pretoria: Academia.

Blackwood, K. (2014). *Benefits of creating an organizational learning culture.* www.biv.com/article/2014/9/benefits-creating-organizational-learning-culture/.

Bolstad, R., Gilbert, J., McDowall, S., Bull, A., Boyd. S., & Hipkins, R. (2012). *Supporting future-oriented learning and teaching: A New Zealand perspective.* Retrieved from www.educationcounts.govt.nz/publications/schooling/109306.

Booyse, J. J., le Roux, C. S., Seroto, J., & Wohuter, C. C. (2011). *A history of schooling in South Africa: Method and context.* Pretoria: Van Schaik Publishers.

Britt, A. (2015). *6 steps to creating a learning culture – and why you should.* Retrieved from www.lynda.com/articles/6-steps-to-learnng-culture.

Brodie, K., Lelliot, A., & Davies, H. (2002). Forms and substance in learner-centred teaching: Teachers' take-up from an in-service programme in South Africa. *Teaching and Teacher Education, 18*, 541–559.

Brown, P., & Scase, R. (1997). Universities and employers: Rhetoric and reality. In Smith, A., & Webster, F. (Eds), *The postmodern university: Contested visions of higher education in society.* Buckingham: SRHE and Open University Press.

Capra, F. (1985). Criteria of systems thinking. *Futures,* October, 475–478.

Chisholm, L. (Ed.) (2004). *Changing class: Education and social change in post-apartheid South Africa.* Cape Town: HSRC Press.

Coe, R., Aloisi, C., Higgins, S., & Major, L. E. (2014). *What makes great teaching?* Retrieved from www.suttontrust.com/wp-content/uploads/2015/01/DEVELOPING_TEACHERS-FINAL.pdf.

Commonwealth of Learning. (2000). *An introduction to open and distance learning.* Retrieved from www.col.org/sitecollectiondocuments/odlintro.pdf.

Costa, A., and B. Kallick. (1995). *Assessment in the learning organization.* Alexandria, VA: ASCD.

Council on Higher Education. (2007). *The national policy framework for teacher education and development in South Africa.* Retrieved from www.che.ac.za.

De Kadt, D. (2010). Why human capital matters. *The Journal of the Helen Suzman Foundation, 59*, 3–9.

De La Harpe, B., & Radloff, A. (2000). Informed teachers and learners: The importance of assessing the characteristics needed for lifelong learning. *Studies in Continuing Education, 22*(2), 169–182.

Department of Education. (2008). *The design of the continuing professional teacher development (CPTD) system.* Retrieved from www.sace.org.za/upload/files/CPTD%20Design%20doc%20draft%20version%2013A%201006081.pdf.

Evans, L. (2002). What is teacher development? *Oxford Review of Education, 28*(1), 123–137.

Garcia-Morales, V. J., Llorens-Montes, F. J., & Verdu-Jover, A. J. (2007). *Influence of personal mastery on organizational performance through organizational learning and innovation in large firms and SMEs.* Retrieved from www.elsevier.com/locate/technovation.

Gay, G. (2000). *Culturally responsive teaching: Theory, research, and practice.* New York: Teachers' College Press.

Glossary of Education Reform (2013). *The glossary of education.* Retrieved from edglossary.org/professional-development/.

Goleman, D., & Senge, P. (2014). *The triple focus: A new approach to education.* Florence, MA: More than Sound.

Green, W., Parker, D., Deacon, R., & Hall, G. (2011). Foundation phase teacher provision by public higher education institutions in South Africa. *South African Journal of Childhood Education, 1,* 109–122.

Hammonds, B. (2006). *What's your 'mental model' about teaching?* Retrieved from http://leading-learning.blogspot.com/2006/05/whats-your-mental-model-about-teaching.html.

Harich, J. (2014). *Systems thinking.* Retrieved from www.thwink.org/sustain/glossary/SystemsThinking.htm.

Henderson, L., Putt, I., & Coombs, G. (2002). *Mental models of teaching and learning with the www.* Retrieved from www.ascilite.org/conferences/auckland02/proceedings/papers/063.pdf.

Heystek, J., & Lethoko, M. (2001). The contribution of teacher unions in the restoration of teacher professionalism and the culture of learning and teaching. *South African Journal of Education, 21*(4), 222–228.

Holloway, J. H. (2001). The benefits of mentoring. *Educational Leadership, 58*(8).

Howe, C., Tolmie, A., Anderson, A., & Mackenzie, M. (1992). Conceptual knowledge in physics: The role of group interaction in computer-supported teaching. *Learning and Instruction, 2,* 161–183.

Jerald, C. D. (2009). *Defining a 21st century education.* Retrieved from www.cfsd16.org/public/_century/pdf/Defininga21stCenturyEducation_Jerald_2009.pdf.

Jih, H., & Reeves, T. (1992). Mental models: A research focus for interactive learning systems. *Educational Technology Research & Development, 40,* 39–53.

Johnson, S., Hodges, M., & Monk, M. (2010). Teacher development and change in South Africa: A critique of the appropriateness of transfer of northern/western practice. *Compare: A Journal of Comparative and International Education, 30*(2), 179–192.

Jakobsdottir, S., Mckeown L., & Hoven, D. (2010). Using the new information and communication technologies for the continuing professional development of teachers through open and distance learning. *NMC Horizon Report: 2013 K-12 Edition.* nmc.org/publications/2013-horizon-report-k12.

Jones, N. A., Ross, H., Lynam, T., Perez, P., & Leitch, A. (2011). Mental models: An interdisciplinary synthesis of theory and methods. *Ecology and Society, 16*(1), 46. www.ecologyandsociety.org/vol. 16/iss1/art46/.

Kea, C., Campbell-Whatley, G. D., & Richards, H. V. (2006). *Becoming culturally responsive educators: Rethinking teacher pedagogy.* National Center for Culturally Responsive Educational Systems. Arizona US: Arizona State University. www.nccrest.org/Briefs/Teacher_Ed_Brief.pdf.

Kovach, J. V. (2014). Leadership in the "classroom". *The Journal for Quality and Participation, 37*(1), 39–40.

Ling, L. Y. (2003). Underpinnings of teachers' professional development: A new conceptualization of field experience. *Asia Pacific Education Review, 4*(1), 11–18.

Malaysian Qualifications Agency. (2010). *Guidelines to good practices: Open and Distance Learning.* Retrieved from. www.mqa.gov.my/garispanduan/GGP%20ODL.pdf.

McFarlane, D. A. (2011). The leadership roles of distance learning administrators (DLAs) in increasing educational value and quality perceptions. *Online Journal of Distance Learning Administration,* IV (I). www.westga.edu/~distance/ojdla/spring141/McFarlane141.html.

Nakabugo, M. G., & Sieborger, R. (2001). Curriculum reform and teaching in South Africa: Making a paradigm shift. *International Journal of Educational Development, 21*(1), 53–68.

News24. (2014). Corporal punishment violates children's rights – SAHRC. 29 May 2014. Retrieved from www.news24.com/Archives/City-Press/Corporal-punishment-violates-childrens-rights-SAHRC-20150429.

Onwu, G. O. M., & Sehoole, C. T. (2011). *Why teachers matter: Policy issues in the professional development of teachers in South Africa.* Retrieved from http://aadcice.hiro shima-u.ac.jp/e/publications/sosho4_2-10.pdf.

Organization for Economic Cooperation and Development (OECD). (2009). *Creating effective teaching and learning environments: First results from TALIS.* Retrieved from www.oecd.org/berlin/43541636.pdf.

Perraton, H. (2000). *Open and distance learning in the developing world.* London: Routledge.

Pitsoe, V. J., & Maila, M. W. (2012). Rethinking continuing professional teacher development within the open distance learning framework. *International Journal of Technology and Inclusive Education (IJTIE), 1*(1). Retrieved from www.infonomics-society.org/IJTIE/Rethinking%20Continuing%20Professional%20Teacher%20Development%20within%20the%20Open%20Distance%20Learning%20framework.pdf.

Quattlebaum, S. (2012). *Why professional development for teachers is critical.* Retrieved from http://evolllution.com/opinions/why-professional-development-for-teachers-is-critical/.

Ravhudzulo, A. (2003). "Nobody is listening": The attitudes of teachers towards professional development by distance. *Progressio, 25*(1), 76–85.

Rodriguez, V. (2013). The potential of systems thinking in teacher reform as theorized for the teaching brain framework. *Mind, Brain and Education, 7*(2), 77–85.

Rodriques, S. (Ed.). (2005). *International perspectives on teacher professional development: Changes influenced by politics, pedagogy and innovation.* New York: Nova Science Publishers.

Runhaar, P., & Sanders, K. (2015). Promoting teachers' knowledge sharing. The fostering roles of occupational self-efficacy and human resources management. *Educational Management Administration & Leadership* (1–20). Sage.

Scheerens, J. (Ed.) (2010). *Teachers' professional development. Europe in international comparison. An analysis of teachers' professional development based on the OECD's teaching and learning international survey (TALIS).* A secondary analysis based on the TALIS dataset. European Union.

Senge, P. (1990). *The fifth discipline: The art and practice of the learning organization.* New York: Doubleday/Currency.

Senge, P. M. (2006). *The fifth discipline: The art and practice of the learning organization* (2nd Ed.). London: Random House.

Skerlavaj, M., Stemberger, M. J., Skrinjar, R., & Dimovski, V. (2007). Organizational learning culture – the missing link between business change and organizational performance. *International Journal of Production Economics, 106,* 346–367.

South African Council of Educators. (2011). *About professional development and research.* Retrieved from www.sace.org.za/Professional_Development/jit_default_24.Profes sional_Development.html.

Taylor, M., Yates, A., Meyer, L. H., & Kinsella, P. (2011). Teacher professional leadership in support of teacher professional development. *Teaching and Teacher Education, 27,* 85–94.

The Horizon Report (2013). K-12 Edition. Retrieved from nmc.org/publications/2013-horizon-report-k12.

Thomas, D., & Brown, J. S. (2011). *A new culture of learning: Cultivating the imagination for a world of constant change.* Lexington, KY: CreateSpace?

UNESCO. (2001). *Teacher education through distance learning: Technology, curriculum, evaluation, cost.* Paris: UNESCO.

UNESCO. (2002). *Open and distance learning: Trends, policy and strategy considerations.* Paris: UNESCO. http://unesdoc.unesco.org/images/0012/001284/128463e.pdf.

Villegas, A. M., & Lucas, T. (2002). *Educating culturally responsive teachers.* Albany, NY: State University of New York Press.

Villegas-Reimers, E. (2003). *Teacher professional development: An international review of the literature.* Retrieved from www.unesco.org/iep.

Wei, R. C., Darling-Hammond, L., & Adamson, F. (2010). *Professional development in the United States: Trends and challenges.* Dallas, TX: National Staff Development Council.

Wei, R. C., Darling-Hammond, L., Andree, A., Richardson, N., & Orphanos, S. (2009). *Professional learning in the learning profession: A status report on teacher development in the United States and abroad.* Dallas, TX: National Staff Development Council.

Welch, T. (2002). Teacher education in South Africa before, during and after apartheid: An overview. In Adler, J., & Reed, Y. (Eds), *Challenges of teacher development: An investigation of take-up in South Africa.* Pretoria: Van Schaik.

Welch, T., & Gultig, J. (2002). *Becoming competent: Initiatives for the improvement of teacher education in South Africa 1995 to 2002.* Paper presented at Pan-Commonwealth Conference, Durban July. Retrieved from http://citeseerx.ist.psu.edu/viewdoc/download?doi=10.1.1.458.9640&rep=rep1&type=pdf.

Wolhuter, C. C. (2006). Teacher training in South Africa: Past, present and future [online]. *Education Research and Perspectives, 33*(2), 124–139. Retrieved from: http://search.informit.com.au/documentSummary;dn=200703101;res=IELAPA ISSN: 0311-2543.

3 Cultural strategy for developing a knowledge-based economy in the Global South

The case of Tanzanian higher education

George L. Kahangwa

Introduction

For several decades, multilateral organisations and international institutions, such as the Organisation for Economic Cooperation and Development (OECD) and the World Bank (WB), have been urging nations to develop knowledge-based economies (KBEs), one key element of which is reforming higher education policies and practices (OECD, 1996, 2007; World Bank, 2002, 2008). The urge to develop KBEs is an international and global phenomenon that has occurred in various cultures. Scholars (e.g. Fairclough, 2001; Jessop, 2004; St George, 2006) have argued that, to create KBEs, international organisations and institutions use a variety of strategies, including a *cultural strategy* involving discourse and/or semiosis. KBEs also require the development and use of technology to be a part of the culture in a country (Munro, 2000), and it promotes ideologies both implicitly and explicitly (St George, 2006). KBE development further entails mobility of individuals between countries (Isaakyan & Triandafyllidou, 2013). All these elements have the potential to contribute to the relevance and cultural sustainability of higher education reforms in the Global South (Soini & Birkeland, 2014).

This chapter draws from the key findings of a doctoral dissertation (Kahangwa, 2013), focusing on cultural strategies within KBEs. It employs the critical cultural political economy of education (CCPEE) theoretical framework (Robertson, 2009) to analyse the cultural strategies underlying the development of the dominant models of KBEs through higher education reforms. The analysis focuses on discourse, technology, ideology and mobility. The use of cultural strategies to construct KBE is examined in the context of Tanzanian higher education. The core question addressed here is which (or whose) cultural strategy is applied in efforts to build KBEs. The aim is to identify key elements and propose an alternative model that is more relevant to Tanzania and other countries in the Global South.

Predominant models for KBE development

The urge to develop KBE has led to the formulation of different models, and several multilateral and international organisations have designed their own models or frameworks. The most widely used is the WB (2008) model, which has four pillars. The first pillar is an economic incentive and institutional regime capable of supporting the efficient generation of new knowledge and using existing knowledge. The second pillar is a dynamic Information and Communication Technology (ICT) infrastructure that can facilitate effective communication, dissemination and processing of information. The third pillar is a sound education system that produces highly educated and skilled human capital that can create, share and utilise knowledge (World Bank, 2008). The fourth pillar is an efficient innovation system composed of firms, research centres, universities, think tanks, consultants and other organisations that can tap into knowledge, assimilate and adapt it to local needs and create new technology (Utz, 2006).

The OECD's KBE model entails benefitting from ICT, harnessing the potential for innovation and technology diffusion, enhancing human capital and realising its potential, evaluating economic situations and fostering firm creation and entrepreneurship (OECD, 1996). Another KBE model is that used by the Australian Bureau of Statistics (ABS, 2002), which comprises three core dimensions: innovation and entrepreneurship, human capital and ICT. The innovation and entrepreneurship dimension includes research and knowledge creation, knowledge networks and flows, innovation, entrepreneurial activity and support for innovation. The human capital dimension includes the stock and flow of skilled people, investment in human capital, lifelong learning and access to education and training. The ICT dimension entails infrastructure and access to internet connection and ICT demand and supply. The model also has two supporting dimensions: context and economic and social impact (Trewin, 2002). The context dimension involves business environments and effectively functioning markets, which are preconditions for successful KBEs (Trewin, 2002). The economic and social impact dimension is based on the assumption that a KBE has to impact the economy and society. The economic and social impact dimension includes gross domestic product (GDP) per capita, labour productivity, employees' earnings and unemployment rates.

The Asia–Pacific Economic Co-operation (APEC) also has a model. It addresses business environments, innovation systems, human resource development and ICT infrastructure (APEC, 2000).

In terms of structure, the WB, OECD and ABS models all share common components: innovation, ICT and human resources. The ABS (2002) model's business environment context dimension is similar to the economic and incentive regime mentioned in the WB model. The business environment dimension appears also in the APEC (2000) model. Economic and social issues are common to both the OECD and ABS models. However, unlike the other models, the ABS model of KBE addresses how knowledge impacts the economy and society. Additionally, the models use significantly different indicators. For instance, as Daugeliene (2004) explains, the four pillars in the WB model are indicators of the performance of KBEs, while the OECD model outlines what has to be done to develop a KBE. The next section traces the cultural strategies advocated by these KBE models.

Elements of a cultural strategy for KBE development

One element of a cultural strategy in the models for KBE development is the use of language and discourse. Proponents of KBE use a specific language that not only changes how academics in higher education institutions think and act but also requires them to make a choice about how to think and act. For instance, when the WB (2002) model argues that KBE enables countries to be competitive, it is suggesting that the culture developed amongst individuals, organisations and countries is competitive rather than cooperative, thus implying that countries may not attain economic prosperity if they cooperate. In the Global South, it is not appropriate to use a cultural strategy that focuses on competitiveness at the expense of cooperation, as efforts to attain economic prosperity require cooperation among peoples and countries, since the economies of the weak can be strengthened by working together. Other discourses regarding KBE development include education as a product or social service, knowledge as a commodity or public good, digital divides (which create more social differences) and e-learning (which creates another avenue for the provision of education) (see Fairclough, 2005; Jessop, 2004). Such discourses pose a challenge in the Global South; they require people either to change the conventional ways of thinking about and providing education or to embrace both the conventional and modern KBE-related educational paradigms.

Another element of a cultural strategy for KBE construction is an emphasis on technology. KBE requires the development and use of technology (Munro, 2000), an aspect of material culture (Smith, 2002), because ICT is crucial for economic prosperity. The kind of technology that is advocated for in the WB model, ICT, is a high form of technology that entails the use of complex gadgets predominantly produced by high- and middle-income countries. While it is important for countries in the Global South to begin to develop and use ICT, it is difficult to define a focus. To perform well as a KBE, high levels of consumption and ICT use are required (World Bank, 2002), but the WB model of KBE does not encourage countries in the Global South to produce their own ICT. Further, the culture of using ICT to develop a KBE favours the economy of a producer country more than that of a non-producer country, as producer countries have more citizens with access to ICT (internet, computers, cell phones, etc.). In addition, in the WB model, the technological indicators of KBE include the scope of a country's ICT manpower, pricing and penetration in households, business, government and e-commerce, all of which reflect the efficiency and effectiveness of knowledge and information distribution in the economy. Good scores on these indicators call for improvements in ICT network infrastructures and social networks. Unfortunately, most of these indicators not only are biased towards treating ICT simply as a tool for knowledge/information distribution but also involve costs for consumers.

ICT is an industry with numerous manufactured goods, which, when marketed well, contribute to revenue earning. The indicators in the WB KBE model do not consider this fact. The model could be improved if it included additional indicators that address income earned by producers, such as those involving the production of ICT gadgets in a country and a country's ICT sales in the local and global markets. In other words, if the KBE pillar of ICT was looked at in terms of knowledge production, the following indicators should be considered: ICT hardware and software production and export, the number of data processing jobs in a country, useful information retrieval and the use of telecommunication in sustainable development (Ernberg, 1999). It can be improper to use internal ICT consumption indicators to tell the extent to which an economy is a KBE while ignoring indicators related to internal ICT production. Economically, the indicators of internal consumption are misleading; the right ones are internal production: that is, the extent to which a country produces ICT products internally. Again, what matters is not just the presence of ICT in a country, but also what information is given and communicated and whether the kind of technology used is affordable, efficient and effective.

In the OECD model, ICT is considered crucial for diffusion and distribution of knowledge. Unfortunately, this view is problematic, as it does not consider alternative methods of knowledge distribution. In addition, the model uses how much a country pays for technology as an indicator of KBE development, but does not include international transfers of knowledge through employment and foreign personnel, consulting services, foreign direct investments and intra-firm transfers (OECD, 1996, 2007).

Unlike the previous two models, the ABS model considers ICT in terms of supply and demand (Trewin, 2002). This model is applicable to low-income countries (LICs) because it considers the importance of turning a country into a supplier of ICT products rather than a mere consumer. The APEC model emphasises ICT infrastructure (APEC, 2000).

All four models have weaknesses regarding the way they present technological issues and the indicators of KBE development. For instance, the models have been criticised for privileging Western science and technology. In a review of the WB model, Robertson (2009) noted that KBE is inclined to science and technology disciplines. So are the APEC and OECD models. Such a bias devalues humanities and social science disciplines, which may lead to a dearth of these subjects in higher education.

Ideologies are another part of a cultural strategy for KBE development. They feature in the WB (2008) model, especially in the supportive economic incentives and institutional regimes pillar, which is informed by neo-liberalism. The indicators in this pillar include the influence of globalisation on a country and its economic performance, which show the extent to which a country has a regulatory environment and policies that allow a KBE to flourish. Such policies and regulations include openness to global trade, few restrictions on imports and licensing and intellectual property rights (IPR) protection, which are neo-liberal in nature. Indeed, neo-liberalism has been the most common ideology used to develop KBEs (see Telo, 2002). It involves, for instance, reducing the involvement of the government in the provision of higher education, allowing the market to control education provision and forcing universities to compete among themselves (St George, 2006). This approach is supported by the WB model, which favours the market and individualism as means to construct KBEs. The model also proposes the creation of an institutional regime that supports an open market and an innovation system that allows research fund sources to be diversified by engaging the private sector. According to Olssen and Peters (2005), such trends in higher education have culminated in the replacement of IPR protection with a culture of open intellectual inquiry in universities.

Such ideologies have influenced higher education policies in the Global South, where several countries, including Tanzania, have implemented higher education policies that aim to deregulate the industry and protect IPR. For example, one of Tanzania's policies reads as follows:

> Intellectual property right (IPR) today commands much attention globally than ever before. The knowledge-led economy is based on the protection of intellectual property (IP) products. Intellectual property protection facilitates technology development and transfer within/from outside a nation.
>
> (SUA, 2005, p. 1)

According to this statement, IPR is a key element of KBEs, which is why IPR has to be protected. The statement corresponds with the WB model, which claims that IPR protection indicates how much a country's economy has developed into a KBE. Policies protecting IPR, which are in favour of few restrictions and thus support the neo-liberal model of deregulation and free markets, have been criticised by different scholars because they are seen as a strategy used by high-income capitalist countries to achieve more economic gains by extending their reach across borders (Robertson, 2009). With few restrictions on imports, countries are required to open their internal markets to foreign goods. Thus, goods from powerful economies overwhelm the internal markets of LICs, dominating over local goods. Moreover, critics argue that such policies privilege the power of the market over state regulations and cause poor economic performance, particularly in LICs (Green, Little, Kamat, Oketch, & Vickers, 2007).

Neo-liberalism has contributed to the marketisation and commercialisation of university research, the entrepreneurial nature of universities and academic capitalism (Bok, 2003; Canaan & Shumar, 2008; Kenway, Bullen, & Robb,

2004). In Tanzania, commercialisation is explicitly mentioned in educational policies that support the development of KBE. For example, the national research and development policy states: "This policy emphasizes on innovation and commercialization of research results which are key in bringing about economic growth while at the same time solving societal problems" (MCST, 2010, p. 9). With its neo-liberal outlook, the statement presents a shift from considering research results (knowledge) as a public good to considering them as a private good with commercial value. If countries in the Global South are taking or will continue to take a neo-liberal approach to developing KBEs, they will adopt aspects of Western culture, such as the marketisation of education. However, as much as the Global South might be in need of IPR protection and entrepreneurship in education, it cannot afford to lose its culture of open intellectual inquiry and view of education as a public good.

Another ideological approach to the construction of KBEs is neo-corporatism, which basically allows negotiations between the public, the private sector and labour unions (Jessop, 2004). Thus, the state cooperates with employers and employees. Under this ideological approach, the state plays a mediating role in integrating the interests of various powerful groups, particularly those representing labour and capital. The government also intervenes in economies in order to moderate market forces and protect social priorities. In this way, neo-corporatism allows social partnership, consensus decision making and constructive engagement or full involvement of 'stakeholders', including workers and other interest groups at the national, industrial and enterprise levels. Neo-corporatism is further characterised by relatively high taxation rates, highly developed national infrastructures and considerable public expenditure on social services. Finland, which is said to have set a good example in developing KBE, has used a neo-corporatism approach to KBE construction (Jessop, 2004). Finland also follows a welfare state politico-economic framework for constructing KBE, as opposed to an American Silicon Valley model, which is neo-liberal oriented (Castells & Himanen, 2002). Thus, Finland's approach corresponds with the approach adopted by the European Union (EU) at its Lisbon summit in 2000, when it "aimed to become a leading KBE in the world whilst protecting the European social model and developing modes of meta-governance based on social partnership rather than pure market forces" (Telo, 2002). Such an approach suggests that KBE can be constructed without deregulating markets (as proposed in the WB model of KBE and the US's approach). In the Global South, this ideological approach has not been adopted by countries attempting to develop KBEs.

A third ideological approach to KBE construction is neo-statism (Jessop, 2004), which has been adopted by countries such as Singapore (Boyd & Ngo, 2005). In this approach, the national state strategically plans and directs the expansion of higher education (St George, 2006). The state that follows neo-statism sponsors the economic system while allowing the economy to conform to the market's rules. The state also organises knowledge production and utilisation networks and facilitates collective appropriation and redistribution of the benefits of such networks. In doing so, it manages tensions between the intellectual commons and intellectual property and redesigns the relationship between economic and extra-economic issues related to knowledge (St George, 2006).

Fourth, KBEs can be constructed in a neo-communitarian way (Jessop, 2004). This ideology allows the operation of non-profit self-governing organisations working for public interests. These civil societies are included in a third sector, with the other two sectors being state-led and market-led (Fyfe, 2005). The use of this approach to construct KBE can allow the third sector to provide higher education in a non-profit making manner.

KBE development entails the cultural component of mobility, which includes intercultural education (Bennett, 2009). Mobility has predominantly involved the movement of students and teachers from the Global South to the Global North or Europe (Kotsi & Agiomirgianakis, 2013). This trend has to be reversed if the Global South is to develop KBE at a pace equivalent to that of the Global North. One such effort is the newly introduced Intra-Africa Mobility Scheme, which focuses on the spread of ICT use across Africa. The scheme was launched by the European Commission in collaboration with the African Union (EU, 2016).

General critiques of KBE construction

In literature, criticism of approaches to KBE development ranges from critiques of their definitions and models to issues with the indicators that are used to determine whether an economy is knowledge based. For instance, the definitions of various approaches are said to lack clarity and consistency (Carlaw, Oxley, Walker, Thorns, & Nuth, 2006). Smith (2002) argues that all economies are in some way based on knowledge and so it is difficult for a single economy to be directly based on producing and distributing knowledge and information products. Moreover, the definition of knowledge in KBEs does not correspond with the philosophical definition of knowledge (Usher, 2002), which states that knowledge is that which is proved and a justified true belief.

According to Robertson (2009), indicators of KBEs are not appropriate measures of the contribution of knowledge to the economy. Godin (2006) argues that the indicators measure only input and activity, but they do not measure the output and impact of knowledge, which are very important. The indicators in the innovation system pillar of the WB model do not determine the cost of knowledge production and revenue earned from it. Moreover, most of the indicators in the WB model only identify what it may take to build a KBE; they do not show the extent to which an economy is based on knowledge. Second, the KBE indicators in the dominant models (e.g. WB's model) do not measure the relationship between the pillars of KBE (e.g. innovation, education and ICT) and economic prosperity (Robertson, 2009). Specifically, the human development index, which the KBE indicators in the WB model draw from, is inadequate for measuring development (Robertson, 2009). Likewise, according to Pyatt, the living standard measurements used by the WB model are unreliable due to major errors (as cited in Robertson, 2009). Moreover, the use of GDP (as in the ABS model) to measure the impact of knowledge is inaccurate since GDP is a result of many things. As explained by Trewin (2002), GDP is influenced by many factors other than knowledge creation and utilisation. Thus, it is difficult to establish a cause–effect relationship between knowledge/KBE and the indicators used in the ABS model.

Another criticism of the indicators used in the models is that they only cover a narrow scope of knowledge-related issues. For instance, according to the OECD (1996), the indicators of research and development expenditure and research personnel used in its model are unable to draw a full picture of what KBEs are. In addition, patents are sometimes used as indicators of KBE, which is problematic because not all applications of knowledge are patented and not all patents are equally significant. In that sense, the dominant KBE models have been criticised for not covering all the knowledge needed in an economy. Not all forms of knowledge are measurable and therefore their impacts cannot be identified.

Additionally, the indicators used in the models are not new. For instance, the indicators in the OECD model are a continuation of what the organisation was investigating long before it began to advocate for KBEs. Investments in higher education are expected to produce innovative, creative and entrepreneurial individuals, who are regarded as the engines of new economies, yet such investments cannot be considered valid indicators (Robertson, 2009).

An additional critique of KBEs is that the commodification of electronic knowledge tends to increase inequality as those who cannot afford to buy are denied access to knowledge (Subortzky, 2000). Moreover, developing KBEs through education privileges the economic value of education over its other functions (Robertson, 2009). Thus, KBE excludes other ways of thinking about education, including as a way for individuals to develop their social and cultural knowledge. Similarly, its proposition to increase the use of education to serve market interests eclipses the social and cultural purposes of education (Naidoo, 2003). There is uncertainty that economies around the world are truly knowledge based, as explained in the dominant models; scholars are still divided on whether this change has actually occurred or it is just a fashionable rhetoric (Fairclough, 2005). In other words, the empirical evidence that a global KBE has been developed is still very weak, and there is no evidence that capital can be infinitely substituted for manual and/or skilled labour (Peters, 2001).

Another line of criticism of KBE development is that the highly skilled human resources that are called for in the dominant models of KBE can be drained, as evidenced by the large numbers of workers moving to different countries (Kolodko, 2014). Thus, using the number of highly skilled individuals that have been trained in a country as an indicator of a KBE is inaccurate. A good indicator of the presence of highly skilled individuals in a country and their contribution to the economy is the relative number of highly trained individuals/graduates within each economic sector. Additionally, it may be beneficial to use one of the OECD model's indicators, the employment of engineers and technical personnel in an economy, to determine the quality and use of human resources. However, this indicator may be biased towards the science and technology fields.

In summary, the KBE models discussed in this chapter fail to consider national context and the impact of knowledge. The discourses about KBE in these models may not target a country's developmental needs; they privilege the interests of foreign groups, have negative effects upon academic practices, do not bring any new ideas or processes to the Global South and perpetuate neo-liberalism.

Need for an alternative cultural strategy in low-income countries

Given all the weaknesses pointed out in previous sections, the dominant models of KBE and the cultural strategies they use (especially that used in the WB model) are not designed in a way that allows them to be helpful to LICs in the Global South. Therefore, LICs need to design suitable KBE models of their own. Each country should consider its cultural issues, national development priorities and public interests when creating these alternative models. Specifically, higher education policies targeting KBE construction need to respond to national needs and positively impact academic practices rather than simply adopting the ideologies in the dominant models of KBE.

Unlike the dominant models, which are focused on the service sector, alternative models should treat knowledge as a facilitator in all economic sectors that allows every sector to benefit from the production and application of knowledge. In addition, in a country such as Tanzania, the concept of a KBE can be adapted to support the development of the agricultural sector, which is the backbone of the country's economy, natural resources and industrialisation.

Alternative models should avoid biasing higher education towards the economy. When this has happened in the past, KBEs have neglected the social and cultural purposes of education (Robertson, 2009). Economic progress is not the only priority; societies need to address challenges such as diseases, environmental problems and injustice. It might therefore be useful to the Global South if alternative models allow higher education to focus on what Talisayon (2006) calls knowledge-based development (KBD), or economic, social and natural development based on knowledge creation and application.

Further, Global South models should refrain from using consumption indicators (such as those used in the WB model) to measure KBEs and instead use indicators of internal production and earnings from knowledge distribution.

This would respond to some of the criticisms that were raised earlier and be a common-sense approach to measuring KBEs; when an economy is based on agriculture, we do not measure it by the extent to which we consume food, and likewise, it is misleading to determine the extent to which an economy is knowledge based by looking at, for example, the number of telephone users. Because KBEs are supported by internal production, for an LIC like Tanzania to benefit from a KBE, it must be a producer and supplier of knowledge products rather than a disadvantaged consumer. Thus, LICs should, for example, invest in local firms producing ICT software and hardware or inventing tools derived from original research. Alternative models' indicators of the production, distribution and application of knowledge should also measure the extent to which knowledge is supportive of the country's primary sectors (e.g. the use of irrigation technology to support agriculture). Likewise, publication of articles in journals should be used to share knowledge with a broad audience rather than serve as an indicator of a country's competitiveness. For that matter, the indicators should be able to tell the extent to which an economy is knowledge based, not simply what KBE requires.

Based on the arguments it raises, this chapter proposes an alternative model for KBE/KBD (see Figure 3.1). This model suggests a shift from the view

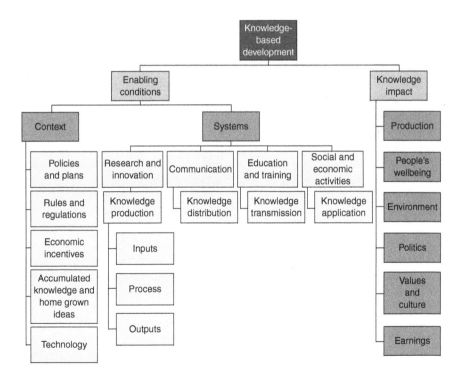

Figure 3.1 An alternative model of KBE/KBD for countries in the Global South.

that knowledge serves economic purposes only (KBE) to the view that knowledge has other uses, adapting Talisayon's (2006) idea of KBD. The proposed model is underpinned by the hypothesis that there are conditions that enable KBE and the eventual impact of knowledge on development. In the alternative model, these conditions involve the context of the country and areas or systems related to the processes through which knowledge is produced and utilised (knowledge-related systems). In other words, for a KBE to succeed in a country, it must take into account all the economic sectors in the country, the specific needs of the country, national policies and the legal context.

In the case of Tanzania, where neo-liberalism has had adverse impact on national development, there is a need for a new economic model with a different ideology, such as one prioritising social justice to ensure the equity, rights, access, redistribution, recognition and participation of all (Fraser, 1996; Miller, 1999). Tanzania needs to consider other approaches to the construction of KBE that are more suitable for its needs, such as neo-corporatism, neo-communitarianism and neo-statism. Indicators in the context could include the integration of social justice into national policies and the extent to which the country's needs are met by its policies.

In the context of a country, the elements for KBE development are supportive policies and plans, rules and regulations, control of and solutions for issues such as the draining of resources (direct and indirect), knowledge looting through IPR and other means, economic incentives, the legal framework of a country, accumulated knowledge and internal production of ideas and technology, especially ICT. Together, these elements create a conducive environment for the production and distribution of knowledge. In particular, policies and plans that focus on the needs and interests of a particular country address the problem discussed above: that the WB model of KBE does not allow higher education in Tanzania to meet national needs and interests.

Knowledge-related systems (see Figure 3.1) include research and innovation systems (for knowledge production), communication systems (for knowledge distribution), education and training systems (for knowledge transmission) and social and economic activity systems (for knowledge application).

The research and innovation system

Knowledge production involves inputs, processes and outputs or products. Inputs include intellectuals (knowledgeable and highly skilled individuals), funding (public/state, community and private funds), equipment, institutions (research centres, intellectual power houses, think tanks, high-technology industries, schools and colleges), knowledge agendas and knowledge stock. The process of knowledge production has to do with the development of available knowledge, search for new knowledge (OECD, 1996), internal research, creation of ideas and two-way knowledge transfer. The outputs of knowledge production are discoveries, inventions, innovations, blueprints, research reports, journal articles, technological devices/gadgets, ideas, education materials (education and training services, publications/books and equipment) and other intellectual works. These elements are equivalent to the innovation system in the WB model of KBE. Thus, knowledge production occurs within the research and innovation system, which produces knowledge and transforms it into new, usable materials, products, devices or processes.

Knowledge communication system

Knowledge distribution or dissemination involves transmitting knowledge to a number of people and providing inputs for problem solving (OECD, 1996). There are many channels through which knowledge can be distributed to acquirers and users, including publications, conferences, workshops, patents, exhibitions, displays, press releases, media and advertising, the internet, outreach programmes such as extension services in all sectors and incubation centres. Therefore, knowledge distribution is much aided by ICT within the knowledge communication system.

Education and training system

Knowledge transmission and acquisition (and deepening; Kozma, 2008) involves training, educating and developing or enhancing individuals' capacities (OECD, 1996). It entails formal schooling, informal education, universal lifelong learning, e-learning (which requires ICT), study tours, the media (air time can be filled with useful knowledge), learning experiences, skill acquisition (by actors in different sectors) and education level. Knowledge transmission therefore takes place within the education and training system.

Social, economic and natural sector system

Knowledge application and utilisation require the use of knowledge in socioeconomic and natural sectors (Talisayon, 2006) ranging from primary to quinary sectors. Knowledge application can be indicated by the use of new techniques in different sectors that are important in a country (e.g. techniques related to agriculture, livestock, etc.). These sectors require the social and cultural application of knowledge, production of knowledge, integration of knowledge into individuals' lives and free disclosure of knowledge, which makes it hard to trace.

Socioeconomic impact of knowledge

KBD is reflected in the outcomes and/or impact of knowledge on economic and social endeavours. This impact is determined by the social and economic benefits experienced by a country as a result of knowledge. Specific indicators of the economic impact of knowledge include revenue from knowledge products/outputs, benefits resulting from the utilisation of 'old' knowledge in different sectors, socioeconomic benefits that are a result of new knowledge and discoveries, the output of high-technology industries and their contribution to the economy, the number of jobs provided by high-technology and knowledge-intensive sectors (e.g. education and communication) and the contribution of knowledge-intensive sectors to GDP. Indicators of social gains include wellbeing, political progress (e.g. democracy) and health attributable to knowledge.

The alternative model proposed in this chapter suggests that KBE/KBD occurs as a result of the impact of knowledge on the economic production of goods and services in all economic sectors and aspects of human life. Such a suggestion aims to address the problem that the dominant models of KBE do not measure the usefulness of knowledge that has been produced and distributed. Further, unlike the WB model, which does not consider the impact of knowledge, the alternative model adopts the view that KBE/KBD is reflected in the impact of knowledge upon socioeconomic endeavours, including culturally sustainable development. Furthermore, knowledge impact in the alternative model is considered in terms of the components of knowledge production, distribution, transmission and application systems. The outputs of such systems are properly indicated as well. There must be appropriate indicators of knowledge production across the pillars of KBE/KBD. For instance, drawing from Ernberg (1999), indicators of the ICT pillar include ICT software production, ICT export, local ICT production, internal supply of ICT, the number of data processing jobs, retrieval of useful information and use of telecommunication for sustainable development.

The alternative model also considers countries' own science and technology sectors rather than prioritising Western science and technology. Further, the model has no bias towards science and technology or against other fields of knowledge. Although countries need to have scientists and technologists, the economy is not based solely on these disciplines; other areas of study are just as socio-economically relevant. Students should not be denied access or have limited access to these subjects in higher education, as this will have negative impacts, including negative financial effects.

As suggested earlier, the alternative model should also observe the principles of social justice, consider all groups of people and value the contributions of all disciplines to human development. Thus, alternative indicators include higher education enrolment in all disciplines. Moreover, the extent to which knowledge is disseminated to and is used by the majority (as opposed to blind growth fanaticism) is indicated, as is the extent to which a country has knowledge-intensive sectors. The broad purpose of higher education is emphasised in the alternative model.

A balance of social, cultural and economic interest in all efforts to attain KBD is necessary for culturally sustainable development. Thus, the alternative model takes into account the impact of knowledge on the various social and economic fields in a country (beyond the production, distribution, transmission and application of knowledge). It therefore requires alternative indicators of KBE that can accurately measure the impact of knowledge on sustainable development, not only economic growth. Since indicators such as GDP cannot sufficiently measure the contribution of knowledge to an economy, and since GDP is influenced by many factors other than knowledge, figures resulting from statistical multivariate analysis of different variables contributing to GDP are used to estimate, for example, the amount that research and development returns to the economy compared to other variables that are not directly related to knowledge. Similarly, the correlation between variables related to knowledge and economic growth has to be considered when calculating indicators, as does the possibility that some knowledge-related variables contribute to social development rather than economic growth (Kolodki, 2014).

In the alternative model, KBE involves various types of knowledge, including local, non-commercial and non-patentable knowledge. Therefore, it emphasises cultural sustainability as a way to explore and explain key elements *from within* the complex cultural and economic context of Tanzania and the Global South (Soini & Birkeland, 2014). All economies are knowledge based but differ in the extent to which knowledge plays a role in the local culture and economy.

References

Australian Bureau of Statistics. (2002). *Measuring a knowledge-based economy and society.* Retrieved from www.ausstats.abs.gov.au/Ausstats/free.nsf/Lookup/4F8E59034103 E624CA256C230007DC05/$File/13750_aug%202002.pdf.

Bennett, M. J. (2009). Defining, measuring, and facilitating intercultural learning: A conceptual introduction to the intercultural education double supplement. *Intercultural Education, 20*(S1–2), 1–13.

Bok, D. (2003). *Universities in the market place: The commercialization of higher education.* Princeton, NJ: Princeton University Press.

Boyd, R., & Ngo, T. (2005). *Asian states: Beyond the developmental perspective.* London: Routledge.

Canaan, J. E., & Shumar, W. (2008). *Structure and agency in the neo-liberal university.* New York: Routledge.

Carlaw, K., Oxley, L., Walker, P., Thorns, D., & Nuth, M. (2006). Beyond the hype: Intellectual property and the knowledge society/knowledge economy. *Journal of Economic Survey, 20*(4), 633–690.

Castells, M., & Himanen, P. (2002). *The information society and the welfare state: The Finnish model.* Oxford: Oxford University Press.

Daugeliene, R. (2004). *Peculiarities of knowledge-based economy assessment: Theoretical approach.* Retrieved from www.calculemus.org/lect/07pol-gosp/dyn-cyw/.../lisbon-strat.pdf.

Ernberg, J. (1999). Empowering communities in the information society: An international perspective. In D. Richardson & L. Paisley (Eds), *The first mile of connectivity* (pp. 191–211). Retrieved from www.fao.org/WAICENT/FAOINFO/SUSTDEV/Cddirect/Cdre0025.htm.

European Union. (2016). *Intra-Africa mobility scheme.* Retrieved from https://eacea.ec.
europa.eu/intra-africa/funding/intra-africa-academic-mobility-scheme-2016_en.

Fairclough, N. (2001). The dialectics of discourse. *Textus, 14*(2), 3–10.

Fairclough, N. (2005). Discourse in the process of social change: 'Transition' in
Central and Eastern Europe. *British and American Studies, XI,* 9–34.

Fraser, N. (1996). *Social justice in the age of identity politics: Redistribution, recognition, and
participation.* Retrieved from www.intelligenceispower.com/Important%20E-mails
%20Sent%20attachments/Social%20Justice%20in%20the%20Age%20of%20
Identity%20Politics.pdf.

Fyfe, N. (2005). Making space for neo-communitarianism? The third sector, state and
civil society in the UK. *Antipode, 37*(3), 536–557.

Giroux, H. A. (2002). Neo-liberalism, corporate culture, and the promise of higher
education: The university as a democratic public sphere. *Harvard Educational Review,
72*(4), 425–463.

Godin, B. (2006). The knowledge-based economy: Conceptual framework or buz-
zword. *Journal of Technology Transfer, 31*(1), 17–30.

Green, A., Little, A., Kamat, S., Oketch, M., & Vickers, E. (2007). *Education and
development in a global era: Strategies for successful globalisation.* London: Department
for International Development.

Greenblatt, S., & Zupanov, I. (2009). *Cultural mobility: A manifesto.* Cambridge: Cambridge University Press.

Guruz, K. (2011). *Higher education and international student mobility in the global knowledge economy.* Albany, NY: State University of New York Press.

Isaakyan, I., & Triandafyllidou, A. (2013). *High-skill mobility: Addressing the challenges of
a knowledge-based economy at times of crisis.* Retrieved from http://hdl.handle.net/
1814/27706.

Jessop, B. (2004). Critical semiotic analysis and cultural political economy. *Critical
Discourse Studies, 1*(2), 159–174.

Kahangwa, G. L. (2013). *The influence of knowledge-based economy imaginary on higher education policies and practices in Tanzania* (doctoral thesis). University of Bristol, UK.

Kenway, J., Bullen, E., & Robb, S. (2004). The knowledge economy, the techno-
preneur and the problematic future of the university. *Policy Futures in Education, 2*(2),
330–349.

Kolodki, G. W. (2014). *Whither the world: The political economy of the future.* Hampshire: Palgrave Macmillan.

Kotsi, F., & Agiomirgianakis, G. (2013). Mobility of higher education students in
Europe: The south–north differences. *International Journal of Education Economics and
Development, 4*(3), 233–254.

Kozma, R. B. (2008). *ICT, education reform, and economic growth: A conceptual framework.*
White Paper, retrieved from http://support.intel.co.jp/content/dam/www/public/
us/en/documents/brochures/kozma-wp1-conceptual-framework.pdf.

MCST (2010). *The National Research and Development Policy.* Retrieved from http://
drp.muhas.ac.tz/Documents/Research_Information/The%20National%20
Research%20and%20Development%20Policy.pdf.

Miller, D. (1999). *Principles of social justice.* London: Harvard University Press.

Munro, D. (2000). The knowledge economy. *Journal of Australian Political Economy,
45,* 5–17.

Naidoo, R. (2003). Repositioning higher education as a global commodity: Opportunities and challenges for future sociology of education work. *British Journal of Sociology of Education, 24*(2), 249–259.

Organisation for Economic Cooperation and Development. (1996). *Knowledge-based economy*. Retrieved from www.oecd.org/dataoecd/51/8/1913021.pdf.

Organisation for Economic Cooperation and Development. (2007). *Staying competitive in the global economy*. Retrieved from www.oecd-ilibrary.org/industry-and-services/staying-competitive-in-the-global-economy_9789264034259-en.

Olssen, M., & Peters, M. A. (2005). Neoliberalism, higher education and the knowledge economy: From the free market to knowledge capitalism. *Journal of Education Policy*, *20*(3), 313–345.

Peters, M. (2001). National educational constructions of the 'knowledge economy': Towards a critique. *Journal of Educational Inquiry*, *2*(1), 1–22.

Robertson, S. (2009). 'Producing' the global knowledge economy: The World Bank, the knowledge assessment methodology and education. In M. Simon, M. Olssen, & M. A. Peters (Eds), *Re-reading education policies: A handbook of studying the policy agenda of the 21st century* (235–256). Rotterdam: Sense Publishers.

Smith, K. (2002). *What is the 'knowledge economy'? Knowledge intensity and distributed knowledge bases*. United Nations University, Institute for New Technologies, Discussion Paper Series, 2002–2006.

Soini, K., & Birkeland, I. (2014). Mapping the scientific discourse of cultural sustainability. *Geoforum*, *51*, 213–223.

St George, E. (2006). Positioning higher education for the knowledge based economy. *Higher Education*, *52*(4), 589–610.

SUA (2005). *Sokoine University of Agriculture Institutional Intellectual Property Rights Policy*. Morogoro: University Press.

Subotzky, G. (2000). Complementing the marketization of higher education: New modes of knowledge production in community-higher education partnerships. In A. Kraak (Ed.), *Changing modes: New knowledge production and its implications for higher education in South Africa*. Cape Town: Human Sciences Research Council Press.

Talisayon, S. D. (2006). *99 paradigm shifts for survival in the knowledge economy: A knowledge management reader*. Paranaque City: Centre for Conscious Living Foundation.

Telo, M. (2002). Governance and government in the European Union. In M. J. Rodrigues (Ed.), *The new knowledge economy in Europe* (242–272). Cheltenham: Edward Elgar.

Trewin, D. (2002). *Measuring a knowledge-based economy and society: An Australian framework*. Retrieved from http://unpan1.un.org/intradoc/groups/public/documents/apcity/unpan020309.pdf.

Usher, R. (2002). A diversity of doctorates: Fitness for knowledge economy. *Higher Education Research and Development*, *21*(2), 143–153.

Utz, A. (2006). *Fostering innovations, productivity and technical change: Tanzania in the knowledge economy*. Washington, DC: The World Bank Institute.

World Bank. (2002). *Constructing knowledge societies: New challenges for tertiary education*. Washington, DC: The World Bank Institute.

World Bank. (2008). *Measuring knowledge in the world's economies: Knowledge assessment methodology and knowledge economy index*. Retrieved from http://siteresources.world bank.org/.

4 Culturally responsive qualitative research

Issues and ethics

Gunilla Holm and Elina Lehtomäki

Introduction

In this chapter we discuss the strengths and weaknesses of using various qualitative research methods in culturally diverse settings. We explore which aspects are most important when a researcher wants to conduct culturally responsive research. The essence of qualitative research in education is to be able to draw close to children, students, teachers, parents and others involved; in this way, researchers may capture their experiences, ideas, views, voices, meanings and emotions, as well as discerning the reasoning behind the participants' actions or behaviours. We highlight this closeness to people who experience learning and education in the examples and cases discussed in this chapter. Because the idea for this book emerged during our African–Finnish North–South–South collaboration project, which applied Geneva Gay's (2010, 2013) culturally responsive education approach, our focus is on how qualitative research is conducted in diverse cultural contexts while acknowledging and respecting cultural diversity. We discuss the qualitative research's potential for exploring various issues that are relevant and important to the participants. We are interested in conducting research without imposing our own priorities; instead, we wish to respond to the participants' needs and values in a culturally sensitive way.

This discussion on the use of qualitative research methods in education resonates with the ongoing search for solutions to the largest and most persistent challenges in educational development in Africa. According to the UNESCO Regional Office in Dakar in 2015, these challenges include girls' low school enrolment rates compared to boys, high drop-out rates among both girls and boys (42 per cent of schoolchildren leave school early) and youth who lack the necessary skills for employment. The Seychelles is the only African country to have reached the 2015 Education for All targets (World Education Forum, 2000), while 31 of the 54 countries in Africa are considered to be likely to attain these goals by 2020. Representatives of several African countries and the African Union have demonstrated their commitment to the implementation of the United Nations' global sustainable development goals (SDGs) – including SDG 4, on high-quality education for all (United Nations, 2015) – by designing and adopting a strategy for the continent-wide development of education (African Union, 2016). The policy-level goals of inclusion and equity aim to improve the quality of education and to address (1) girls' participation in school, (2) school drop-out rates and (3) youth who lack skills for employment. This study seeks to examine the factors that culturally responsive qualitative research can offer for solving these challenges in diverse contexts.

Underpinning qualitative research in education is the understanding of the critical role social and cultural contexts play in defining quality and relevance. Equally important is how we as researchers approach children, students, teachers, parents and others involved with education and learning. One example of this is a quality improvement project in Malawi that Kendall, Kaunda and Friedson-Rideneur (2015) discuss in which they applied a "respectful partnership" that focussed on school–community relations. In that project, building trust was key to identifying what learners and their families and communities expected, valued and required in school–community relations and elsewhere. The researchers stressed how their respectful approach to listening to those who are silenced or marginalised in society transformed their previous perceptions of what matters in debates about education and learning.

In qualitative research, we strive to conduct culturally responsive or culturally sensitive research, although the particular aspects we need to be especially sensitive to might vary from situation to situation. For some research participants, for example, gender, race, language, class, religion, age, sexuality or disability might be most important, while for others, regional belonging or age might matter most. In order for the research to be conducted in an ethically sound manner, researchers need to have a well-attuned sensitivity 'radar' so that they may pick up what the participants consider to be most important and necessary to focus on. Likewise, what researchers consider to be a cultural aspect may differ depending on the situation. At times, politics or human rights might play a larger role than certain aspects such as gender or religion. In a segregated community, for instance, race might be the most sensitive issue at a desegregated school, while the most sensitive cultural aspect at a segregated school might be religion or social class.

In this chapter, we will mainly focus on culturally responsive aspects in data-collection methods such as interviews, participant observations, illustrations and photography and will offer a few examples of research in diverse contexts. We will also explore the role of the researcher, in addition to determining which roles the participants can play in order to make the research more culturally responsive.

Drawing close to people's lives: sensitivity and responsiveness

In much empirical qualitative research, the goal of the researcher is to develop a close and trusting relationship with the study participants. Within ethnographic studies, the researcher traditionally spends a year or more living in the setting he or she is researching. In recent years, however, it has become more common for researchers to claim that they have conducted ethnographic studies when they have actually spent only a few weeks in the setting with the participants. Developing a trusting relationship with participants who are very different is challenging; it requires the researcher to be sensitive to what the participants find to be important in their lives. The researcher must ask: Could any common traits or experiences serve as a bridge to the participants? Reflexivity on the part of the researcher is essential. The development of this trust can be seen as a two-way street. In order to get close to people, for example, researchers must also give something to the participants that is of value to them: this might be as simple as spending time and expressing one's interest, but it might also entail lending one's expertise to help solve problems. For researchers in the field of education, this might mean sharing information about schools or how best to help participants' children with their homework, among other possibilities.

Certain characteristics of the group or individuals who are being studied can make it more difficult to draw closer to their lives. When studying children in a preschool, for example, it can be difficult to find common experiences or traits that will help the researcher to connect to the young children. Many good examples exist in the research literature on the proper role to assume when studying children. In Van Ausdale and Feagin's study (2001), for instance, Van Ausdale assumed the role neither of a child nor a teacher, but of an adult who did not interfere in the children's activities; nor did she tell the teachers what the children did. In this way she was able to obtain the trust of the children, who then behaved in the same way with her as they did with their fellow pre-schoolers. Other researchers have engaged children in taking an active part in the data-collection process, for example through the use of drawings (Einarsdottir, Perry & Docket, 2009).

Having the ability to listen attentively is a key skill in culturally responsive research. In Tuomi, Lehtomäki and Matonya's study on Tanzanian university students with disabilities (2015), the interviewees stated that they were keen to participate and that they enjoyed the opportunity to discuss their experiences and lives. The students also stated that the interviewer was the first person they had encountered to ask them about how they experienced their university studies and how they had succeeded – despite the limited resources that were available – in overcoming a variety of challenges.

Sharing the same habitus with the participants can be both advantageous and disadvantageous. In Holm, Londen and Mansikka's study (2015) of Swedish-speaking teenagers' views about what it means to belong to Finland's

Swedish-speaking minority group, the researchers (who themselves belonged to the same group) found that the teenagers opened up very easily because of their sense of a shared experience. These experiences included both good experiences and negative experiences such as harassment. The teenagers also automatically assumed that the researchers knew what they were talking about, however, and felt no need to elaborate on what they perceived to be common sense. It can also be more difficult for the researcher to view data from a new angle, due to his or her familiarity with the data.

Another example of shared habitus may be found in Chang's (2013) study of highly educated Taiwanese women who had married Finnish men and were now living in Finland. Because Chang was in the same situation as the women whom she studied, this led the Taiwanese women to share their experiences with the researcher in a way that assumed she knew what they were referring to when they compared family and work life in Taiwan and Finland. The women told their life stories during study sessions, some of which lasted up to six hours. We should bear in mind, however, that it can also be difficult for a researcher who is completely on the inside to know how much things have to be elaborated upon in order for outsiders to understand the results.

Different ways of overcoming the challenges related to one's status as an outsider or insider include engaging in close collaboration between researchers from the outside (from different cultures and contexts) and the committed involvement of the research participants. One example of researcher collaboration is Okkolin's (2013) study of highly educated Tanzanian women who had completed degrees in higher education. The researcher benefitted both from the close collaboration with her Tanzanian colleagues in identifying and contacting the interviewees and from the motivation of the research participants: highly educated women who valued the research topic and interview themes. Another example is Posti-Ahokas's (2014) research using empathy-based stories with female secondary-school students in Tanzania: a group that is traditionally at risk of dropping out. Together with her Tanzanian colleagues and students, she developed the stories that she used as motivating introductions in the research. These stories drew from previous research findings, the reality of secondary schools and from ongoing debates in the media on the failure of secondary education in Tanzania.

Unequal power relations

As researchers concerned with culturally responsive research, it is important for us to be aware of our own position. The researcher is always in a position of power, even if the participants act as co-researchers or participating researchers in the data-collection and analysis portions of the study. The research would not be conducted and the data would remain uncollected if the researcher had not made the initial decision to conduct the study. Because the participating co-researchers are collecting data for the researchers, the latter hold a position of power in relation to the former (Gibson, 2005; Holm, 2008). Ultimately it is the researcher who decides and is responsible for what is disseminated and published (Holm, 2014). While power differences in qualitative research will always exist, the issue is more a matter of what the researcher does with that power difference.

In many countries, politics and power relations can challenge or regulate research and the publication of findings. Exhibiting cultural responsiveness within research not only requires having an understanding of the contexts, it also requires identifying whose views and experiences have been excluded. In Morrow and Pells's broad sociological study (2012) on poverty and human rights as experienced by children in different countries (including Ethiopia and India), the researchers used a variety of qualitative methods and local languages and they engaged children in the research process. Their study thus succeeded in explaining the processes that underlie the many challenges related to injustice and inequality; the authors showed how children found strategies for survival that provided new information for policy design and implementation.

Another example of unequal power relations may be found in the study that Katsui, Lehtomäki, Yehualawork Malle and Chalklen (2016) conducted in Ethiopia, where the advocacy of human rights is strictly forbidden by law. In such cases, any research that demonstrates students' experiences of (often extreme) marginalisation may be harmful or even dangerous to the research participants; the researchers thus had to carefully consider how best to report and protect the interviewees. Although research participants may be aware of the risks involved, the consequences of a research report cannot be foreseen; as a result, the researchers, whether they are from outside or inside the country, may have no way to protect the study participants.

As Harper (2003) points out vis-à-vis unequal power relations and the taking of photographs, academic researchers can take photographs of homeless people, but homeless people cannot walk into researchers' offices and take photographs of them. Some researchers try to balance these power differences by asking their potential participants to act as co-researchers during the data-collection process. This is fairly common when using photography as a data collection method (Holm, 2008, 2014; Majumbar, 2011). The participants can then take photographs that will exemplify the topic under consideration; they can also write about their interpretations of the photographs. Another possibility is for the researcher to interview the participants about the photographs (Holm, 2008).

The use of photovoice is one possible approach for equalising power differences. In this method, the participants can take photographs of what they consider to be a problematic situation; they then analyse them together with the researcher in order to accomplish a change or improvement of some kind. Wang (2005), among others, has used this approach many times in what resembles action research but is more focussed on the needs of the participants. According to Howes and Miles (2015), photography offers the

possibility of reducing the power imbalance between researchers and participants. It also offers tools to the participants to explore their educational contexts and highlight aspects of injustice as they experience it.

When conducting interviews, the power relationship can be levelled
somewhat by making the interview more of a discussion; in such cases, the
researcher also shares his or her experiences. This method is sometimes used
in feminist research (Hesse-Biber, 2014). It is also common that, after transcribing and analysing the interviews, the researcher will return to the interviewees with the results in order to ask them if the researcher had interpreted
their responses as they had intended. One approach that has proven successful
in reducing power differences is the use of participant engagement in the
research. When using this approach, researchers collect data with the participants (for example, students, school communities and young people) in order
to produce knowledge that can then be used to inform local decision makers.
After sharing their findings with the decision makers, the researchers then
return to the participants to inform them about the process results (Flecha,
2011; Lehtomäki et al., 2014).

Ethical requirements

The misuse of researchers' power positions can cause serious ethical breaches.
In a multi-sited international study of how best to benefit from the consumption potential among the poor (living on 3 dollars a day), for example, Lindeman and colleagues (2010) only had a few weeks to gather the ethnographic
data they needed in each country. Among other things, this caused the
researchers to surreptitiously take photographs of people's homes (despite the
fact that the inhabitants did not want their impoverished homes to be photographed) and of women who did not want to be photographed for religious
reasons.

Culturally responsive research requires the researcher to engage in a discussion with the participants about what is possible and desirable to do in the
research and what is off limits. This requirement holds both for the research
questions and the data-gathering process and for the dissemination of the
results. Participants do not always understand what, exactly, it means for the
results to be disseminated at academic conferences and published in academic
journals. Promising confidentiality is not always enough; nor is it always possible to do so. If a studied community or group is small and unique, for
example, it can be difficult to promise confidentiality. In studies that use
photography, for instance, the participants often take photographs of their
lives; all possible identifiers (such as photographs of particular buildings or
people) then have to be removed if people do not agree to have their photographs published. It is not enough that just a few students in a study of a
school or class (or their parents) give their permission, however, since other
students may be identifiable based on the photographs that their fellow
students have published. The only possibilities in such cases include not

publishing any identifying characteristics or photographs, or excluding those who do not give their permission to publish any identifying data.

Exhibiting ethical conduct in research that spans cultures requires researchers to be "honest in the negotiation of relations between the researcher and the researched" (Honan, Hamid, Alhamdan, Phommalangsy, & Lingard, 2013, p. 396). Governments in the Global South are also beginning to regulate research licences and to require ethical-committee approval in order to protect the dignity of their citizens, which has been common practice in the Global North for quite some time. Honan and colleagues (2013) recommend that both researchers and ethical committees should reflect on critical ethical issues in cross-cultural research by asking questions such as 'How does one show respect in the cultural setting that we have chosen for this research?' and 'In this cultural context, how do people understand written and informed consent?'

Results that researchers find interesting and important can be potentially harmful to study participants. Once we have disseminated our results, we no longer have control over how they are interpreted – or perhaps even purposely misinterpreted. Even if the researcher has discussed any potential harm that may come from the study with the participants, it is the former's responsibility to foresee (as much as possible) and prevent any potential problems that may happen to the latter. It is also necessary to view the potential problems from both the researchers' and the participants' perspectives and situations.

Qualitative research can be politically sensitive because it may reveal issues that tend to be overlooked in policy-guided monitoring and reporting. It is thus important to engage in reflections on one's role as a researcher and the research participants' potentially critical situations due to the existence of power relations (Baily, Shah & Call-Cummings, 2016). Yet qualitative research results may offer alternatives that can contribute to the desired policy objectives, such as enhancement of the quality of education. For instance, in a study on teachers and teacher development in Ethiopia, Abebe and Wolde-hanna (2013) interviewed classroom teachers and head teachers in diverse rural and urban contexts across the country in order to explore which types of continuous development the people valued and participated in. Their findings indicated several issues that are commonly overlooked in planning and reporting on professional development activities, such as the important roles that experienced teachers play in exhibiting supportive leadership and in guiding newly recruited teachers.

Qualitative research also has the potential to create new approaches to transformations and processes by inquiring into diverse stakeholders' perspectives. To both investigate and develop teacher-education students' understanding of inclusive pedagogies through practice, Florian and Spratt (2013) developed a framework for conducting observations of learning and teaching in schools combined with tasks for reflections. Instead of following predefined guidelines to applying inclusive pedagogies, the student teachers were instructed to reflect on their observations and their own practices from both the learners' perspectives and their own, with an emphasis on equity and equality in learning.

Suspicion of outsiders

As discussed in more detail in the section below on researcher characteristics, situations in which a researcher is a complete outsider – with starkly different characteristics in terms of gender, class, race, gender, religion and language – can elicit suspicion on the part of the potential study participants. They may wonder 'Why is a complete stranger interested in us? Are we somehow considered strange? What do they want from us?' It is often the case that showing interest in and listening to individuals will break down barriers over time. The act of being persistently present and choosing sides when necessary can form strong relationships. In many cases, suspicion towards outside researchers is based on previous experiences of being exploited by outsiders. It is not uncommon for researchers to promise benefits to the communities or individuals who are being studied, for example, only to leave these communities as soon as they have gathered enough potentially interesting data.

Gatekeepers can be protective of the people who are to be studied, but they might also be afraid of being studied. In a study of a school for pregnant and parenting teenage girls, Holm (1995) received permission to study the school without difficulties, but she encountered teachers who were reluctant to participate in the study and a gatekeeping principal who wanted to control what the students shared, and in what ways. Interestingly (and surprisingly), the poor and middle-class black girls were those who were most interested in participating. They opened up to the researcher quickly, despite major differences in terms of race, language, religion and educational background. The white Catholic girls, in contrast, were the most suspicious, despite being white (like the researcher) in a city that was segregated by race and had a school system that had been desegregated by court order. The white girls were a minority in the school, however, and in that sense were in a weaker power position than their black peers.

In most parts of Africa, children with disabilities have traditionally remained at home (where they are overprotected or hidden), since impairments are often associated with shame. Marginalisation and exclusion in education further worsen the situation; as a result, research on the education of Africans with disabilities is still rare. Recognising this marginalisation and exclusion, Eide and his colleagues (2011) trained and involved research assistants with disabilities in order to conduct studies in diverse communities throughout southern Africa. Through collaborative research, they succeeded in highlighting several experiences of exclusion from the inside.

An increasing number of studies in the African context have given voice to those who are targeted by education-development policies; these studies also cover issues of equality, equity and inclusion. In Warrington and Kiragu's study (2012) in Kenya, for instance, the girls whom they interviewed were outspoken about their situations, stating that the boys were favoured; mean-while, their families stressed the economic and cultural reasons that favoured the education of boys. In these contexts, as Unterhalter (2012) has demon-strated, girls are often silenced by their families, teachers and society; without a voice, their needs can hardly be met in terms of educational development. Due to the existing sociocultural power structures, it may be difficult for researchers to negotiate and acquire permission for conducting research. Yet various researchers have reported how the interviews and stories that are used in data collection have enabled girls and women to analyse their own experi-ences and to feel empowered (e.g. Posti-Ahokas, 2013; Posti-Ahokas & Lehtomäki, 2014; Posti-Ahokas & Okkolin, 2015).

One alternative to the researcher being an outsider is for researchers to use available data. Stories that teachers, students or persons who are marginalised in education write or tell may offer rich material for research that aims to understand different meanings and values (Turnyansky, Tuval, Mansur, Barak, & Gidron, 2009). One example is Lehtomäki and Hukkanen's study (2015), which analysed comics that were produced by people with disabilities and their family members at workshops organised by artists. The comics were used to empower the participants, who had the freedom to choose any issues of importance in their daily lives and were given instructions about ways to illustrate those topics. Many of the participants chose to express their experi-ences of encountering barriers to learning and exclusion from education. With their permission, the researchers then analysed the comics in light of inclusive education development. Through the comics, the people with disabilities and their family members (some of whom were illiterate) were offered a powerful means for communicating their messages and their suggestions for removing barriers to learning (World Comics Finland, 2010).

Researcher characteristics

The researcher needs to reflexively and continuously keep track of his or her own position vis-à-vis power and various cultural aspects. In many places in the world, a white researcher is in a more privileged position than a person of colour; the fact that a researcher is white, however, might also prevent him or her from gaining access to certain kinds of information within communities of colour (and vice versa for black researchers in white communities).

It might take a long time to build up relations of trust in interview-based and participant-observation-based studies in situations where the researcher is perceived to be different in terms of race, ethnicity, class, gender, language, religion, sexuality or disability (Holm, 1995). It will also be difficult for researchers if they study ethnic or religious groups who have hostile relations to their own. A few classic studies have been conducted, however, that show that it is possible for a researcher to study a group that is very different from his or her own. Alan Peskin (1986), for example, spent 18 months among a small fundamentalist Christian community in the United States, where he studied the community's school as an alternative to public schools. He immersed himself as an outsider (being Jewish himself) within the community, where he conducted interviews with teachers, parents and students. He also participated in the church's activities, even though he was not a fundamentalist Christian. He won the trust of the community and was able to gain valuable, respectful and rare insights into an otherwise fairly closed community.

Study situations in which researchers and participants speak the same language will also create an automatic bond, especially if the study participants are members of a language minority group. The participants will then assume that the researcher understands what they are talking about. To some extent, researchers and participants seem to have a shared understanding of the world in such cases, although language is only one characteristic. For many others, identities such as gender or religion might be more important than language (Holm et al., 2015).

To a certain extent, a researcher must be like a chameleon in adjusting to the research participants' world. While aspects like colour and gender cannot be adjusted, with both social class and religion, one's own circumstances can be pushed into the background. If a researcher who comes from a middle or upper-middle-class background is studying people who live in very poor circumstances, for example, it will be an affront to them to flaunt his or her expensive designer clothes and jewellery in the research setting. Likewise, if a researcher who would normally dress in jeans is studying a business community or upper-class parents, it then becomes necessary to dress according to the local customs (Holm, 1995; Holm & Farber, 2005).

Situations in which a female researcher studies an all-male community (or vice versa) can also be difficult, depending on the community's attitudes and values. Power relations can be obvious in these cases, and gatekeepers become even more crucial. In order for researchers to gain access, they may have to consider what they could offer, such as methods or tools, for the participants or their communities to investigate their own situations, values and meanings (Flecha, 2011; Turnyansky et al., 2009).

Discussion

Conducting culturally sensitive and responsive research is an ethical, respectful way to engage in research. The necessity for a culturally responsive approach to research became very clear during our collaborative North–South–South project on culturally responsive education between Finland, Ghana, South Africa and Tanzania. Even though many issues remain the same, independent of where the research is conducted, many issues are unique to the specific sociocultural contexts. Gender, class, ethnic and religious issues can be barriers or gate-openers in research that is related to schools, families and education. Any differences, for example, in gender, class and religion between the researcher and the study participants are important for gaining access and developing trust. Likewise, power differences and confidentiality are key issues in culturally responsive research. Conducting culturally sensitive and responsive research requires a strong reflexive attitude on the part of the researcher. Doing collaborative research with the participants is a way to secure a balanced and sensitive research approach that will put the needs of the participants at the forefront.

Conducting culturally sensitive and responsive qualitative research may offer new perspectives to both teacher-education students and practitioner researchers, tools for reflexive professional development and possible ways to bring research back to children, students, teachers, teacher educators and other educational stakeholders. In essence, culturally responsive research means "learning with the world and its people" (Maguth & Hilburn, 2015). In this chapter, we have discussed the means and tools that are available for *doing research with people*.

References

Abebe, W., & Woldehanna, T. (2013). *Teacher training and development in Ethiopia: Improving education quality by developing*. Oxford: Young Lives, Oxford Department of International Development (ODID), University of Oxford. Retrieved from www.younglives.org.uk/files/working-papers/yl-wp103-abebe-woldehanna.

African Union. (2016). *Continental Education Strategy for Africa 2016–2025, CESA 16–25*. Adopted by the African Union in Addis Ababa, Ethiopia, 31 January 2016. Retrieved from www.au.int/en/pressreleases/19702/african-union-heads-state-and-government-adopts-continental-education-strategy.

Baily, S., Shah, P., & Call-Cummings, M. (2016). Reframing the center: New directions in qualitative methodology in international comparative education. In A. W. Wiseman and E. Anderson (Eds), *Annual review of comparative and international education 2015: International perspectives on education and society*, vol. 28 (139–164). Bingley, UK: Emerald Group.

Chang, C.-C. (2013). *Highly educated Taiwanese women seeking a self-acceptable social position in Finland*. (Doctoral dissertation, University of Helsinki.) Retrieved from http://urn.fi/URN:ISBN:978-952-10-9371-5.

Eide, A. H., Loeb, M. E., Nhiwatiwa, S., Munthali, A., Ngulube, T. J., & van Rooy, G. (2011). Living conditions among people with disabilities in developing countries. In A. H. Eide and B. Ingstad (Eds), *Disability and poverty: A global challenge* (55–70). Bristol: The Policy Press.

Einarsdottir, J., Perry, B., & Dockett, S. (2009). Making meaning: Children's perspectives expressed through drawings. *Early Child Development and Care*, *179*(2), 217–232.

Flecha, R. (2011). The dialogic sociology of education. *International Studies in Sociology of Education, Special Issue: Education for Social Inclusion*, *21*(1), 7–20.

Florian, L., & Spratt, J. (2013). Enacting inclusion: A framework for interrogating inclusive practice. *European Journal of Special Needs Education*, *28*(2), 119–135.

Gay, G. (2010). *Culturally responsive teaching: Theory, research, and practice*, 2nd ed. New York: Teachers College Press.

Gay, G. (2013). Teaching to and through cultural diversity. *Curriculum Inquiry*, *43*(1), 48–70.

Gibson, B. E. (2005). Co-producing video diaries: The presence of the 'absent' researcher. *International Journal of Qualitative Methods*, 4(3), Article 3. Retrieved from www.ualberta.ca/~ijqm/backissues/4_4/pdf/gibson.pdf.

Harper, D. (2003). Reimagining visual methods: Galileo to neuromancer. In N. K. Denzin and Y. S. Lincoln (Eds), *Collecting and interpreting qualitative materials* (176–198). Thousand Oaks, CA: Sage.

Hesse-Biber, S. (2014). Feminist approaches to in-depth interviewing. In S. Hesse-Biber (Ed.), *Feminist research practice: A primer* (182–232). London: Sage.

Holm, G. (1995). Handled but not heard: The managed lives of teenage mothers. *International Journal of Qualitative Studies in Education*, 8(3), 253–254.

Holm, G. (2008). Visual research methods: Where are we and where are we going? In S. Hesse-Biber and P. Leavy (Eds), *Handbook of emergent methods* (325–341). New York: Guilford.

Holm, G. (2014). Photography as a research method. In P. Leavy (Ed.), *The Oxford handbook of qualitative research* (380–402). Oxford: Oxford University Press.

Holm, G., & Farber, P. (2005). Cultural competence: College students learn through academic service-learning. In H. Helve and G. Holm (Eds), *Contemporary youth research: Local expressions and global connections* (121–132). Hampshire, UK: Ashgate.

Holm, G., Londen, M., & Mansikka, J.-E. (2015). Interpreting visual (and verbal) data: Teenagers' views on belonging to a language minority group. In M. Griffiths, D. Bridges, & P. Smeyers (Eds), *International handbook of interpretation in educational research methods* (753–782). Dordrecht: Springer Science.

Honan, E., Hamid, M. O., Alhamdan, B., Phommalangsy, P., & Lingard, B. (2013). Ethical issues in cross-cultural research. *International Journal of Research & Method in Education*, 36(4), 386–399.

Howes, A., & Miles, S. (2015). Representation and exploitation: Using photography to explore education. In S. Miles and A. Howes (Eds), *Photography in educational research: Critical reflections from diverse contexts* (1–18). London: Routledge.

Katsui, H., Lehtomäki, E., Yehualawork Malle, A., & Chalklen, S. Questioning human rights: The case of education for children and youth with disabilities in Ethiopia. In S. Grech and K. Soldatic (Eds), *Disability in the Global South: The critical handbook* (187–198). Amsterdam: Springer.

Kendall, N., Kaunda, Z., & Friedson-Rideneur, S. (2015). Community participation in international development education quality improvement efforts: Current paradoxes and opportunities. *Educational Assessment, Evaluation and Accountability*, 27, 65–83.

Lehtomäki, E., & Hukkanen, S. (2015). Tanzanian girls and women with [dis]abilities claim their right to education. In F. Kiuppis and R. Sarromaa Hausstätter (Eds), *Inclusive education: Twenty years after Salamanca* (231–250). New York: Peter Lang.

Lehtomäki, E., Janhonen-Abruquah, H., Okkolin, M., Posti-Ahokas, H., Tuomi, M., & Palojoki, P. (2014). Research to engage voices on the ground in educational development. *International Journal of Educational Development*, 35, 37–43.

Lindeman, S., Halme, M., Kallio, G., Kourula, A., Lima-Toivanen, M., & Korsunova, A. (2010). Doing ethnographic research among low-income people in emerging markets. *Proceedings of the 3rd Qualitative Research Conference*, University of Vaasa, Finland. ISBN 978-952-476-309-7.

Maguth, B. M., & Hillburn, J. (2015). Introduction. The state of global education: Learning with the world and its people. In B. M. Maguth and J. Hillburn (Eds), *The state of global education: Learning with the world and its people* (1–10). New York: Routledge.

Majumbar, A. (2011). Using photographs of places, spaces and objects to explore South Asian women's experience of close relationships and marriage. In P. Reavey (Ed.), *Visual methods in psychology: Using and interpreting images in qualitative research* (69–84). New York: Psychology Press.

Morrow, V., & Pells, K. (2012). Integrating children's human rights and child poverty debates: Examples from young lives in Ethiopia and India. *Sociology, 46*(5), 906–920.

Okkolin, M.-A. (2013). *Highly educated women in Tanzania – Constructing educational well-being and agency.* (Doctoral dissertation.) *Jyväskylä Studies in Education, Psychology and Social Research*, 483. Jyväskylä, Finland: University of Jyväskylä.

Peshkin, A. (1986). *God's choice: The total world of a fundamentalist Christian school.* Chicago: University of Chicago Press.

Posti-Ahokas, H. (2013). Empathy-based stories capturing the voice of female secondary school students in Tanzania. *International Journal of Qualitative Studies in Education, 26*(10), 1277–1292.

Posti-Ahokas, H. (2014). *Tanzanian female students' perspectives on the relevance of secondary education.* PhD Diss., University of Helsinki. Retrieved from https://helda.helsinki.fi/handle/10138/45346.

Posti-Ahokas, H., & Lehtomäki, E. (2014). The significance of student voice: Female students' interpretations of failure in Tanzanian secondary education. *Gender and Education, 26*(4), 338–355.

Posti-Ahokas, H., & Okkolin, M.-A. (2015). Enabling and constraining family: Young women building their educational paths in Tanzania. *International Journal of Community, Work and Family.* http://dx.doi.org/10.1080/13668803.2015.1047737.

Tuomi, M., Lehtomäki, E., & Matonya, M. (2015). 'As capable as other students': Tanzanian women with disabilities in higher education. *Disability, Development and Education, 64*, 32–39.

Turnyansky, B., Tuval, S., Mansur, R., Barak, J., & Gidron, A. (2009). From the inside out: Learning to understand and appreciate multiple voices through telling identities. *New Directions for Teaching and Learning, 118*, 39–47.

United Nations. (2015). *Sustainable Development Goals.* Retrieved from www.un.org/sustainabledevelopment/sustainable-development-goals/.

Unterhalter, E. (2012). Inequality, capabilities and poverty in four African countries: Girls' voice, schooling, and strategies for institutional change. *Cambridge Journal of Education, 42*(3), 307–325.

Van Ausdale, D., & Feagin, J. R. (2001). *The first R: How children learn race and racism.* Plymouth: Rowman & Littlefield Publishers.

Wang, C. (2005). *Photovoice. Social change through photography.* Retrieved from www.photovoice.com/method/index.html.

Warrington, M., & Kiragu, S. (2012). 'It makes more sense to educate a boy': Girls 'against the odds' in Kajiado, Kenya. *International Journal of Educational Development, 32*, 301–309.

World Comics Finland. (2010). *Grassroots comics by disabled people: Report January–February 2010.* Retrieved from http://comics-with-attitude.blogspot.fr/2012/01/v-behaviorurldefaultvmlo_03.html.

World Education Forum. (2000). *The Dakar framework for action. Education for all: Meeting our collective commitments.* Adopted by the World Education Forum in Dakar, Senegal, 26–28 April 2000. Retrieved from http://unesdoc.unesco.org/images/0012/001202/120240e.pdf.

Part II

Multidimensional and comprehensive approaches to learning

5 Incorporating cultural and linguistic diversity in Information and Communication Technology in education in Kenya

Suzanne Adhiambo Puhakka

Language, culture, and ICT

Cultural diversity can be seen as having a variety of different ideas, customs, and social behaviour. Some scholars (e.g. Gay, 2013; Inglis, 2008; Terry & Irving, 2010) have argued the need for countries to address cultural dimensions when administering education in diverse societies if learning is to take place effectively. Cultural diversity is as necessary as biodiversity for the survival of mankind, and this can be seen in the United Nations Educational, Scientific and Cultural Organization (UNESCO) Universal Declaration on Cultural Diversity, adopted in 2001, which supports cultural cohesion in societies (UNESCO, 2002). Cultural diversity brings with it certain responsibilities, such as the responsibility to ensure that different groups are respected and treated fairly and equally within a given organization, group, or society. Furthermore teachers who play a vital role in their students' education have an unequivocal responsibility to address the cultural environments of their learners (Piquemal, 2004).

Diversity is a rich resource that should be preserved and understood as it provides possibilities for meaningful comparative learning in any society and across the globe (Herring, 2009). In order to understand cultural diversity, one needs to have a basic definition for what constitutes a culture. One description of culture is as a common system of decorum and combination of cognitive constructs and understanding that are learned by socialization (Perso, 2012).

This chapter discusses the use of ICT in primary education in Kenya and suggests ways in which cultural responsiveness can be incorporated. Chapter 44 of the current constitution in Kenya promotes respect and recognition for cultural diversity (Kenya Law Reform Commission, 2015). However, the history of inter-tribal hostility and violence which has existed in Kenya for a combination of reasons such as land distribution, unequal distribution of resources, unemployment, and poverty has led to many misconceptions such as "acknowledging cultural differences being equated to tribal prejudice" (Bale & Sang, 2013; Njuguna, 2011). Furthermore, as a consequence of colonialism many Kenyans view their own cultures as being primitive and education is seen mostly as a way to eradicate these perceived primeval African cultural practices. This is the mentality that colonialists wanted Africans to adopt. "Education is a westernization concept and not a learning concept": this attitude has been passed down for generations (Sobania, 2003; Tarimo, 2008).

Culture and language in Kenya

Language contains the culture and history of communities (Boroditsky, 2010; Geng, 2010). A clear embodiment of the language diversity found in Sub-Saharan Africa can be observed in Kenya (Bowden, 2007; Dwivedi, 2014; Heine & Nurse, 2000). The language environment in Kenya is heterogeneous, with the country having between 43 and 72 indigenous languages depending on whether one is dividing along tribal lines or dialects distributed among the 41 million inhabitants (Republic of Kenya, 2009; Ogechi, 2009). The diversity in the population is seen in linguistic diversity, ethnic diversity, as well as racial diversity. The native languages are categorized in three main groups as Bantu, Nilotic, and Cushitic. The Bantu languages of the people, e.g. Agikuyu, Abaluhya, Akamba, Aembu, and Ameru, are spoken by approximately 62 per cent of the population. The Nilotic languages of the Dholuo, Akalenjin, Aturkana, and Amaasai people are spoken by 30 per cent, while the Cushitic languages of the Somali, Oromo, and Rendille form an ethnic minority spoken by less than 5 per cent of the people (Lewis, Simons, & Fennig, 2015). Cultural identity in Kenyan society is formulated within the home environment. Although the people are referred to as Kenyan, there is no single culture that can be identified as the Kenyan culture.

In traditional society, education and culture were embedded. The Luo people, for example, believed that education is a process that takes place from the birth to death of a person, a continuous process spread throughout the entire life. Initial learning took place in the family setting where the children learnt about their responsibilities in the home, and, as they grew older, they learnt their responsibilities at the societal/tribal level. The oldest persons were the teachers and the learners were expected to follow what they taught without question. One factor of traditional Luo teaching was that specialized education was not open to all; skills were passed from one generation to the next along family lines for example in the case of traditional healers and medicine men. The primary goal of traditional education was to teach the children to become socially conforming adults (Ocholla-Ayayo, 1976).

If we compare this traditional learning model to today's schooling systems we see that the current practices do not explicitly teach norms and beliefs expected of the person with respect to their culture. Rather, learners are encouraged to be critical thinkers and to question everything for the sake of educational progress. Therefore, a child coming from a Luo home that is still using the authoritarian approach for socialization may find it difficult to adjust as a critical thinker questioning what the teacher is teaching at school, whether the criticism is constructive or not. A teacher should be in a position to support this child and this can only take place if the teacher is aware of the child's cultural background. In order for cultural diversity to be acknowledged in the classroom, teachers need to be educated on cultural issues that affect learning.

Language in education in Kenya

During the nineteenth century with the coming of the missionaries and the spread of Christianity, early reading instruction to children and adults was taught in the indigenous African languages with the sole purpose of ensuring that the natives could translate the Bible into their respective traditional languages (Mojola, 2002). The use of the English language in schools was introduced at the beginning of the twentieth century, and this was done after discussions and decisions were made at the 1909 missionary conference in an effort to enable the missionaries to work better with the local communities (Anderson, 1984; Capon, 1952; Omulokolii, 2004). However, a commission set up by the government known as the Phelps-Stokes Commission (1924) recommended the use of African indigenous languages as languages of instruction and the teaching of English as a second language. This commission also recommended that the Kiswahili language be taught in the Kenyan coastal region only to those people for whom it was a mother tongue. These recommendations were never put into practice effectively (Kioko & Muthwii, 2001).

In the post-colonial period, Kenya adopted the use of the English language as the official language, which consequently led to its dominance. The Kenyan education system continued to face challenges over which language would be used for learning, especially in the early grades (1–3). The local languages are not accorded significant status as higher status is accorded to the English language, which is spoken proficiently by less than 20 per cent of the people as a second language (Crystal, 2003; Dwivedi, 2014; Lewis et al., 2014). There is a constant dilemma on what language should be used to teach early reading instruction. While the consensus is growing that the children's mother tongue is the way to go, it is practically challenging to use the mother tongues because the local languages do not have print material that can be used for teaching and learning. Furthermore many educators have not understood the impact of language in early learning (Liddicoat, 2007; Puhakka, 2015; Trudell & Piper, 2014).

Lack of consideration of the language issues in the school curriculum has led to poor learning outcomes (Agalo & Mbai, 2015; Kioko, 2015). Unfortunately, this is a situation that is reflected in many countries in Sub-Saharan Africa. The 2003 Biennial Meeting of the Association of the Development of Education in Africa was a critical meeting that spearheaded the acknowledgement of the significant role of mother-tongue education in early learning. Research (e.g. Cordeur, 2014; UNESCO, 2003) has shown that the use of a child's mother tongue in education is paramount in ensuring the success of the child's literacy acquisition. There are more than 2,000 indigenous languages spoken in Africa (Heine & Nurse, 2000). This means that linguistic diversity is not a new concept; what is new, however, is how to incorporate this linguistic diversity in the education curriculum.

In 2014, Minister Jacob Kaimenyi issued a directive that all primary schools should start teaching in the mother tongue under a new language policy (Omwenga, 2014). The Sessional Paper of 2012 states: "The language of the catchment area (mother tongue) shall be used for child care, pre-primary education i.e. nursery schools and kindergartens and in the education of lower primary children (class 1–3)." This policy has long been in existence theoretically but has not been implemented because of the lack of reading material and methodology training for teachers on how to teach reading in the indigenous languages (Bunyi, 2001; Trudell & Piper 2014).

Language is necessary for communication in the classroom in any given school. It is the medium by which teachers convey their message to the learners. Without language, learners would not understand what they are taught (Benson, 2004; Polias, 2004). Language plays a vital role in acquisition of reading skills and further development in becoming proficient readers, and today, researchers and educational professionals agree that initial literacy skills in the classroom must be taught with regard to the respective languages the pupils speak (Aro & Wimmer, 2003).

ICT language and culture

ICT (Information and Communication Technology) can be defined as a comprehensive term to describe digital media, communication gadgets, radio, television, mobile phones, computers and their networks, hardware and software, and satellite systems. The big leap in technological development has led to reduced costs, consequently leading to increased use of ICT in many aspects of every day communication, enhancement of economic growth as well as education (Kinuthia, 2009; Obayelu & Ogunlade, 2006; Sife, Lwoga & Sanga, 2007).

Several theories are linked to the use of ICT in education, such as the information processing theory, the technology enhanced learning theory, the social construction of technology, and Robert Gagne's conditions of learning and technological determinism (Gagne, Briggs, & Wager, 1992; Miller, Galanter, & Pribram, 1960; Oudshoorn, & Pinch, 2003; Smith & Marx, 1994). Learning theories are important to help us understand how people learn and, therefore, enable us to design effective teaching methodologies. Because ICT has become an integral part of education and learning, education practitioners should embrace theories that support the use of ICT in learning. But we should not embrace ICT for the sake of ICT. That is focusing only on networking and information dissemination. The role of ICT should be to enhance the knowledge of learners.

With the world of ICT evolving every day and with the complex situations concerning language, culture, and education in Kenya, and the international pressure to use ICT for the advancement of education, the curriculum developers in Kenya have the challenging task of finding solutions for how to use ICT successfully and in a culturally sensitive way for the Kenyan pupil (Muinde, 2009). When technology (in this case, computers) first arrived, the most important issue was learning to use the computer, and technology or science in itself was not viewed as having a cultural perspective.

However, views have long existed suggesting that cultural practices of any society revolve around its technological foundation (Smith & Marx, 1994). As the use of ICT environments advanced, it became apparent that language and culture were an inherent part of using the tools, because people began using computers for communication such as writing and receiving emails and more recently in teaching and learning in classroom settings. The big question remains: "How can ICT be used in a culturally sensitive way and, at the same time, incorporate language diversity?" The Geneva Declaration of the Global Forum of Indigenous Peoples and the Information Society states:

> Information and Communication Technology (ICT) should be used to support and encourage cultural diversity and to preserve and promote the language, distinct identities and traditional knowledge of Indigenous peoples, nations and tribes in a manner which they determine best advances these goals. The evolution of the information and communication societies must be founded on the respect and promotion of the rights of Indigenous peoples, nations and tribes and our distinctive and diverse cultures, as outlined in international conventions. We have fundamental and collective rights to protect, preserve and strengthen our own languages, cultures and identities.
>
> (United Nations Permanent Forum on Indigenous Issues, 2003)

Challenges of accommodating cultural and linguistic diversity with ICT in primary schools

Schools in Kenya, whether linguistically homogeneous or heterogeneous, display cultural diversity. Unfortunately, the Kenyan school curriculum has not succeeded in incorporating diversity into everyday learning, despite researches and documentation by scholars (Elischer, 2008; Ogechi, 2009). This may be due to the fact that everyone is aware that cultural diversity should be part of the school system but nobody knows how it can be embedded into the curriculum (Maina, 2003).

Many studies in Kenya (e.g. Bunyi, 2001; Gakure, Muria, & Kithae, 2013) continue to show the devastating state of the teaching profession and how many teachers lack specialized training, especially in the area of early education (class 1–3) and language learning. Already faced with these obstacles, it is difficult to imagine how these teachers would incorporate ICT in their classrooms, not to mention provide culturally responsive education. Complex terminologies in ICT learning, coupled with the fear of technologies, makes teachers unwilling to embrace ICT tools (Cakir & Yildirim, 2013; Ilomäki, 2008). Still, the teachers' gender and age can easily contribute to their rejection of new policies. Not understanding what is expected of them and their pupils can lead to a fear of failure and a resistance to change based on comfort in familiar patterns or methods, but all these are issues that can be overcome through appropriate training (Crump, Logan, & McIlroy, 2007).

Another challenging issue is the lack of effective education development programmes and curricula to support existing policies. For example, in Kenya there is a language policy that encourages the use of indigenous languages as the languages of early instruction, and yet English still is used dominantly in early learning. This in part is due to lack of practical methodologies that can support multilingual learning and unavailability of learning support material in the local languages (Ogechi, 2003; Trudell and Piper, 2014).

Kenya has in place a national ICT policy framework and implementation strategy in principle, with the section on information technology stating that the Kenyan government will support "the use of ICT in schools, colleges, universities and other educational institutions in the country so as to improve the quality of teaching and learning" (Ministry of Information and Communications, 2006). The policy is commendable for factoring in issues concerning gender, in-service training for teachers and developing and improving local content. It also has incorporated measurable outcomes and listed various challenges in its implementation. Unfortunately, the policy has failed to address issues on language learning and cultural diversity (Dean, 2011).

Non-governmental organizations (NGOs), government institutions, and other organizations have developed numerous initiatives to promote ICT in education in Kenya. The Ministry of Education (MOE) has established an ICT unit. To facilitate the unit, the Ministry of Education, Science and Technology (MOEST) a branch of the MOE, coordinates and mobilizes funds through a trust fund, a registered consortium that operates as an NGO in Kenya. It works as an umbrella organization for various partner organizations from the public, private, and civil society sectors and its chairman is the permanent secretary of the Ministry of Education in Kenya. Its primary objective is to mobilize funds for the sole purpose of setting up computer laboratories in all Kenyan primary and secondary schools over 4–5 years.

Other initiatives include computers for schools – Kenya aims to provide 16,000 computers in over 531 educational institutions; train well over 3,106 head teachers and their deputies, ICT teachers, and other teachers; sensitize educational administrators and policy makers; and develop curricula on ICT competence. The New Partnership for Africa's Development's e-schools initiative aims to provide graduating students with ICT skills. Each e-school in Kenya is equipped with computers that are interconnected through local area networks (LANs). The individual LANs are then linked via satellite to form a wide area network that stretches across the continent. The Regional

African Satellite Communication Organization, with the support of the International Telecommunication Union, designed, assembled, and launched a satellite into orbit to support the e-Africa Commission's activities. There is also the Network Initiative for Computers in Schools, a consortium of NGOs involved in ICT in the education sector in Kenya, which coordinates member activities related to computer equipment sourcing, refurbishment, distribution, installation, training, maintenance, networking, connectivity, and use of ICT as a tool within the formal and informal sectors (Wambui & Barasa, 2007).

Several evaluations and assessments of these ICT programmes have been made (e.g. Njagi & Oboko, 2013). In a general sense, these initiatives are a step in the right direction. However, so far there are no effective methodologies that can be used to evaluate the success rate of these initiatives and most often information on the achievements of the ICT trust fund is unavailable.

The current infrastructure in Kenya especially in the rural areas does not support the effective use of ICT (especially in schools) due to the high cost of ICT infrastructure support as well as the high cost of computers, android tablets, and the like. Besides, in a country where 50 per cent of the population lives below the poverty line, use of ICT is not among the most urgent issues to be resolved. Further still, linguistic and cultural dimensions have not been given enough attention in the ICT initiatives; many applications that are imported to Africa are developed and based on western cultures (Madzingira, 2001; Okello & Ndirangu, 2010).

The future of ICT in Kenyan education: what does the future hold?

Endeavours by the Kenyan government geared towards improving ICT access or the use of ICT in education have faced and continue to face numerous challenges such as poor infrastructure, lack of resources, lack of adequate teacher training in ICT among others. For example, a heavily funded plan to introduce mobile computer laboratories in public schools has yet to take off even after a budgetary allocation due to many issues related to mismanagement and corruption (Hennessy et al., 2010). Furthermore there are other problems facing Kenyan children in school such as hunger and illness, and there are always ethical questions associated with the justification for equipping a child with an expensive ICT gadget before the child's basic needs are met. Nonetheless the society is steadily embracing technology tools and their applications. Strategies showing the effectiveness of ICT need to be developed, if language and cultural dimensions are to be effectively taken into account in ICT.

Available teacher training curricula need to be improved to include cultural and language perspectives, because language and culture are paramount for any education and learning to take place. The most efficient classroom teachers are those who accept and acknowledge their pupils cultural diversity

(Colombo, 2005; Guild, 1994; Joy & Kolb, 2009). It is possible that language and cultural issues in education have been neglected because most people see them as innate characteristics that will in one way or another find their way into the student's learning progress. Hence, tools to measure their success or failure do not really exist in the African context. The development of effective cultural assessment tools requires that all stakeholders work together (Kumas-Tan, Beagan, Loppie, Macleod, & Frank, 2007).

Government policies that are developed to support ICT in education should be supported with practical methodologies and curricula in the school and classroom setting. They should also support systems such as in-service teacher education to enable constructive administration. African languages and cultures need to be accorded the status they deserve. There needs to be a resocialization so that people can view their cultures as attributes to be honoured.

A key point that should not be overlooked is that effective use of technology in the classroom can only be achieved through competent teachers. Teachers should be educated appropriately on both the pedagogical methodologies and practical aspects of using ICT in and out of the classroom via culturally sensitive approaches so that they develop confidence in their abilities and the efficacy of the technology. In this way, they will view ICT not as an adversary but rather as a learning enhancement tool (Ertmer, Ottenbreit-Leftwich, Sadik, Sendurur, & Sendurur, 2012). Incorporating language and culture is an eventuality that, when embraced sooner rather than later, allows us to begin the process of developing and improving technology learning tools.

References

Agalo, J., & Mbai, C. (2015). Chasing international language: Genesis of language of curriculum in Kenya. *International Journal of Education Learning and Development*, *3*, 1–7.

Anderson, K. (1984). *Church history and theology*. Nairobi: Evangel.

Aro, M., & Wimmer, H. (2003). Learning to read: English in comparison to six more regular orthographies. *Applied Psycholinguistics*, *24*, 621–635.

Bale, J., & Sang, J. (2013). *Kenyan running: Movement, culture, geography and global change*. New York: Routledge.

Benson, C. (2004). The importance of mother tongue-based schooling for educational quality. *Education for All Global Monitoring Report (2005): The quality imperative*. Retrieved from http://unesdoc.unesco.org/images/0014/001466/146632e.pdf.

Boroditsky, L. (2010). Lost in translation. *The Wall Street Journal*. Retrieved from www.wsj.com/articles/SB10001424052748703467304575383131592767868#U30 1072366249K2H.

Bowden, R. (2007). *Africa south of the Sahara*. Chicago IL: Heinemann Library.

Bunyi, G. (2001). Language and educational inequality in primary classrooms in Kenya. In M. Heller & M. Martin-Jones (Eds), *Voices of authority: Education and linguistic difference* (77–100). Westport, CT: Ablex.

Cakir, R., & Yildirim, S. (2013). ICT teachers' professional growth viewed in terms of perceptions about teaching and competencies. *Journal of Information Technology Education: Innovations in Practice, 12*, 221–237.

Capon, M. G. (1952). *A history of Christian co-operation in Kenya.* Nairobi: Christian Council of Kenya.

Colombo, M. W. (2005). *Empathy and cultural competence: Reflections from teachers of culturally diverse children.* Retrieved from https://journal.naeyc.org/btj/200511/ColomboBTJ1105.pdf.

Cordeur, M. (2014). *Mother tongue education provides essential basis for sound education.* Stellenbosch University. Retrieved from www.sun.ac.za/english/Lists/news/Disp-Form.aspx?ID=1289.

Crump, B. J., Logan, K. A., & McIlroy, A. (2007). Does gender still matter? A study of the views of women in the ICT Industry in New Zealand. *Gender, Work & Organization, 14*, 349–370.

Crystal, D. (2003). *English as a global language.* Cambridge: Cambridge University Press.

Dean, C. (2011). *Understanding diversity and seeking unity in the Kenyan educational context.* Retrieved from www.strathmore.edu/ethics/pdf/DeanCatherineUnderstandingDiversity.pdf.

Dwivedi, A. V. (2014). Linguistic realities in Kenya: A preliminary survey. *Ghana Journal of Linguistics, 3*, 27–34.

Elischer, S. (2008). Ethnic coalitions of convenience and commitment: Political parties and party systems in Kenya. *German Institute of Global and Area Studies (GIGA), Working Papers, 68.* Retrieved from SSRN: http://ssrn.com/abstract=1114123.

Ertmer, P. A., Ottenbreit-Leftwich, A. T., Sadik, O., Sendurur, E., & Sendurur, P. (2012). Teachers' beliefs and technology integration practices: A critical relationship. *Computers & Education, 59*, 423–435.

Gagne, R., Briggs, L., & Wager, W. (1992). *Principles of instructional design* (4th Ed.). Fort Worth, TX: HBJ College.

Gakure, R., Mukuria, P., & Kithae, P. (2013). An evaluation of factors that affect performance of primary schools in Kenya: A case study of Gatanga district. *International Journal of Nursery and Primary Education, 1*, 1–11.

Gay, G. (2013). Teaching to and through cultural diversity. *Curriculum Inquiry, 43*, 48–70.

Geng, X. (2010). Cultural differences influence on language. *Review of European Studies, 2*, 219–222.

Guild, P. (1994). The culture/learning style connection. *Educating for Diversity, 51*, 16–21.

Heine, B., & Nurse D. (2000). *African languages: An introduction.* Cambridge: Cambridge University Press.

Hennessy, S., Onguko, B., Harrison, D., Ang'ondi, E. K., Namalefe, S., Naseem, A., & Wamakote, L. (2010). *Developing the use of information and communication technology to enhance teaching and learning in East African schools: Review of the literature.* Cambridge: University of Cambridge and DFID.

Herring, C. (2009). Does diversity pay? Race, gender, and the business case for diversity. *American Sociological Review, 74*, 208–224.

Ilomäki, J. (2008). *The effects of ICT on school: Teachers' and students' perspectives* (Doctoral Dissertation). University of Turku, Finland.

Inglis, C. (2008). *Planning for cultural diversity.* Paris: UNESCO.

Joy, S., & Kolb, D. A. (2009). Are there cultural differences in learning style? *International Journal of Intercultural Relations*, *33*, 69–85.

Kenya Law Reform Commission. (2015). *Constitution of Kenya, 44. Language and culture.* Retrieved from, www.klrc.go.ke/index.php/constitution-of-kenya/112-chapter-four-the-bill-of-rights/part-2-rights-and-fundamental-freedoms/210-44-language-and-culture.

Kioko, A. (2015). *Why schools should teach young learners in home language.* British council. Retrieved from www.britishcouncil.org/voices-magazine/why-schools-should-teach-young-learners-home-language.

Kioko, A. N., & Muthwii, M. J. (2001). The demands of a changing society: English in education in Kenya today. *Language, Culture and Curriculum*, *14*, 201–213.

Kinuthia, W. (2009). Educational development in Kenya and the role of information and communication technology. *International Journal of Education and Development Using Information and Communication Technology (IJEDICT)*, *5*, 6–20.

Kumas-Tan, Z., Beagan, B., Loppie, C., MacLeod, A., & Frank, B. (2007). Measures of cultural competence: Examining hidden assumptions. *Academic Medicine*, *82*, 548–557.

Lewis, M. P., Simons, G. F., & Fennig, C. D. (Eds) (2015). *Ethnologue: Languages of the World*, Eighteenth edition. *Languages of Kenya. An Ethnologue Country Report.* Dallas, TX: SIL International. Online version. Retrieved from www.ethnologue.com.

Liddicoat, A. J. (Ed.) (2007). *Language planning and policy: Issues in language planning and literacy.* Clevedon, UK: Multilingual Matters.

Madzingira, N. (2001). *Culture, communication and development in Africa.* Zimbabwe: IDEP.

Maina, F. (2003). Integrating cultural values into the curriculum for Kenyan schools. *Opinion papers* (120). Nairobi: Kenyan Government.

Miller, G. A., Galanter, E., & Pribram, K. H. (1960). *Plans and the structure of behavior.* New York: Holt, Rinehart & Winston.

Ministry of Information and Communications. (2006). *National information and communications technology (ICT) policy.* Retrieved from www.ist-africa.org/home/files/Kenya_ICTPolicy_2006.pdf.

Mojola, A. O. (2002). Bible translation in Africa. What implications does the new UBS perspective have for Africa? An overview in the light of the emerging new UBS translation initiative. *Acta Theologica Supplementum*, *2*, 202–213.

Muinde, F. N. N. (2009). *Investigation of factors affecting the adoption of information and communication technologies for communication of research output in research institutions in Kenya* (Doctoral dissertation). School of Information Management, Victoria University of Wellington, Wellington, New Zealand. http://researcharchive.vuw.ac.nz/bitstream/handle/10063/1417/thesis.pdf?sequence=1.

Njagi, R., & Oboko, R. (2013). A monitoring and evaluation framework for the integration in ICTs in teaching and learning in primary schools in Kenya. *Journal of Education and Practice*, *12*, 21–28.

Njuguna, G. K. (2011). *Breaking the culture of ethnic hostility in Kenya: A national reconciliation strategy* (Doctoral thesis). Asbury Theological Seminary.

Obayelu, E. A., & Ogunlade, I. (2006). Analysis of the uses of information and communication technology for gender empowerment and sustainable poverty alleviation in Nigeria. *International Journal of Education and Development Using Information and Communication Technology* (IJEDICT), *2*, 45–69.

Ocholla-Ayayo, A. B. C. (1976). *Traditional ideology and ethics among the southern Luo.* Uppsala: Offset.

Ogechi, N. O. (2003). On language rights in Kenya. *Nordic Journal of African Studies, 12*, 277–295.

Ogechi, N. O. (2009). The role of foreign and indigenous languages in primary schools: The case of Kenya. *Stellenbosch Papers in Linguistics PLUS, 38*, 143–158.

Okello, J. J., & Ndirangu, L. K. (2010). *Does the environment in which ICT-based market information services (MIS) projects operate affect their performance? Experiences from Kenya.* Paper presented at the Joint 3rd African Association of Agricultural Economists (AAAE) and 48th Agricultural Economists Association of South Africa (AEASA) Conference, Cape Town, South Africa (September 2010).

Omulokolii, W. A. (2004). The early history of church cooperation and unity in Kenya. *Africa Journal of Evangelical Theology, 23*, 145–160.

Omwenga, G. (2014). Use local languages, insists minister. *Daily Nation*, 3 March 2014. Online edition.

Oudshoorn, N., & Pinch, T. (2003). *How users matter: The co-construction of users and technology.* Cambridge, MA: MIT.

Perso, T. F. (2012) *Cultural responsiveness and school education, with particular focus on Australia's First Peoples: A review and synthesis of the literature.* Menzies School of Health Research, Centre for Child Development and Education, Darwin Northern Territory.

Piquemal, N. (2004). Teachers' ethical responsibilities in a diverse society. *Canadian Journal of Educational Administration and Policy, 32*, 1–19.

Polias, J. (2004). *Language and learning in the KLAs and the implications for curriculum writers.* Retrieved from http://education.qld.gov.au/literacy/docs/language-learning.pdf.

Puhakka, C. S. A. (2015). *Digital solutions for multilingual learning environments: The case of GraphoGame™ adaptations in Kenya.* Jyväskylä, Finland: University of Jyväskylä.

Republic of Kenya. (2009). *2009 Kenya population and housing census.* Retrieved from: https://international.ipums.org/international/resources/enum_materials_pdf/enum_instruct_ke2009a.pdf.

Sife, A. S., Lwoga, E. T., & Sanga, C. (2007). New technologies for teaching and learning: Challenges for higher learning institutions in developing countries. *International Journal of Education and Development Using Information and Communication Technology (IJEDICT), 3*, 57–67.

Smith, M. R., & Marx, L. (1994). *Does technology drive history? The dilemma of technological determinism.* Cambridge, MA: MIT.

Sobania, N. (2003). *Culture and customs of Kenya.* Westport, CT: Greenwood.

Tarimo, A. S. J. (2008). *Politicization of ethnic identities. The common good in Kenya.* Ethics at Noon presentation, 7 April 2008, Markkula Center for Applied Ethics, Santa Clara University.

Terry, N. P., & Irving, M. A. (2010). *Cultural and linguistic diversity: Issues in education.* Dubuque: Kendall Hunt.

Trudell, B., & Piper, B. (2014). Whatever the law says: Language policy implementation and early-grade literacy achievement in Kenya. *Current Issues in Language Planning, 15*, 4–21.

UNESCO. (2002). Universal declaration on cultural diversity. A vision a conceptual platform a pool of ideas for implementation of a new paradigm. A document for the World Summit on Sustainable Development. *Cultural diversity series* no. 1.

UNESCO (2003). *Language vitality and endangerment*. Retrieved from http://portal. unesco.org/culture/en/ev.php-URL.

United Nations Permanent Forum on Indigenous Issues. (2003). *Declaration and pro-gramme of action of the global forum of indigenous peoples and the information society*. Retrieved from www.un.org/esa/socdev/unpfii/documents/ips_genderand_ icts_en.pdf.

Wambui, M., & Barasa, E. (2007). ICT: Dawn of a new era. *Elimu News*: a newsletter of the MoEST.

6 Relevance of schooling in Tanzania

Educational leaders' perspectives on economically disadvantaged families

Aneth Komba

Introduction

Since independence, Tanzania has acknowledged the necessity of educating its citizens as a way of overcoming ignorance and combating poverty. Hence, education policies have been always structured with the aim of ensuring the quantity, quality, equality and efficiency of the education system. Consequently, the sector has annually received a substantial share of resources from the national cake. For example, from 2002–2003 to 2011–2012, the education sector's budget has ranged from 15.1 to 19.8 per cent (United Republic of Tanzania (URT), 2011). The Tanzanian government has implemented various policies and programs to ensure universal basic education, including the 1977 and early 2000s Universal Primary Education Program, Primary Education Development Programs (PEDP phase I, 2002–2006 and phase II, 2007–2011) and Secondary Education Development Program (SEDP phase I, 2004–2009 and phase II, 2010–2015).

In all of these policies and programs, education is cited as a means of combatting the three national archenemies: poverty, ignorance and disease. These initiatives have resulted into a number of positive outcomes, including rapidly increasing the enrolment in primary and secondary schools (URT, 2010b). Indeed, the government's efforts have largely aimed at supporting the various global declarations and international policies which emphasize achieving universal basic education. Yet, the education sector is still experiencing a number of challenges, including truancy, dropout and poor learning outcomes, whereby many children complete primary schooling without acquiring basic literacy and numeracy skills.

Dropout has remained a challenge. The government statistics for 2012 show that less than 1 per cent of pupils in primary education but almost 37 per cent of pupils in secondary education dropped out (URT, 2014a). The dropout rate at secondary education is significantly higher compared to primary schools. The frequently mentioned reasons for truancy and dropout in primary and secondary schools, as identified in the government's Basic Education Statistic reports, include truancy, pregnancy, death, inability to meet basic needs, illness, parental illness, misbehaviour, early marriage and nomadic families. For example, in 2011 the leading factors for dropout in primary schools were truancy (75.5 per cent) followed by a lack of basic needs (5.4 per cent) and in secondary schools truancy (72.7 per cent) and an inability to meet basic needs (13.9 per cent) (URT, 2012).

The achievements and challenges that have been revealed in Tanzania education development initiatives are similar to those cited in the 2015 Education For All global monitoring report (UNESCO, 2015). Yet, the global monitoring report notes that several countries were still experiencing challenges in ensuring primary school completion, providing quality education and ensuring that the education which is provided is relevant to the needs of the intended population. Regarding primary school attainment, the report cited poverty as the key factor contributing to low primary school completion (UNESCO, 2015). Notably, the primary school attainment rates of children from poor households were low compared to those from the average population, which requires further attention in the low-income countries, including Tanzania.

In the Tanzanian education policy context, education is regarded as a key to life and the only way that will enable individual Tanzanians to employ the available resources innovatively to create wealth (Galabawa, 2005). Education is also among the basic human rights, hence the various educational national and international policy statements emphasizing the need to ensure that basic education is accessible to and compulsory for all. The UN Sustainable Development Goal 4 defines quality education for all as a global goal (UN, 2015). The basis of all of these policies lies in the argument that investment in education is associated with a number of benefits to both the nation and the individual. Therefore, education of children from economically disadvantaged families requires attention.

In Tanzania 'economically disadvantaged families' mean families deprived of decent human life due to lack of resources and lack of ability to acquire basic human needs (URT, 1998). These families have low per capita income and are therefore categorized as families living in poverty. It is worth noting here that Tanzania is among the developing countries with a high level of poverty, as evidenced by indicators identified in the 1998 Tanzanian poverty eradication strategy, which include high illiteracy rate, poor health services, high mortality rate, homelessness, poor housing, low income, unemployment and poor living conditions in the rural areas (URT, 1998). Poverty still remains a big challenge in country, especially in rural areas (URT, 2010a).

This chapter explores the perspectives of educational leaders in five Tanzanian regions on how economically disadvantaged families value schooling and perceive its relevance. The term 'educational leaders' covers three levels: regional and district level educational leaders and school-level heads. 'Teacher' refers to primary school-level teachers who have no managerial, leadership or administrative duties. The point of departure is that educational leaders and teachers have the potential to make education culturally responsive (Gay, 2013) and contribute to the relevance and thereby to cultural sustainability (Soini & Birkeland, 2014) in education.

The problem

Research and educational policies maintain that investment in education is a valuable and relevant form of investment and is among the key strategies for reducing poverty (see for example Galabawa, 2005, URT 2001; Zymelman, 1973). In Tanzania, studies have shown that education is associated with both social and private benefits (Galabawa, 2005). It has been noted that, when other things remain constant, investment in education in Tanzania yields a higher return than any other form of investment (Galabawa, 2005; Omari, 1999). Indeed, the previous research in Tanzania and elsewhere suggests that there is a positive correlation between income and education, even in the informal sectors. However, to be able to enjoy the benefits of education, individual pupils, students and their parents need to invest their resources in the form of money and time. Parents are required to pay the direct and indirect costs of education and also to sacrifice their children's contribution to the family wellbeing or income by working i.e., the opportunity costs of schooling. Similarly, children need to devote time and effort, tolerate the various difficulties associated with schooling and also sacrifice their participation in other quick-earning activities.

Covering the opportunity costs of schooling might be a difficult decision for the economically disadvantaged families to make. However, economically disadvantaged families' decisions to sacrifice these resources are largely dependent on the various expected benefits of education after graduation. Little is known, however, about how families perceive this long-term investment. The findings in my previous research (Komba, 2013) indicated that most of the children from economically disadvantaged households were less committed to school and that pupils' commitment to school was associated with seven factors: (1) family poverty; (2) families' level of education; (3) parents' attitudes, values and interests regarding their children's education; (4) family structural constraints; (5) parents' monitoring of children; (6) home rules; and (7) parent/child socialization and conversation on educational matters. These findings have guided this study to problematize the relevance and cultural responsiveness of education. Here the focus is on teachers, educational leaders and educational officers at the school, district and regional levels who are responsible for addressing the educational needs and expectations of children coming from economically disadvantaged families. Their work is to implement government policies at the levels of school, district and region, and, therefore, they are supposed to be well-informed regarding the needs and expectations of the consumers of the education service in their area of work.

Theoretical framework

The concept relevance of schooling has been divided into two sub-concepts: the personal relevance referring to learning experiences which are either directly applicable to the personal aspirations, interests, or cultural experiences of the students; and the life experiences i.e., the experiences that are connected to real-world issues, problems and contexts (GPE, 2013). On the other hand, personal relevance is defined as the meaning, value and usefulness of the education experienced by the students (Posti-Ahokas, 2014, p. 70). Henceforth, in the context of this study, education's relevance is defined broadly to mean the value and usefulness of education as perceived by the end users of education services; that is, the parents and children, who are referred to here as families. The author maintains that families will regard education as 'relevant' if, upon graduation from primary or secondary school, the students have acquired the knowledge and skills that meet their aspirations, allowing them to solve their day-to-day problems, successfully engage in community activities and productively use the available resources to liberate themselves from poverty. Similarly, the word 'value' in the definition of relevance is understood as the extent to which education is perceived by economically disadvantaged families as something important and useful in their day-to-day activities. Indeed, education, which is perceived by the end users as being relevant, is also valuable. Hence, this kind of education would motivate economically disadvantaged parents willingly to forego present consumption for future benefits and invest their limited financial resources as well as sacrifice and bear the opportunity, direct and indirect costs of their children's schooling. The evidence from previous literature indicates that government investment in primary and secondary education does not guarantee the automatic consumption of the service by the end users. Parents play a determining role in whether or not their children enrol in school, attend regularly, are committed to school and complete a given cycle of education (Lloyd & Blanc, 1996; Willms, 2003). In the context of this study, parents are regarded as the duty-bearers for inputs to the school organization. Hence, their perceptions concerning the relevance and value of education are vital in contributing to their children's schooling.

The study draws on the human capital theory (HCT) and expectancy theory of motivation. In the HCT, investment in education is seen as a way to improve national economic growth as well as individual wellbeing (Harobin, Smyth, & Wiseman, 1970). Hence, investment in education is perceived as central to a long-term strategy for sustainable economic, social and political development. The evidence from the literature indicates that the social rate of returns on investment in primary education is high, which justifies government intervention in its provision; similarly, investment in education is associated with the private rate of returns which justifies families' investment in their children's education (Galabawa, 2005; Harobin et al., 1970). However, for investment in education to be successful in terms of attracting consumers, the government's statements on the benefits and relevance of education, as usually stated in national level educational policies, and expectations should tally with those of the families. The differences between the government's statements and families' perceptions may act as an obstacle to the families' level of consumption of education.

Another theory used in this study is the expectancy theory of motivation, which is commonly used in organizational research. This theory explains behavioural choice, i.e., why individuals choose one behavioural option over others. The theory is used to explain the views of educational officers, educational leaders and teachers regarding how economically disadvantaged families decide which of the various different kinds of investment is the best choice for them and how families' perceptions of schooling are energized, directed and maintained (Pareek, 2004). The two components of this theory were used to inform this study. First, the process of choosing a particular type of investment is directed by the families' belief regarding the future benefits of that form of investment. This implies that, under *Ceteris Paribus* conditions, when economically disadvantaged families choose to invest in education or other income-earning activities, they weigh and select an investment alternative which is perceived to make a significant contribution to their children's future lives. Among other perceived benefits, this may include improving children's future lives either in the formal or informal sectors and hence reducing the family's level of poverty. Second, families' motivation to invest in their children's education is a function of the three components of Vroom's 1964 expectancy theory i.e., expectancy, instrumentality and valence (Vroom, 1995). This relationship is summarized mathematically as follows: economically disadvantaged parents' motivation to invest in their children's schooling $= \sum$ Expectancy $\times$ Instrumentality $\times$ Valence.

Expectancy is a subjective probability of getting an outcome (Pareek, 2004, p. 225). In this study, expectancy means the views of educational officers, educational leaders and teachers regarding children's subjective probability that their efforts at school will lead to the desired outcomes, for example, whether a child believes that attending school regularly and working hard will enable him/her to perform better at school, pass the final examinations and proceed to the next levels of education. A child is likely to have two kinds of belief: first, attending school regularly and working hard at school will allow one to perform better at school and pass the final examination (expectancy probability of 1); or regular attendance at school and working hard is not associated with improved performance and passing the final examination i.e., even if a child attends school regularly and works hard, his/her efforts will not result in any positive outcomes (expectancy probability of 0).

Instrumentality is a perceived a performance–reward relationship (Pareek, 2004, p. 225). In this study, it is regarded as the views of educational officers, educational leaders and teachers concerning the families' belief that children's schooling is associated with children's future success in life. Parents are likely to hold two kinds of belief: first, that, even if they spend the resources they have on investing in their children's education, their children, upon graduating, will still remain poor in the village (instrumentality probability of 0); or investing in their children's education financially and sacrificing their children's contribution to the family will provide an opportunity for the children to learn skills that will enable them to succeed in life and reduce their level of poverty (instrumentality probability of 1).

Valence refers to the value that the individual personally places on the rewards (Pareek, 2004). In this study, valence is used to explain the views of educational officers, educational leaders and teachers concerning the value that families attach to the existing outcomes of schooling. Basically, expectancy theory in this study is used to explain the perceptions of educational officers, educational leaders and teachers regarding why parents choose to invest in other income-earning activities than education.

Methodology

In Tanzania, the formal education system comprises two years of pre-primary education, seven years of primary education, four years of junior secondary (O-level), two year of senior secondary (Advanced level), and three or more years of tertiary education i.e., $2+7+4+2+3+$ (URT, 1995). This study focuses on the relevance of primary education and O-level secondary education. A qualitative research approach using a multiple embedded case study design (Scholz & Tietje, 2002; Yin, 2008) is employed to investigate perceptions of educational leaders and teachers.

Data were collected in five regions of Tanzania: Morogoro, Iringa, Rukwa, Mbeya and Katavi. The regions were selected using convenience sampling due to the limited time available but also because of the regions being easily accessible at the time of this study (Miles & Huberman, 1994). Within each region, a stratified sampling strategy was used to obtain one rural and one semi-urban district. In each district, schools were purposefully selected on the basis of four criteria: serving economically disadvantaged families; location in remote rural areas; dropout, truancy and cases whereby several class seven graduates who were selected to join secondary schools never reported to school; and poor performance in the national primary and secondary school examinations. Using these criteria, 200 secondary and primary schools were selected. Due to heavy rains, more than 75 per cent of the selected schools were not easily accessible and alternative schools were visited based on the recommendation of the district educational officers (DEOs) and regional educational officers (REOs). Educational officers were knowledgeable and familiar with those schools that were reachable at that time.

Research participants, educational leaders and teachers were selected using purposeful and convenient sampling. The sample size was determined in the field and not at the prior data-collection stage. Hence, data were collected until a saturation point was reached, i.e., there was no new information coming out from the interviews. The researcher visited 15 primary schools and 15 secondary schools, interviewed 5 REOs, 20 DEOs, 30 heads and 40 teachers. Hence, in total, the study employed a sample of 95 participants. In each region, the researcher adhered to research ethics, including obtaining research clearance from the regional administrative secretaries. This clearance was presented to the district administrative secretaries and the regional and district educational officers. In every district studied, the DEO or a member from the office volunteered to escort the researcher to the schools studied. In the school, the DEO or representative introduced the researcher to the heads, who introduced the researcher to the teachers. All participants were asked for their permission to participate in the study, to have the interview conversation recorded and for the recorded information to be used in communicating the findings to a wider audience.

Data were collected between February and June 2014 using individual interview, focus group interview, classroom observation and documents. Interviews were conducted with heads of primary and secondary schools while focused group discussion (FGD) was conducted with teachers and educational officers at the level of regions and district. In all these groups, the researcher used open-ended questions which enabled the participants to open up and speak as much as possible on what they think regarding families' perceptions on the relevance of schooling. At each of the primary schools visited, the researcher observed classroom sessions and pupils' exercise books. Documents reviewed in the sampled schools included attendance records and records regarding students who were selected to join secondary schools.

Data collected through documents were analysed using content analysis. Interview and FGD data were transcribed verbatim, reduced by deleting information that seemed irrelevant to the study and displayed in a matrix. In the matrix, it was possible to identify clearly the various themes that emerged from each of the participants and groups studied. The matrix facilitated both within and between case analysis and enabled the researcher to count covertly the frequency of occurrence of similar responses. Finally, conclusions were drawn and were verified using data from observations and documents. Being a qualitative study, the findings cannot be generalized to the wider population but only to the studied cases (case-to-case transfer) and may be transferred and applied in contexts similar to that used in this study (Miles & Huberman, 1994; Yin 2008).

Results and discussion

The participants were asked to explain disadvantaged families' understandings of the value and relevance of primary and secondary schooling and to provide indicators to justify their responses. What was evident from all the school level teachers, heads, district and regional education officers studied was that the majority of economically disadvantaged parents in the locations studied seemed to devalue education, never regarding it as necessary, relevant or valuable. According to them, the major reason for this is the families' failure to realize the positive benefits that children enjoy through successfully completing their schooling, i.e., what are the overall returns of investing in children's education. In the locations studied, the majority of the children drop out at primary and secondary school or decide not to attend secondary school because of their family's estimation of the cost and returns of education, which suggest that the costs outweigh the benefits. The participants described how, since the expansion of secondary schools, several students have been selected to join these schools, yet they have been performing so poorly that the majority of them never proceed beyond ordinary level secondary schools. Due to this tendency, the parents may have been discouraged by the idea that their children will simply waste four years in school and, in the end, fail and remain in the village empty handed. Thus, the data imply that the economically disadvantaged families in the areas studied perceive investing in secondary education as a wasted investment in terms of time and other family resources. Similarly, since children who graduate at form four remain poor in the village, education was perceived to be irrelevant to the needs of the society.

The participants provided five indicators to support their arguments: (1) parents' unwillingness to bear the opportunity, direct and indirect costs of schooling; (2) parents' reluctance to support school activities and their children's education; (3) families' perceptions regarding the value and returns from schooling compared to those from other kinds of investment; (4) families' tendency purposefully to hinder teachers' efforts to encourage schooling; and (5) parents' tendency purposefully to urge their children to ensure that they fail the primary school leaving examination. These findings are described below.

Parents' unwillingness to bear the opportunity, direct and indirect costs of education

The educational officers and educational leaders reported that parents from economically disadvantaged families were not ready to bear the opportunity, direct, and indirect costs of education. In this regard, the children were expected to support the families' activities, such as farming, taking care of siblings, grazing animals and participating in other economic activities to subsidize the family income. For example, the participants in two regions studied noted that the majority of the boys drop out of school and go to graze cows and sell tomatoes. The following was reported by the REO:

> There is greater absenteeism among boys who participate in grazing cattle. When they have grazed cattle for a year, they are given a bull. Hence, grazing for two years means two bulls, which can be used as a workforce. In most cases, these children will never return to school, even if you pursue them using legitimised rules and regulations. For example, parents with children who drop out of or miss school are fined, yet parents are ready and willing to pay these fines rather than send their children back to school.
>
> (FGD, regional education officer)

In the same manner, the head of a secondary school in another region had this to say:

> another challenge is during the tomato harvesting period, male children participate in tomato selling rather than going to school. There is a lot of truancy during the tomato harvest season and, at the end of the season, some boys decide completely to disappear from school.
>
> (Interview, headteacher)

These quotations suggest that the educational officer at regional and school levels assumed that education was valued less by parents than bulls and farming. With reference to HCT, these statements suggest that parents are unaware of the fact that sending their children to school inevitably means sacrificing their children's contribution to the family, or they may be aware yet unprepared to shoulder the opportunity costs of schooling. On the other hand, referring to the expectance theory of motivation, the quotations can be interpreted as representing instrumentality and valence, thus the probability of parents sending their children to school is zero, meaning that they believe that investment in their children's education is unassociated with any positive outcomes and thus valueless. Through their children's participation in other activities, parents witness various immediate benefits yet have never witnessed students from their village benefitting from schooling. Hence, families choose to invest in other income-earning activities. Similarly, the first quotation suggests that having rules and laws to monitor children's schooling is useless when the implementers of those laws and rules are ignorant of the benefits of what is being enforced. Notably, the effectiveness of educational laws and rules depends greatly on stakeholders' understanding of the purpose and benefits of what is being enforced (Komba, 2012).

In light of this perception, it is worth considering the many reasons for parents' tendency to encourage students' truancy and dropout, a key one of which is poverty, directly associated with parents' inability to finance their children's education and poor school outcomes. The poor educational outcomes, according to the school-level teachers and heads interviewed, raise complaints by both primary and secondary school teachers. The secondary school teachers revealed that several students had graduated from class seven while still unable to read and write but, surprisingly, they had been selected to attend secondary education. Hence, the secondary school teachers thought that the primary school teachers were not doing their job properly. On the other hand, the primary school teachers thought that they were doing their job well, as the majority of schools had a 100 per cent transition rate from primary to secondary level. Sadly, the primary school teachers noted that these students were not being properly taught at secondary school, a factor which leads the majority to fail at form four. In the same manner, the secondary school teachers blamed the government, noting that it is impractical for a school to have a 100 per cent transition rate; i.e., a situation whereby all pupils in standard seven pass and go on to secondary school. Notably, some of the pupils who were selected to attend secondary school obtained very low marks in their leaving examination, yet were enrolled in secondary school and automatically failed at the end of secondary education. It is thus imperative for educational leaders at all levels to work cooperatively to address the poor educational outcomes. Equally important is the need to provide a wider opportunity for class seven graduates so that those who do not perform well academically can join the world of vocational education rather than proceeding to secondary education.

To understand and verify the remarks of the REO, DEO, heads and class level teachers regarding poor school outcomes, the researcher undertook several classroom observations in the primary schools visited. Observations revealed that several standard seven students who were about to graduate from their primary schooling were unable to read and write. This means that pupils and families had invested for seven years in schooling yet pupils were unable to acquire the basic literacy and numeracy skills, which implies poor quality primary education especially in rural schools. From these findings it can be argued that, in situations where the family resources are scarce, parents will most likely not opt to invest their few resources in an unprofitable endeavour. This finding calls for the need to use transactional management and leadership styles whereby educational leaders at all levels will promote families' compliance through both rewards and punishments (Yukl, 1999). In the context of this study, the reward that could stimulate families to send their children to school is good schooling outcomes upon children's graduation. Transaction leadership theory works on the premise "I invest in this business and you provide me with gains on my investment". This theory precisely explains the disillusionment of the parents who do not see their children learn when they invest in schooling.

Parents' reluctance to support schools' activities and their children's education

The educational leaders interviewed at the levels of the school, district and region described how parents were reluctant to contribute to support education development in their villages by providing labour or cash and, in some areas, were unwilling to help the schools to combat truancy and dropout. For example, parents refused to participate in constructing teachers' houses and hostels, or donating food for their children. It was revealed that this was partially because of the families' poverty. According to the REO and DEO, the construction of the teachers' houses is a common problem, especially in those villages where there is not even a single roofed house. Hence, when the parents were asked to participate in constructing the teachers' houses, they refused, arguing that the teachers receive a salary and hence should construct their own house. The educational officers noted that a lack of teachers' houses means that the region finds it difficult to send teachers to those areas.

This contributes to a shortage of teachers in these areas, which leads to poor school outcomes. All participants in this study noted that the parents also refused to participate in the construction of hostels in secondary schools because they avoid paying the hostel fees and financing their children by providing them with food and other necessities. Some of the school-level informants noted that their schools had hostels, yet the parents did not allow their children to live in a hostel.

> Parents are reluctant to support school activities. Poor partnership between the school and village government is due to a low awareness of the necessity of education.
>
> (Interview, headteacher)

> In this area and in the majority of coastal areas, the parents are willing to contribute to traditional dances. There are traditional dances here called *kigodoro*, which are held during the night. Parents are ready to spend money on these dances rather than contributing to school matters or supporting their children's schooling. In this case, it is difficult for a parent to contribute even 2000 shillings for examinations.
>
> (Interview, headteacher)

> Some schools have hostels but the parents do not want the children to stay in the hostel because they want to avoid the responsibility of paying for the cost of food.
>
> (FGD, district education officer)

The findings indicate that there was a poor partnership between the schools and the families, whereby all responsibilities were left to the teachers. Notably, according to the teachers, heads, REOs and DEOs the parents did not encourage their children's schooling or advise them to read and work hard at school. Indeed, the participants interviewed insisted that economically disadvantaged parents are so unaware of their children's educational progress that some of them do not even know which class their children are attending. The parents' reluctance to support their children could be explained by poverty and their ignorance regarding the future benefits of education for their children and the community. Poverty encourages families to focus their attention on immediate needs and returns such as food, hence it is hard to expect that parents will contribute to construct houses for teachers who receive salaries.

Families' perceptions regarding the value and returns from schooling compared to those from other kinds of investment

The heads reported that there were several cases whereby secondary school students wrote to the headteachers asking to drop out of school. The secondary school heads assumed that these students preferred to participate in other activities such as fishing, small businesses, farming, etc. In addition, the heads noted that the parents supported their children's views and wanted the school authorities to allow their children to drop out of school for other economic activities. In the same manner, the heads of primary and secondary schools reported that there was a common tendency whereby primary school pupils who pass class seven national examinations fail to report to secondary school for various reasons, one being their unwillingness to proceed to secondary education. It was evident that most of the pupils who fail to report to school remain in the village and engage in other income-earning activities. The DEOs described how they imposed penalties on parents whose children failed to report to secondary school and they pointed out that the majority of disadvantaged families do not willingly send their children to secondary school but children are sent to school simply because the parents are scared of the government imposing penalties.

The findings show the need for flexible schooling i.e., allowing children/ youth to work and study. Similarly, this finding indicates that children and their parents compare the time required to invest in education and that required to invest in other activities. Since investing in education takes time before one sees a return, the children and their parents opt for an investment with a quicker return. This means that the families were unaware that investment in education is a long-term investment and it takes time before one can witness the benefits. Using the expectancy theory of motivation, the finding suggests that the children and their parents had an expectancy probability of zero regarding schooling. Schooling is perceived as a long-term investment, which is not associated with relevant immediate tangible positive benefits. Hence, it is obvious that one cannot dare to agree to bear the double loss i.e., investing in education and facing a loss in terms of wasted time and family resources. In this regard, the parents and their children were motivated to invest their resources and energy in quick income-earning activities with tangible outcomes.

According to the views of the educational leaders studied at the school, district and regional levels, it may be concluded that the families had an expectance, instrumentality and valence probability of 1 regarding investment in quick income-earning activities. From the HCT perspective, education is perceived to be a long-term investment; hence for individuals with low capital education is not competitive as the return on the investment is low. The HCT also supports the transactional management theory that individuals are motivated to work hard after evaluating the rewards associated with their efforts.

Families' tendency purposefully to hinder the teachers' efforts to encourage schooling

The educational leaders and teachers reported that the parents in the areas studied regarded teachers as enemies. They hated the teachers, who were in the front line of enforcing rules regarding attendance and children learning at school. It was noted that teachers of this kind were punished by their houses and farms being burnt down. In one region, the REOs described how, in three districts, the teachers' houses were burnt down because the teachers were using various strategies to ensure that all of the children who had dropped out returned to school. In addition, the heads told of several conflicts that had arisen between teachers and families because of this.

In three of the regions studied, the DEOs, teachers and heads noted that parents used witchcraft as a weapon to combat the teachers' efforts to promote children's schooling. Notably, once a teacher appears to be curious and follows up children's attendance or advises pupils to work hard in order to pass their primary school leaving examination, the parents start to hate them and take revenge on them by torturing them using witchcraft. Several types of witchcraft performed against teachers were reported, including raping female teachers and male teachers' wives through witchcraft, getting teachers out of their beds and making them sleep outside their house during the night, and causing teachers illness and other odd events; for example, a teacher cooked a chicken for some visitors, and when she was ready to serve the dish, she found her cooking pot completely empty. These behaviours indicate that parents consider education to be irrelevant, which leads them to devalue and punish those who provide it. As a result, the teachers asked to be transferred and, hence, their children had a chance to continue playing truant, as there was no one else to encourage and insist on their school attendance. This further contributes to poor learning outcomes.

Parents' tendency purposefully to urge their children to ensure that they fail the primary school leaving examination

In the locations studied, according to teachers, heads, DEOs and REOs, the parents had a tendency to urge their children to ensure that they failed the final national class seven leaving examination. Notably, the parents used vivid examples of children who attended secondary education for four years and failed to proceed with further education and compared these with those who dropped out of school or refused to proceed with secondary education and participated in other income-earning activities. From their examples, the students could gather that those who drop out engage in other economic activities succeed economically compared to those who attend school.

> The parents in these areas behave very strangely. During the class seven examination period, parents deliberately sit down with their children, give them examples of children who passed the standard seven examination, attended secondary school for four years, and finally returned to the village empty-handed. They also give examples of children who failed or dropped out of school. These remain in the village and farm or do

business that enables them to construct their own house, own oxen, get married and have children.

(FGD, district educational officer)

Parents deter their children from doing well in the class seven leaving examination. They tell them that, if they pass the examination, then this will mean that their parents will have to sell their cattle to finance their children's education. We work hard. We prepare our pupils before the examination and, based on our informal assessment before the examination, we know which pupils will pass it, yet it is very surprising that, after the examination, the students whom we expected to do well simply fail. When we ask them, they tell us openly that their parents urge them to provide the wrong responses in the examination so that they will fail.

(FGD, teachers)

This finding further illuminates the earlier observation that investment in education in the areas studied is seen as a waste of the children's time and the parents' scarce resources, as it is not associated with any positive returns. According to the expectancy theory the parents and their children had an expectancy and valence probability of zero.

The heads of primary schools and teachers explained further that, in some areas, when the results were posted and the parents of those children who had passed the examination were congratulated by their fellow parents, it was normal to find that, instead of the parents being happy, they responded by wondering why they were being congratulated rather than commiserated with. It was reported that the parents whose children had passed the examination know that this automatically means that they will be required to buy uniforms and make a number of financial contributions. The findings confirm that most of the parents were happy when their children failed because they knew that they would not be required to pay for their education. Hence, this finding clearly indicates that parents' comparison of children who attend school with those who remain in the village suggests that the latter succeed more than the former. According to primary school heads and teachers, this implies that the economically disadvantaged families studied disregard education compared to other forms of investment. Indeed, to these parents, a family's investment in education is pure consumption rather than investment. In terms of expectancy theory, the families had an expectancy, instrumentality and valence probability of zero. In this situation, one cannot expect parents to make any effort to invest in their children's schooling.

Conclusion

The findings according to the educational officers, educational leaders and teachers studied show that economically disadvantaged families were more likely to invest in other income-earning activities rather than education. The reason for this tendency is based on the expected result of investing in education. Notably, it can be assumed that families would be willing to send their children to school if they believed that education was valuable, relevant to the children's personal life and will eventually help them to minimize poverty at the family level. These findings suggest the incongruity regarding the value and relevance of primary and secondary schooling in Tanzania between the families, the government and the international educational regulations and policy statements The various national and international policies on education (such as, for example, the Universal Declaration on Human Rights proclaimed by the UN General Assembly in 1948; the 1961 Addis Ababa conference; the 1990 Jomtien (Thailand) conference; the 2000 Dakar framework for action; the World Summit Millennium Development Goals; the Tanzania 1995 and 2014 Education and Training Policy; the Tanzanian primary and secondary educational development programs; and the Tanzanian 2025 development vision) stipulate that education is every person's fundamental birthright. In these policies, education is recognized as a basic human right, on the assumption that it is associated with a number of benefits, including its contribution to economic growth as well as improving health and reducing poverty. For example, the Primary Education Development Program phase II (URT, 2001) noted the following:

> Tanzania has consistently focused its development strategies on combating ignorance, disease and poverty. Investment in human capital is recognised as central to improving the quality of life of Tanzanians and the reduction of poverty.
>
> (URT, 2001 p. 1)

Basically, the ultimate aims of education in the various educational policies are the provision of skills and knowledge to people that will help them to fight poverty at both the individual and national levels. Indeed, the policies highlight the need to provide quality education as a pre-requisite for society's economic and political development. In contrast, the findings from this study suggest that, according to the educational officers, educational leaders and teachers studied, disadvantaged families seem to believe that education adds to the family's level of poverty for the following reasons: (1) it is associated with opportunity, indirect and direct costs, which are unbearable for families, as these costs increase the family's poverty level; (2) investment in education requires families to sacrifice their resources, yet this sacrifice is not associated with any profit upon the children' graduation so this means a waste of the family's scarce resources; and (3) education is a long-term investment, yet its profits are yet to be realized by disadvantaged families.

The contradictions in the reported perceptions and the education policy statements regarding the value and relevance of education between the provider and the end users of education mean less consumption of the service by the end users. This contradiction might be explained by the common tendency in developing countries whereby policies are implemented without involving the key implementers. The findings of this study support Posti-Ahokas's (2014) argument that educational policies are inadequately considering families and communities as active partners in policy implementation. The evidence suggests that educational policies have been implemented on the assumption that all parents recognize the role of schooling and perceive its value and relevance as per the policies' guidelines. As noted earlier, parents in these locations see no return on their investment, due to low quality schooling; hence they do not see its value. From the human rights perspective, one could support disadvantaged families' perceptions by posing the following question: "why should parents value education if the return on their investment is nil?" In the same line the current inflexible administrative arrangements in aligning school attendance to the demands of families contribute to parents' tendencies to devalue education. For example, parents need their children to support them on various household chores, suggesting that in the Tanzanian context children are also serving as the family workforce. In the previously discussed case, children missed school so as to engage in tomato harvesting. There is a need to look into possibilities for a flexible timetable so that during important family events pupils could be on holiday, say like a potato harvesting holiday.

Furthermore, what transpired from the field is that families, upon witnessing little benefits associated with children's schooling, concluded that schooling is irrelevant, resulting in devaluing schooling and discouraging their children from attending school and in some cases encouraging them to perform poorly in national examinations. Hence a comparison of the families' perceptions as explained by the educational leaders studied vs. the government and national policy statements regarding the value and relevance of education suggests that there is some variance. While the government and national education policies believe that schooling is a valuable, useful means of eradicating poverty, economically disadvantaged families regard education as irrelevant and a contributor to increased family poverty levels. This begs the question of how to make education more relevant and culturally responsive.

Recommendations

The educational leaders' experiences of collaborating with economically disadvantaged families and learning about their perceptions concerning the relevance of primary and secondary schooling suggest that families devalue education, considering it a consumptive form of investment which is not associated with profit and is irrelevant in assisting them to reduce poverty. Along the same lines, the findings show that calculating economically disadvantaged parents' motivation to invest in their children's schooling using the formula given previously, gives an answer of zero. This means that the economically disadvantaged families' expectancy, instrumentality and valence probability to invest in their children's schooling is zero. This explains why disadvantaged families prefer to invest in phenomena other than education. In this regard, there is a need to review the current strategies and find ways to reverse this situation.

The study claims that education needs to increase its relevance to economically disadvantaged families. Finding and implementing sustainable ways to assist the families to bear the direct, indirect and opportunity costs of their children's education are necessary. This means, according to Gay (2013), that we not only acknowledge the conditions of poverty and cultural differences, but teach to and through them. This could be achieved by introducing a flexible education system whereby children work and attend school. Another way is to prepare a school calendar which accommodates important family economic activities. Second, the quality of schools serving rural communities should be improved so that they produce graduates who can either progress to other levels of education or can use the skills gained in school to bring about changes in their own life or community: i.e., there is a need to ensure that the education provided is relevant to the needs of the community.

The current tendency whereby the majority of children who attend secondary education graduate without showing evidence of having acquired the necessary skills to enable them to improve their life and simply remain in the village poorer than before they went to the school demotivates parents, lowering their expectancy, instrumentality and valence probability, and as a result contributes to their tendency to devalue education. Third, an alternative route to formal education would be useful in enabling those children who do not graduate from primary school with sufficient marks to be selected formally to attend vocational education. Fourth, there is a need to reconsider seriously the benefits associated with engaging families in implementing educational policies. Families should not be taken as an empty vacuum to be fed with policy-makers' knowledge, but rather involving families should be considered a resource which might contribute to the provision of culturally responsive education.

References

Galabawa, J. (2005). *Returns to investment in education: Startling revelations and alternatives before Tanzanians*. Professorial Inaugural Lecture Series, No 45. Dar es Salaam: University of Dar es Salaam.

Gay, G. (2013). Teaching to and through cultural diversity. *Curriculum Inquiry, 43*(1), 48–70.

Global Partnership for Education (GPE). (2013). *The value of education*. Retrieved from www.globalpartnership.org/content/value-education-plain-text-version.

Harobin, G. W., Smyth, R. L., & Wiseman, J. (1970). Voucher for education: Reply and counter reply. In M. Blaug (Ed.), *Economics of education: Selected readings* (360–372). London: Penguin Books.

Komba, A. A. (2012). The effectiveness of school rules and sanctions in managing pupils' schooling among Tanzanian's economically disadvantaged pupils. *Journal of Adult Education, 1,* 61–76.

Komba, A. A. (2013). Are economically disadvantaged children in Tanzania committed to primary schooling? Korean Educational Development Institute (KDEI) *Journal of Educational Policy* (KJEP), *10*(1), 63–82.

Lloyd, C., & Blanc, K. (1996). Children's schooling in Sub-Saharan Africa: The role of fathers, mothers and others. *Population and Development Review, 22*, 265–298.

Miles, B., & Huberman, A. (1994). *Qualitative data analysis: An expanded sourcebook,* 2nd Edition. London: SAGE.

Omari, I. (1999). The relationship between education and income in poverty alleviation strategies. In J. Galabawa (Ed.), *Basic education renewal research for poverty alleviation* (66–103). Dar es Salaam: KAD Associates.

Pareek, U. (2004). *Understanding organizational behaviour.* New Delhi: Oxford University Press.

Posti-Ahokas, H. (2014). *Tanzanian female students' perspectives on the relevance of secondary education.* PhD Thesis. University of Helsinki.

Scholz, R. W., & Tietje, O. (2002). *Embedded case study methods: Integrating quantitative and qualitative knowledge.* London: SAGE.

Soini, K., & Birkeland, I. (2014). Mapping the scientific discourse of cultural sustainability. *Geoforum, 51*, 213–223.

UN. (1948). *The universal declaration on human rights.* Retrieved from www.un.org/Overview/rights.html#a1.

UN. (2015). *The Millennium development goals report.* Retrieved from www.un.org/millenniumgoals/2015_MDG_Report/pdf/MDG%202015%20rev%20%28July%201%29.pdf.

UNESCO. (1961). *Conference of African States on the development of education in Africa.* Addis Ababa, 15–25 May 1961. Final Report. Organized and Convened by UNESCO and the United Nations Economic Commission for Africa.

UNESCO. (2000). *The Dakar framework for action education for all: Meeting our collective commitments.* Adopted by the World Education Forum Dakar, Senegal, 26–28 April 2000. Retrieved from www.unesco.at/bildung/basisdokumente/dakar_aktionsplan.pdf.

UNESCO. (2015) *Educational for all 2000–2015: Achievement and challenges.* EFA Global Monitoring Report, UNESCO.

URT. (1995). *Education and training policy,* The Ministry of Education and Culture, Dar es Salaam.

URT. (1998). *The national poverty eradication strategy.* Dar es Salaam: Vice President Office.

URT. (2001). *Primary education development program 2002–2006.* Dar es Salaam, Tanzania: Education and Training Sector Development Program ESDP. Basic Education Development Committee (BEDC).

URT. (2004). *Secondary education development program 2004–2009.* Dar es Salaam, Tanzania: Ministry of Education and Culture.

URT. (2005). *The Tanzania development vision 2025.* Dar es Salaam, Tanzania.

URT. (2006). *Primary education development program II (2007–2011),* Dar es Salaam Tanzania: Education and Training Sector Development Program (ESDP). Basic Education Development Committee (BEDC).

URT. (2010a). *National strategy for growth and reduction of poverty II.* Dar es Salaam, Tanzania: Ministry of Finance and Economic Affairs.

URT. (2010b). *Secondary education development program II 2010–2015.* Dar es Salaam, Tanzania: Ministry of Education and Vocational Training.

URT. (2011). *Basic education statistics in Tanzania (BEST) 2007–2011 – National data.* Dar es Salaam: Ministry of Education and Vocational Training.

URT. (2012). *Basic education statistics in Tanzania (BEST) 2008–2012 – National data.* Dar es Salaam: Ministry of Education and Vocational Training.

URT. (2014a). *Basic education statistics in Tanzania (BEST) 2009–2013 – National data.* Dar es Salaam: Ministry of Education and Vocational Training.

URT. (2014b). *Education and training policy.* Dar es Salaam: Ministry of Education and Vocational Training.

Vroom, V. H. (1995). *Work and motivation.* San Francisco, CA: Jossey-Bass.

WCEFA. (1990) *World conference on education for all: Meeting basic learning needs.* Jomtien, Thailand 5–9 March 1990. The Inter-Agency Commission (UNDO, UNESCO, UNICEF, WB). Retrieved from unesdoc.unesco.org/images/0009/000975/097552e.pdf.

Willms, D. J. (2003). *Student engagement at school: A sense of belonging and participation. Results from PISA (Program for International Student Assessment) 2000.* Paris: Organization for Economic Co-operation and Development OECD.

Yin, R. K., (2008). *Case study research designs and methods.* 4th edition. London: SAGE.

Yukl, G. (1999). An evaluation of the conceptual weaknesses in transformational and charismatic leadership theories. *Leadership Quarterly, 10*(2), 285–305.

Zymelman, M. (1973). *Financing and efficiency in education reference from administration and policymaking.* Boston: Harvard University Press.

7 Culturally situated narratives

Expanding insights and accountabilities

Mona Saleh Alsudis and Venitha Pillay

Introduction

This chapter aims to offer insight into the challenges of negotiating writing and meaning making in diverse cultural worlds. We make a case for the value of culturally situated narrative writing as a methodological tool for meaning making across cultures. We present this chapter as an example of a culturally situated narrative at work. In writing this chapter, our goal is to bring into relief the culturally situated voices at play in the research arena and to suggest that a culturally situated narrative approach may help to traverse this complex yet exciting terrain.

Conceptual platforms

This chapter hinges on two central notions, *culture* and *narrative research*, brought together into a single conceptual space that we refer to as *culturally situated narratives*. Williams (1993) provides a broad, generalised definition of culture: "Every human society has its own shape, its own purposes and its own meaning in every individual mind" (p. 6). Hofstede, Hofstede and Minkov (2010) suggest that culture is what "every person carries within him- or herself; patterns of thinking, feeling, and potential acting that were learned throughout a person's lifetime" (p. 4).

The same authors go on say that:

> *Culture* is a catchword for all those patterns of thinking, feeling, and acting. Not only activities supposed to refine the mind are included, but also the ordinary and menial things in life: greeting, eating, showing or not showing feelings, keeping a certain physical distance from others, making love, and maintaining body hygiene. Culture is always a collective phenomenon, because it is at least partly shared with people who live or lived within the same social environment, which is where it was learned. Culture consists of the unwritten rules of the social game. It is *the collective programming of the mind that distinguishes the members of one group or category of people from others.*
>
> (pp. 5–6, emphasis in original)

Hofstede et al. (2010, p. 12) claim that it is difficult for some individuals or groups to escape culture because children are born into particular groups or communities, and that is how culture reproduces itself. Hence, members of every group inherit the existing values of their social or familial group. The circle of cultural inheritance is unequivocally evident for the women in this study, who were born into a culture that is deeply entrenched and inescapable. The same may be said of the researcher and the research supervisor.

Smith (2001) defines culture as "the intellectual, spiritual, and aesthetic development of an individual, group, or society" (p. 2). He points out that culture constructs the motivations and identity of an individual living within a certain community. As we can see from these various explanations and definitions of culture, it is feasible that identity descends from the culture in which a person lives.

To understand the meaning of religious culture, Ammerman (2003, p. 216) claims that religious identity informs culture. Every culture is shaped by the beliefs and practices of the people living within it. Thus, according to Ammerman, religious identity is demonstrated by actions such as praying or telling people about one's religious and holy experiences. In Saudi Arabia, this type of religious culture is present in the lives of all people. It is a country that is based on Shari'a (Islamic law), and the religious texts of the Quran guide the entire nation.

Saudi culture is vastly different from Western culture; in particular, the Islamic religion has an enormous influence on Saudis. Islamic religious words are frequently found in everyday direct speech. The participants in the study that became the basis of this paper constantly used words such as *Insha Allah*, which means "if God wills it", *Alhamdole Allah*, which means "thank God", and *Masha Allah*, which means "God's will". Muslim people say *Insha Allah* when they intend to do something in the future if God spares them. The Saudi system is different in other ways too. For example, December is not a holiday period, Saudi people do not celebrate New Year in January, and Thursdays and Fridays constitute the weekend.

The Saudi cultural epistemology, along with the Islamic framework, served as the basis for interpreting the data collected in the study that informs this chapter. We suggest that it is only through examination and knowledge of Saudi culture and traditions and the Islamic religion that we can understand and appreciate the lives and successes of the Saudi academic women who participated in the study.

The value of a narrative approach to bring to life the stories of the Saudi women in contexts where they are the 'other' is underscored by Gay (2010, p. 3), who suggests that "stories, are … powerful means for people to establish bridges across other factors that separate them (such as race, culture, gender, and social class), penetrate barriers, and create feelings of kindredness" (p. 3). Taking this idea further, Squire, Andrews and Tamboukou (2008) argue that "what is shared across both event- and experience-centred narrative research, is that there are assumed to be individual, internal representations of phenomena – events, thoughts and feelings – to which narrative gives external *expression*" (p. 5).

In coalescing the embeddedness of culture in the lives of the Saudi women and the appeal of a narrative approach, we offer the notion of culturally situated narratives as a means towards meaning making across cultural boundaries. The value of culturally situated narratives as a method to build a "bridge across ... cultures" (Gay, 2010, p. 3) and its potential for "external expression" was especially appealing, since the student and the participants were outsiders in the contexts in which the results were likely to be read.

Background

This chapter emerges from a broader study in which[1] the author researched the phenomenon of Saudi women becoming academic researchers while living in a conservative religious culture. The purpose of the study was to understand and explain the role of women academics in Saudi Arabia, and how they fulfil their research obligations in a conservative Islamic culture. I used an intrinsic case study design with a sample of four Saudi academics. A sample size of four allowed me to have in-depth conversations with them, as required by the narrative case study method. Hence, the four Saudi women (Salma, Asir, Najd and Hejaz) formed the conceptual group in my case study. By recounting these women's experiences in a culturally situated narrative, the study sought to understand the challenges they have faced and overcome along their academic journeys. The findings revealed that the participants' identities and actions as academic women are inseparable, and that their identities are powerfully shaped by their conservative and religious Saudi culture.

I conducted between three and four conversations with each participant. These sessions were mainly open ended, and gave the women as much space as they wanted to chat about the issues that mattered to them (Travers, 2001). At the same time, the conversations were guided by the study's main research questions. All the conversations were conducted in Arabic, since the participants and I felt more comfortable speaking in our mother tongue. That they spoke with deep conviction and passion about the things that mattered to them suggested to me that they were open with me and spoke from their hearts. In the brief time that I spent with each of them, I witnessed an array of emotions cross their faces and enter the spaces of our conversations. I transcribed the Arabic interviews and then translated them into English. I followed an iterative data collection and analysis approach. After listening to the participants' stories and transcribing and translating the interviews, I interpreted the data by writing their stories as a sequence of readable events. In short, I used a culturally situated narrative approach to present the stories they related to me. Through tuning in to their cultural codes, I felt I was able to understand and interpret with some confidence the nuances of their speech.

It should be noted that few Saudi women would be comfortable having their voices recorded. The younger women I interviewed, Salma and Asir, did not want their interviews to be tape-recorded. This was due to their cultural beliefs and is especially common among conservative and very religious women, who consider recording their voices to be *oura*. *Oura* is a term used to designate something that is extremely private. The established academic women allowed me to tape-record their interviews, probably because they did not feel as bound by cultural laws as did the other two. When I asked Hejaz if she would allow me to record her interviews, she laughed and said, "I don't mind as long as you don't publish them on CNN".

I did not have any difficulty in documenting the conversations, because I took notes while they talked, and I transcribed each interview directly after it took place. This helped me to remember all the details, such as tone of voice, body language and reactions. Copies of the transcripts were shared with the participants for their comments.

Because narratives about Saudi academic women appeared to be absent in academia, I hoped that my culturally situated narratives of the four Saudi academic women, and the interpretations of their experiences through their journeys as academics, would provide valuable insight for the non-Saudi reader. I wanted their stories to be inspiring for other women in similar circumstances. I also wanted the Western world to hear a story about the Middle East from the Middle East. My primary challenge was to make their stories intelligible to an outside world with a vastly different cultural and academic context without compromising the richness of their stories. I also knew that translating their stories from Arabic to English would not be easy, particularly retaining the nuanced and strongly culturally embedded expression and meaning.

I used the stories from all the conversations with each participant in order to present a coherent narrative, especially for a Western reader who is unfamiliar with Saudi culture. The narrative approach allowed me the space to offer the rich details required to give meaning to their stories and for the complexity of their different culture to become meaningful for readers living in other contexts. A culturally situated narrative allowed their stories to move from the shadows to the light. As Clandinin and Connelly (2000) suggest, "narrative inquiry offers the best way to examine particular identities and a society, based upon an individual's narrative" (p. 4).

I found it challenging to represent the Saudi culture clearly through my writing, because I saw writing as a form of communication between me, as the author of my thesis, and the Western reader. So, as a Saudi writer in a Western context, I had to find ways of being accountable to the Saudi women whose stories I told while being intelligible to my potential Western readers. I found consolation in Van Maanen (1988), who explains that "[c]ulture is not strictly speaking a scientific object, but is created, as is the reader's view of it, by the active construction of text" (p. 7). So while I was constructing the text as the writer and was guided by my commitment to be 'true' to their stories, I knew that the reader would be involved in her own act of cultural construction and meaning making of the text. I made peace with that.

Writing about Saudi women in an unknown land

I interpreted the women's stories within the culture in which they live, which I am familiar with, and which cannot be separated from their life stories. In so doing, I did not assume Saudi culture to be homogeneous; rather, I maintained an awareness of its dominant cultures, especially the religious culture, which functions as nationally accepted law in Saudi Arabia. I used my own cultural similarity to embrace their stories and offer depth of meaning.

Avoiding or muting the influence of the participants' culture when writing down their stories would have diluted the strength of those stories. I was deeply aware that my task was to represent the culture of the 'field' that I was researching (Van Maanen, 1988, p. 4). I chose a culturally situated narrative approach to present their stories because "narratives allow researchers to present experience holistically in all its complexity and richness" (Bell, 2002, p. 209). I believe that the "complexity and richness" of narratives affords space for cultural nuances and situatedness to be revealed. Ellis and Bochner (2003) describe narrative inquiry as "stories that create the effect of reality and [show] characters embedded in the complexities of lived moments of struggle" (p. 217). I took direction from Bell (2002) and Ellis and Bochner (2003).

Since I was writing about Saudi women in a non-Saudi academic and cultural context, I needed to write the stories in ways that allowed meaning to be constructed across vast cultural boundaries. I needed to traverse these boundaries myself, as a Saudi woman living and researching in Africa and writing for a mainly Western readership. A culturally situated narrative approach also allowed me to step out of my comfort zone, to step out of and into myself to hear their stories, and to write their stories. It also allowed me to reconnect with myself and come to a better understanding of my own epistemological stance.

Stepping in and out of myself

As described above, I wanted to keep the culture and religious world of the participants alive, but I faced many challenges. One of these was to differentiate my voice from theirs, especially given the common background and culture we share. Chase (2008) describes a similar dilemma:

> For researchers who collect narratives through intensive interviews, a central question is how to treat the interviewee as a narrator, both during interviews and while interpreting them. For all narrative researchers, a

central question revolves around which voice or voices researchers should use as they interpret and represent the voices of those they study.

(p. 58)

I knew I wanted to foreground the voices of the participants. At first I thought it would be easy to write the stories of Saudi academic women, since I am one myself. Yet it was not easy, because "culture is not itself visible, but is made visible only through its representation" (Van Maanen, 1988, p. 3). My writing was an effort towards such representation and to bring this culture to a world that knows little of it.

I had to step out of myself and let the participants 'speak through me', as it were. Yet I knew that it was my voice that readers would hear. To help me through this dilemma, I took a lead from Pillay's (2005) article 'Narrative style: The inseparability of self, style and text', in which she argues that the writer can only write in ways that are true to herself, her history and her identity. That article also led me to understand that, despite the presence of the voices of the participants, my voice would remain discernible. At the same time, it is not possible to separate myself from the stories of the four women, because "narrative research which is based on conversations between people is invariably a process of ongoing negotiation of meaning" (Squire et al., 2008, p. 14). So while I attempted to step out of myself to write their stories, I was always present in the narrative.

At first, the use of narrative inquiry to write the participants' stories was not appealing. However, the literature on narrative enquiry showed that it was an approach that offered space for the expression of emotions, feelings and beliefs intrinsic to Saudi culture. I wanted the women's deepest feelings as they faced the challenges of being women academics in Saudi Arabia to be felt by the rest of the world. For example, it was important to convey the immense difficulty they endured doing research with very limited access to libraries and the internet. Public libraries are mostly for men, and women are allowed limited access on certain days only. Women are not allowed to drive anywhere, so for data collection that required travel they relied on the good-will of a male family member to be their *mahram* (a male family member who may escort a woman in public places). Women may only access laboratories when no males are present. This often means doing research after hours and depending on a man to take one home afterward. Such challenges are alien to most non-Saudi readers.

It was necessary for me to convey with sensitivity the cultural codes by which the women are bound. A Saudi woman is wholly dependent on her family's support. For example, the lives of most Western women academics probably do not include their parents having a role in determining their futures. Stepping out of my culture meant I would not have been able to tell these stories with insight and empathy. It would have been difficult to understand and convey Salma's private sadness in agreeing to study science according to her parents' wishes when she preferred art. It was clear to me that it was not possible for her to defy her family and still have their support. Asir had to comply with her brother's desire that she be married before pursuing graduate studies. She did so; there was no question about it. Being a part of this culture meant that it was possible for me to offer understanding and make no judgements about their decisions.

When I met with the women, I tried not to talk too much or to share similar stories of my experiences or those of other people. It was important to yield the talking space to them, and they welcomed it. The cultural etiquette of small talk and enquiries about our families was mutually understood and accepted. So too, was the ritual of serving sweets and coffee at the start of each conversation. Since the four participants and I shared a similar cultural life and background, it was it easy to encourage their responses – what Jackson and Mazzei (2012) refer to as the "absent presence" (p. 17).

It was also important to write the women's stories from an outsider's perspective. However, I could not do this entirely since I am Saudi myself and share the same culture. It was not feasible to step completely out of myself in my conversations with the women and in writing their stories. Every time I started typing, I found myself present and alive within their stories. This battle was constant, and I found myself moving in and out of the familiarity of hearing and writing about my culture and the challenges of writing for an audience of strangers. Indeed, the culturally situated narrative space allowed me the freedom of this movement in and out of myself: working with the intimately familiar while at the same time writing for a foreign readership. As Ellis and Bochner (2003) argue, "[W]e are inside what we are studying" (p. 216). This awareness formed part of the 'data' of my study, because "as narrative inquirers we work within the space not only with our participants but also with ourselves. Working in this space means that we become visible with our own lived and told stories" (Clandinin & Connelly, 2000, pp. 61–62). As Dillard (2006, p. xi) comments, every time we conduct research, we are researching ourselves in addition to others. Moreover, "[W]e are our narratives. They are not something that can be outside ourselves because they are what give shape to us, what give meaning" (Hendry, 2007, p. 495). Hence, I became part of the story, constantly stepping in and out of myself in order to bring the story to an outside world.

I was aware that I was dealing with people's lives and, at times, their private emotions. Although it was difficult to separate my point of view from theirs, the culturally situated narrative approach allowed me to draw together my and their cultural context and experiences.

Looking inwards

As a Muslim Saudi person, I am accustomed to writing and speaking according to religious concepts. At school, we were taught to support our writing with quotes from the Quran and *Sunnah* (the practice of Islamic law also known as supplications to the Prophet). Thus, the Islamic religion affects me not only spiritually, but also in the way I express myself. If I were to leave my Islamic beliefs and spirit out of my work, then how would I be able to interpret the world around me? For me it would not be possible to connect with my study if my soul were empty. Thus, I decided to embrace my intuition and my spirituality and invite the reader into my world.

I am a Saudi woman in my late thirties. I have been married for 17 years to a supportive Saudi man, and we have three children. I am an artist. I express myself through drawing. I studied fine art and learned how to do sculpture, metal work and to mix colours – skills that taught me patience and creativity. One of my passions is to write poems that remain in my private space. I enjoy writing, and my writing in Arabic flows smoothly. As a postgraduate student, my joy in research and writing in English grew, although this was not easy for me. It was possibly my patience as an artist that helped me to persevere with my studies. My sense of creativity led me to narrative inquiry, for it gives me the scope to create a story that has meaning for me, as well as for the four women participants in the study. I hoped that I would be able to create meaning for the readers too, who I expected would be very different from me and the women interviewed. I found the challenges of using a culturally situated narrative approach and thinking about my research as an artistic creation to be the starting point of my research, rather than an end or a limitation. Instead of signalling an end in my attempt to become a successful researcher, the approach of writing in a foreign language for an unfamiliar audience opened doors for me.

An example of my creative thinking process can be seen in my choice of pseudonyms for the women. Names for the children and family members of the participants were also provided in order to build their 'realness'. For me this was a work of art. I let my pen sail in my imagination and fantasy world. Each of the participants was referred to by the name of a mountain in her region. There was no plan to have the four academic women come from different regions in Saudi Arabia; it just happened that way. Although mountains face extreme conditions, they are known for their stability and glory. Moreover, they produce elements, minerals and useful materials. The academic women who participated in my research possess similar properties. They have produced research and have made useful contributions to their fields despite the many obstacles and challenges they have faced throughout their academic lives. The famous twin mountains, Aja and Salma, lie in the northern region of Saudi Arabia. The name Salma was chosen because it is an internationally recognised feminine name. I gave it to my first participant, because she is from the northern region and has twin daughters. In the southern region, the Asir Mountain is known for its height and the greenery that covers it year round. I named the second participant, who is from the south, Asir. She was known for her forgiving personality and modesty. The Arabic word 'Najd' literally means 'upland' or 'plateau', and was once applied to a variety of regions within the Arabian Peninsula. The most famous of these is the central region in the middle of Saudi Arabia. This became the name of my third participant because she is from that middle region. The fourth participant, an established academic from the western region of Saudi Arabia, was named Hejaz after the biggest mountain in that area. The Hejaz Mountain extends from the north to the south on the west side of Saudi Arabia.

Although writing my thesis was an enjoyable and creative experience with words, I was apprehensive about this significant task. Was I going to be able to present the women's stories with sensitivity and care? My goal throughout the writing of my thesis was not to show a sophisticated level of writing, but rather to share my thoughts, beliefs and experiences, and to offer a small and uncommon glimpse into the world of these Saudi academic women. An additional challenge was that it was not always easy for me to translate from Arabic to English and convey what had been intended. Literal translation often meant losing meaning. Harder still was presenting Saudi women to Western readers, who can be expected to have little understanding of the cultural meanings expressed, even when translated into English.

Arabic and English are very different languages with little in common. English has a different sentence construction than Arabic, which is a Semitic language. Writing in Arabic, a sentence would flow with lilting words; however, translated into English it would often not yield the same qualities. It became useful to translate the meaning of words and not necessarily follow the same language construction. Not every word in Arabic has a direct translation into English, and equivalent words had to be found. The use of equivalent words to translate my or the participants' Arabic thoughts was a useful way out of the quandary. Most importantly, I drew on the ideas of Squire et al. (2008) on how narrative research may assist with the challenges presented by language by focusing on "what narrative does". They suggest:

> [R]esearch that focuses on narrative as an expression of individual experience, or as a mirror of social realities, tends to bypass the language of stories in order to focus on their meanings, or the social positionings they produce or reflect. Approaches that focus on event narratives or narratives in conversation tend to be interested in underlying cognitive structures, or in the social functionings of narrative, 'what narrative does'.
>
> (p. 8)

Expression differs between languages and is also dependent on culture and social conventions. Squire (2013) claims that "narrative involves some reconstruction of stories across times and places, an expression of experience that is not a direct translation of it" (pp. 50–51) and that narrative research is formed from the "broader social and cultural contexts" (p. 51). Therefore, in translating the participants' transcripts, the path of seeking the overall message or meaning of the original text rather than the direct translation of each phrase became a viable approach.

Finally, I wrote my thesis conscious of my identity as a wife, a mother, a woman, a student, an academic and an artist. I found time to write between teaching my children, taking care of my family's needs and affirming my religious commitments. The narrative approach gave me the opportunity to see my writing as part of my artistic self. Through writing my thesis, I feel that I have grown up. I have become more confident in dealing with people; I can talk with people; and I can even facilitate meetings. Although there were times when I thought it was the end of my study and I could not continue, I was able to collect my strength and realise that this kind of documentary project cannot be accomplished overnight.

The years spent doing my PhD have made me a mature woman who can handle problems better than before. I have learnt to think deeply – not only in my study, but even in my daily life – about the needs of every member of my family and my own needs. This study took me from my husband and children at times, but returned me to them stronger. My final joy and affirmation for my choice of narrative inquiry came when my examiners, three women from different worlds, told me how deeply they were moved by my stories of Salma, Asir, Hejaz and Najd, so like them in some ways, so vastly different in others.

A different tale – a vignette written by the supervisor

When Mona came to me as a PhD student she had already had a number of unpleasant experiences at the university. She had initially been declined admission to the PhD programme. No clear reasons were offered. But she was feisty – she requested an explanation and fought the decision. She approached a faculty member who helped her to gain admission and she found herself in a science department in the Faculty of Education. She was subsequently referred to me and relocated to a more appropriate department.

In our first conversation, it was evident that Mona was a determined woman and intellectually strong. Her attitude of not giving up was compelling. She had a clear idea of what she wanted to study, although she lacked confidence. I knew too that her commitment to Islam and her country came from deep within her soul and drove everything she does. It is the centre of her being. With this commitment came a strong awareness of authority and hierarchy.

For me, the question was how I could even begin to understand the world from which she comes. I had been brought up partly as an atheist, partly as a Hindu, and had spent most of my life in the anti-apartheid movement, resisting authority and with little regard for any form of hierarchy. My question was how best to support her through a PhD that is usually an emotional, intellectually challenging and physically draining experience, particularly given our different worlds and backgrounds. Furthermore, she was researching in and writing for a mainly 'Western' audience and a significant African readership. Her readership in South Africa was probably going to be mainly Christian. Universities in South Africa are yet to be free of their colonial history, and in the institution where she was studying, a strong Calvinist tradition continues to prevail (Soobrayan, 2003).

The potential dangers of a pervasive epistemological hegemony that could easily subsume the knowledge traditions of a culture, place and people that have often been portrayed in popular Western media as 'the enemy' hung over us as the study proceeded. Mona needed to be aware of her potential global readership while simultaneously being intensely consciousness of the delicacy of writing about women whose lives are in the main, very private. She too is a private person.

There was little comfort to be found in the literature I read on the challenges of supervision. Martinsuo and Turkulainen (2010) offer detailed, and no doubt valuable, insight into the kinds of support PhD students require. So too does Lindén (2006), in an extensive study of more than 400 postgraduate supervisors. Although much has been written about practical, structural and even emotional support for PhD students from supervisors, little has been said about finding common conceptual spaces that help advance a student through the epistemological quagmire in which she is likely to find herself. The challenge is exacerbated for students and supervisors who come from vastly different worlds, as we did.

Brown (2007) suggests that one of the first problems that supervisors of international students face is the "discrepancy between [the students'] linguistic ability and the level of linguistic competence needed to write the dissertation" (p. 241). Although Mona is not a native speaker of English, her verbal language skills are good. My concern was not language so much, but meaning. A good editor would take care of language matters. But meaning had to be found between the two of us before it could be displayed on the page and her diverse readership could infer its own meanings.

In thinking through the epistemological challenges we faced, I turned to Gough (2001), who wrote, inter alia, about his experiences as an Australian academic working with South African academics. His aim, in part, was to:

> explore some ways in which difference (with particular reference to race, ethnicity, language and location) might be related to individual and/or community dispositions to take up (or to reject) specific research methodologies and epistemologies, and to consider the implications of such differences and dispositions for collaborative transnational research.
>
> (p. 1)

Gough's (2001) focus on people's stories as the foundation for meaning making and analysis was a useful point of entry for the challenges Mona and I faced in making and deriving meaning. In short, he points the way towards narrative inquiry as an available methodological tool, and I surmised that it would be appropriate for Mona and for me.

The plethora of literature on narrative inquiry, a term often used interchangeably with narrative research, points to some level of contestation of its boundaries (if one assumes that such boundaries are present and useful), its validity as a research approach, its rules, its potential for conceptual analysis and therefore epistemology and, to some extent, even its naming. (See Andrews, Squire and Tamboukou (2008) for a good exposition of the debates regarding narrative research.)

I took heart in Webster and Mertova (2007), who point to what narrative inquiry can do rather than what it is. They suggest that narrative inquiry

> studies problems as forms of storytelling involving characters with both personal and social stories. It requires going beyond the use of narrative as rhetorical structure, to an analytic examination of the underlying insights and assumptions that the story illustrates. A key contribution of narrative inquiry is ... [that it] frames the study of human experience.
>
> (p. 4)

The fact that the construction and reconstruction of the stories embedded in Mona's research took place in vastly different social, religious, cultural and academic contexts could be mediated by the flexibility of a culturally situated narrative. Such a narrative would give credibility to individual stories and experiences and to some extent mute the danger of a hegemonic Western discourse subsuming meaning making. It also opened the door for me as her 'first' reader to enact my own cultural contexts through which meaning is constructed, and allowed the complex contexts that colour this study to find room to live alongside each other. The world that Mona knew and shared with the women whose stories she was telling, the intellectual and personal spaces that we shared as researcher and supervisor, and the scholarly world that would mediate her work, could potentially find their niches in a culturally situated narrative approach. Finally, as Mona and I shared many conversations, we found our common space: storytelling, more specifically telling stories as women, what Turnbull refers to as the "interstitial space for meaning making" (Turnbull in Gough, 2001).

Most importantly, I found myself listening to Mona's own stories. It was in this story telling of self that I learned to hear the stories she wrote of others. As women and as mothers we talked about family. We shared funny moments that we have had with our children and our partners. She asked advice when she had health challenges. We talked about the future and the past; we talked about love and hurt. Although I am older, I often did not feel wiser, as Mona's takes on situations were often profound. In these stories I learned to hear both the voice of Mona and the voices of the women she interviewed. In listening to Mona talk, I found a constant refrain: "It is the truth", and I was reminded of Rigoberta Menchú whose insistence on her truth had caused a scholarly storm (see the special issue of Qualitative Studies in Education, 2000 (13)).

In a scholarly world that is characterised by the dominance of grey areas, there were no grey areas for Mona. It became evident that, given the religious and cultural context from whence her stories came, 'truth' is rarely problematised or contested. In 'story-ing' the data, we found that Turnbull's advice was credible: that diverse knowledge traditions can co-exist rather than displace each other (Turnbull in Gough, 2001). Turnbull suggests that the creation of a third, "interstitial" space is necessary for such diversity to be negotiated. We found that space in our mutual love for telling the stories of women who work against the odds. Andrews et al. (2008) point to the openness of epistemological significance that may be derived from narratives. It was this openness and flexibility that allowed Mona and me to travel unexplored epistemological territories without compromising epistemological credibility.

Mona's unwavering conviction of the truth, probably a consequence of her religious convictions, did not sit well with my feminist notion of multiple realities. In debating the nature of truth, I was reminded of Dahlin and Regmi's (2000) study of Nepalese and Swedish students and how each cultural group constructed knowledge. They show that, for Nepalese students, knowledge was closely linked to a social mode of being in keeping with the collectivist culture often found in Eastern societies. On the other hand, the Swedish students described knowledge as being personal − a view that is arguably in sync with the individualistic foundations of Western societies. I was deeply aware that Mona and I probably constructed knowledge differently. Yet we had to find the space to build common understandings and to challenge our individual boundaries.

Mona took the same stance of unassailable conviction when she was asked for clarification of her data and alerted to the possibilities of other interpretations. She explained that jealousy among women academics is a 'reality' and she could not ignore it when the participants related such experiences. I realised that my feminist instincts balked at such stories, and it was unlikely we would agree on such interpretations, but the culturally nuanced narrative space we had agreed on opened its arms to the stories and contexts that these women spoke of. However, this acceptance did not come easily for me.

Since my youth spent in a resistance movement, I have become absorbed into an academic space that speaks to the rigours of research and knowledge production. Despite their possible shortcomings, these 'rigours' could not be discarded. The rigours of data analysis were therefore not negotiable, but the telling of the story was. Sometimes we disagreed on the interpretation of studies described in the literature. For example, when Mona recounted the article she had read about an academic woman who took her baby with her to the laboratory, with undertones of criticism of her motherhood, I cringed. My writings on motherhood found this hard to negotiate. Yet we did negotiate our varied interpretations. We could not agree on the semantic difference between 'similar' and 'the same', and it took some time before this difference, which is self evident in the English language but not so in Arabic, was mutually understood. Mona often pointed to the vast differences between English and Arabic, and their structure and meaning could often find little common ground, if any.

The culturally situated narrative method allowed Mona to write the stories she heard in ways that allowed their construction, deconstruction and reconstruction in different epistemological spaces, while retaining their credibility. It also gave me the space to read with sensitivity and openness about a world that is not familiar to me. My role was to understand her world and guide her to find scholarly paths to recount such stories, not to contest what she expressed. The culturally nuanced narrative space also freed me from my own epistemological chains and allowed me to listen intently. I found that foregrounding our cultural contexts of writing and reading narratives had worked, not just for Mona to write the stories she wanted, but for me to hear her and the stories she wanted to tell with care and sensitivity.

Conclusion

In this paper we have tried to extend Gay's (2010) call for culturally responsive teaching to include culturally responsive research. We believe both are equally important across the globe. We acknowledge that this is not easy to do. In writing this chapter, we sought to offer insight into the challenges we faced and our paths to overcoming them. We suggest that the notion of culturally situated narrative writing offers a conceptual space to explore the possibilities of culturally responsive and responsible research.

Acknowledgments

I would like to acknowledge the Saudi academic women who agreed to be interviewed for my study. I appreciate the fact that Salma, Asir, Najd and Hejaz made time to talk to me and allowed me to publish information about their personal lives and beliefs. Without their stories, I could not have become a narrative researcher; moreover, the learning insights that Professor Pillay and I have addressed in this chapter would not have been discussed or come to light.

Note

1 The major part of the article is written in the first person by the first author (the student), and the vignette near the end is written in the first person by the second author (the supervisor).

References

Ammerman, N. T. (2003). Religious identity and religious institutions. In M. Dillon (Ed.), *Handbook of the sociology of religion* (207–224). Cambridge: Cambridge University Press.

Andrews, M., Squire, C., & Tamboukou, M. (Eds). (2008). *Doing narrative research.* Thousand Oaks, CA: Sage.

Bell, J. (2002). Narrative inquiry: More than just telling stories. *TESOL Quarterly, 36*(2), 207–213.

Brown, L. (2007). A consideration of the challenges involved in supervising international masters students. *Journal of Further and Higher Education, 31*(3), 239–248.

Chase, S. E. (2008). Narrative inquiry: Multiple lenses, approaches, voices. In N. K. Denzin, & Y. S. Lincoln (Eds), *Collecting and interpreting qualitative materials* (3rd ed., 57–94). Thousand Oaks, CA: Sage.

Clandinin, D. J., & Connelly, F. M. (2000). *Narrative inquiry: Experience and story in qualitative research.* San Francisco: Jossey-Bass.

Dahlin, B., & Regmi, M. P. (2000). Ontologies of knowledge, East and West: A comparison of views of Swedish and Nepalese students. *Qualitative Studies in Education, 13*(1), 43–61.

Dillard, C. B. (2006). *On spiritual strivings: Transforming an African American woman's academic life.* New York: State University of New York Press.

Ellis, C., & Bochner, A. P. (2003). Autoethnography, personal narrative, reflexivity. Researcher as subject. In N. Denzin, & Y. Lincoln (Eds), *Collecting and interpreting qualitative materials* (2nd ed., 199–258). Thousand Oaks, CA: Sage.

Gay, G. (2010). *Culturally responsive teaching: Theory, research, and practice.* New York: The Teachers' College Press.

Gough, N. (2001). Educational research in a global economy of knowledge production: What troubles a travelling text worker? In W. Shilton, & R. Jeffrey (Eds), *AARE 2001: Crossing borders: New frontiers in educational research.* Australian Association for Research in Education conference proceedings (1–5). Coldstream, Vic: Australian Association for Research in Education.

Hendry, P. (2007). The future of narrative. *Qualitative Inquiry, 13*(4), 487–498.

Hofstede, G., Hofstede, G. J., & Minkov, M. (2010). *Cultures and organizations: Software of the mind* (3rd ed.). New York: McGraw-Hill.

Jackson, A., & Mazzei, L. (2012). *Thinking with theory in qualitative research (viewing data across multiple perspectives)* (1st ed.). New York: Routledge.

Lindén, J. (2006). The contribution of narrative to the narrative process of supervising PhD students. *Studies in Higher Education, 24*(3), 351–369.

Martinsuo, M., & Turkulainen, V. (2010). Personal commitment, support and progress in doctoral studies. *Studies in Higher Education, 36*(1), 103–120.

Pillay, V. (2005). Narrative style: The inseparability of self, style and text. *Reflective Practice, 6*(4), 539–549. doi: 10.1080/14623940500300723.

Smith, P. (2001). *Cultural theory.* Cambridge, MA: Blackwell.

Soobrayan, V. (2003). Ethics, truth and politics in constructivist qualitative research. *Westminster Studies in Education, 26*(2), 107–123. doi: 10.1080/0140672032000147571.

Squire, C. (2013). From experience-centred to socioculturally oriented approaches to narrative. In M. Andrews, C. Squire, & M. Tamboukou (Eds), *Doing narrative research* (2nd ed., 47–71). Thousand Oaks, CA: Sage.

Squire, C., Andrews, M., & Tamboukou, M. (2008). What is narrative research? In M. Andrews, C. Squire, & M. Tamboukou (Eds), *Doing narrative research* (1–21). Thousand Oaks, CA: Sage.

Travers, M. (2001). *Qualitative research through case studies.* London: Sage.

Van Maanen, J. (1988). *Tales of the field: On writing ethnography.* Chicago: University of Chicago Press.

Webster, L., & Mertova, P. (2007). *Using narrative inquiry as a research method: An introduction to using critical event narrative analysis in research on learning and teaching.* London: Routledge.

Williams, R. (1993). Culture is ordinary. In A. Gray, & J. McGuigan (Eds), *Studying culture: An introductory reader* (5–14). Guildford, UK: Biddles.

Part III

Transforming, empowering and emancipatory experiences in learning

8 Reflections on North–South collaboration in music education

*Sanna Salminen, Pekka Toivanen,
Jaana Virkkala, Sampo Hankama and
Jaana Vahermaa*

Background

The music, education and cultural identity (MECI) network, coordinated by the department of music of the University of Jyväskylä (JyU), has its roots in the North–South higher education programme (which existed between 2004 and 2007, funded by the Ministry of Foreign Affairs in Finland) with the University of Pretoria (UP) as the only partner institution then. However, the first seeds of collaboration between JyU and UP in music education date back to 1998, when the ISME world conference was held in South Africa. Initially, prior to the North–South–South programme (i.e. up to 2007), collaboration existed only between the universities of Pretoria and Jyväskylä.[1] From the very beginning the collaboration has included staff and student exchanges, and some joint intensive periods. During the first years of collaboration, staff members and students from JyU participated in outreach projects in which the UP music department people were also involved. Such activities included, among others, arts and culture teacher training in rural areas of Mpumalanga province. Furthermore, the UP music department was involved with projects such as teacher training in the Sekhukhune district (in Limpopo province) and the former STTEP (State Theater Educational Project) orchestral outreach project for children living in various township areas of Pretoria.

Since Autumn 2007, the overall title for the collaboration projects has been the North–South–South higher education institution network programme (funded by the Ministry of Foreign Affairs and administrated by CIMO – the Centre of International Mobility). In order to bring more focus to the South–South axis, JyU invited UP together with the following new partner institutions to join the new phase of the project:

- North-West University (NWU) – location: Potchefstroom (South Africa)
- Kenyatta University (KU) – location: Nairobi (Kenya)
- University of Botswana (UB) – location: Gaborone (Botswana)
- University of South Africa (UNISA) – location: Pretoria (South Africa)

Up to 2011, the collaboration project included the above-mentioned five African universities plus JyU. The overall title of the project then was 'Music strengthening cultural identity in Southern Africa'.

Since 2011, Africa University (location: Mutare, Zimbabwe) has been a partner institution in this project, which was then renamed MECI (Music, education and cultural identity).The activities within the MECI project have aimed to:

- explore notions of cultural identities through music;
- make African and Finnish students and teachers of music/music education/ cultural education aware of the benefits and challenges of multicultural/ transcultural teaching;
- improve the learning and teaching skills of African and Finnish music and culture educators (including classroom teachers), aiming for in-depth exchange of approaches and ideas;
- boost the cultural identities of music teachers in Africa and in Finland;
- improve the overall quality of music teaching and cultural education in South Africa, Kenya, Botswana, Zimbabwe and Finland; and
- increase cooperation between the different actors and organizations in the fields of cultural education, music and music education in South Africa, Botswana, Kenya and Zimbabwe (and thus strengthen the South–South axis within the project).

The planning concerning the contents and strategies of the MECI project has been done in joint collaboration among the partner institutions, taking into account both the positive and negative experiences from the past. The project phase 2011–2013 has involved, in addition to staff and teacher mobility, various forms of collaboration in the fields of music education pedagogy and research, music technology and its pedagogical and research application possibilities (e.g. in teaching various indigenous musics) as a new area.

This chapter is based on the results gained from a survey that was carried out during the 2012 intensive course, hosted by UNISA. The main reason for our survey was to collect data from course participants related to their experiences and perceptions of activities (both past and present) within the MECI project. The contents of the course programme dealt with topics related to the title of the project – 'Music, education and cultural identity'. Intensive courses, to which each partner institution contributes from their areas of expertise (cultural, pedagogical, research), together with student and staff mobility, are integral parts of activities in all North–South–South projects.

Research methods

The questionnaire was put together in Finland before the intensive course (IC) in South Africa in 2012, and the actual survey was carried out at the end of the IC. The questionnaire contained a section for background information, profession, experience as a music educator and previous attendance on an IC. This section was followed by seven open questions in which the following topics were asked about: expectations of the course, benefits gained from the course, ideas the participants had got, most interesting subjects, how to develop further ICs and the meaning of this kind of collaboration. Questions overlapped with each other in order to enable triangulation, together with observation during the course (Patton 1990, p. 467). There was also a general evaluation rating scale (from poor to excellent) in the questionnaire. The idea of this kind of survey was positively received by all course participants, albeit not everybody participated in it (partly due to schedule overlaps and transport issues).

The total number of course participants was 58, of whom 30 were present throughout the IC. Eleven teachers had attended project ICs more than once, seven of them working in African partner institutions. In total, 27 people (all of whom were present throughout the entire course period) answered the questionnaire: 14 of them were university teachers (Table 8.1) and 13 were students (Table 8.2). Four of the teachers and eight of the students were attending an IC for the first time. Eight teachers had attended an IC at least three times.

In the analysing process the answers were coded according to each participant's status (student, S, or university teacher, U), experience as a music educator in years (y) and previous attendance in intensive courses in times (t). For example S6y1t means student, 6 years of teaching experience, first time participation in IC. All answers were collected into a table, which made it possible to notice connections between the different answers.

Table 8.1 Respondents: university teachers' group

University teacher	Experience in teaching (years)	Participation in ICs (times)
U1	6	1
U2	12	2
U3	15	3
U4	17	1
U5	18	3
U6	21	2
U7	25	4
U8	28	1
U9	29	1
U10	29	4
U11	38	5
U12	40	3
U13	40	3
U14	15	3

Table 8.2 Respondents: university students' group

Student	Experience in teaching (years)	Participation in ICs (times)
S1	–	1
S2	–	1
S3	–	1
S4	–	1
S5	1	1
S6	1	1
S7	2	1
S8	6	1
S9	2	3
S10	3	2
S11	–	2
S12	–	2
S13	–	2

Results

General opinion of the course was positive: 26 per cent of the participants answered excellent, 63 per cent good and 11 per cent ok. The answers of students and teachers were also in line. The survey themes covered the participants' expectations before the IC, what they gained from the course, the meaning of MECI in relation to international cooperation and suggestions for improving ICs.

Expectations before the intensive course

What kind of expectations did the participants have of this intensive course? Along with the rest of the questionnaire, we gathered this information after the course. The answers would probably have been somewhat different, had this been asked before the activities actually started. Despite the bias caused by the timing of this question, we felt that this information gives us a fair idea of the participants' different orientations towards the course. More than half of the respondents, in most cases university teachers, had attended at least one NSS-program's IC in the past. These teachers knew what to expect, and they also had a chance to share in advance their former experiences with the rest of the group from the same university.

First-timers included both students and teachers. Their orientation towards courses topics and activities varied, from having no specific expectations, to quite strong presumptions.

> I thought all that we were going to do is exchange ideas about our (musical) performance practices.

(S5)

I thought it would be a lot of paper presentations. Lots of academic work. Not so much workshops.

(S10)

The most common theme on expectations was the opportunity to share knowledge of music and music education with other attendees from different countries and cultural environments. Related to this theme but a bit more specific, participants expected to learn practical music teaching skills. Networking and making new contacts were also mentioned in many answers as well as academic activities, including paper presentations and research feedback.

To learn different ways to approach music education, learn about other cultures, get something practical to apply to my work.

(S1)

I expected to learn, share and experience other people's ideas and also receive feedback on my research work.

(U9)

Other themes on expectations were attending and participating in musical performances, learning to play musical instruments as well as visits to local schools and sites related to music. Two answers related to attendees' commitment to the course's schedule in general, which appears to be more of a critical remark than an expectation, reminding us of the fact that this question was answered after the course.

What did the participants gain from the course?

To find out what the course participants felt they had benefitted or gained from the course, we asked two somewhat overlapping questions: *What did you gain from this course?* and *What kind of ideas did you get for your work in the future?* The participants came from different cultural and professional backgrounds, so we decided to ask two separate questions with the same focus, enabling the respondents to reflect their experiences from different angles so that their answers would then complement each other.

Most common themes found in these answers were networking ($2 \times S$, $10 \times U$), diverse resources for practical music education ($10 \times S$, $8 \times U$), research skills ($8 \times S$, $9 \times U$) and cultural understanding ($6 \times S$). From a Finnish viewpoint, it seemed that some of the presentations handled culturally, historically and even politically sensitive issues in the context of past and present musical practices in Africa.

I got to know to many lovely people, saw many different ways to have a presentation, new ideas, approaches and influences. I understood so much more about cultural issues, how the background influences your thinking and how sensitive a subject talking about different cultural groups is and the importance of everyone's cultural heritage.

(S1)

A wide knowledge of music theory, different methods of teaching as well as presenting, exposure to a number of instruments, African and western, and networking as well as cultural exchanges.

(S6)

This kind of intensive course with multicultural pedagogical and academic activities exposes the attendants to different cultural views. It would be ideal if these new perspectives and ideas learned on the course, along with practical teaching tools, would eventually benefit the local community of the attendee. It would be very interesting to find out to what extent this kind of transfer actually happens; however, this kind of survey has not yet been carried out.

Article writing and teaching what I've learnt to my friends and students in primary schools as well as practising the conducting, singing and composing of unique sounds and structures.

(S6)

According to the answers given by the participants, a lot of useful information in the field of music education was gained. The majority of respondents ($10 \times S$, $8 \times U$) reported having adopted new practical methods for teaching music and ideas to be used in their future work. These methods included e.g. (1) creative approaches in music education, (2) adding movement to music teaching, (3) choral conducting and singing, (4) teaching African instruments such as mbira, marimbas, drums and percussions, (5) instructing African ensembles or pop bands and teaching hip hop music. Participants also got new material (songs, games) for their lesson plans and new insights about music education in general. Also various music education projects that were introduced during the IC were regarded as interesting, as well as comparing music education methods in different cultures.

Participating in the IC gave many respondents an opportunity to enhance their academic skills. Workshop series for writing articles was popular among the students, whereas university teachers found the event fruitful in terms of having ideas for research, getting encouragement, sharing ideas and engaging in academic discourses ($7 \times S$, $5 \times U$). Also the opportunity to give a presentation was valued, as well as the opportunity to see different ways of presenting a topic ($4 \times S$, $1 \times U$).

With regard to the amount and reliability of the data gathered, there probably would have been a better time and place for answering the questions than the end of the IC. The questionnaire was carried out after the last meeting together, just before the participants were about to say their goodbyes to each other. After the diverse activities during ten intensive days, it must have been quite demanding for many of them to stay focused and reflect thoroughly on all the things that we had learned about music, different cultures and each other.

> To number what I have learned would lead myself to cheat. All I can say is, I have learned more than I expected.
>
> (S9)

What is the meaning of this international cooperation for you?

International collaboration plays a central role in the MECI project. In all answers to the question 'What is the meaning of this international cooperation for you?', the importance of experiences gained from collaboration and reciprocal interaction stood out. Various forms and viewpoints concerning collaboration were brought forward: in some answers, the focus was on cultural interaction, in others the bias was towards research collaboration. In some cases, the emphasis was on dialogue between pedagogy and musicianship, whereas some informants found the development of their own identity within cultural interaction to be very important.

In more than 90 per cent of the answers given, the issues of international cooperation and interaction stood out clearly and felt important (12 students out of 13 and 13 teachers out of 14). Under those concepts were mentioned, for example, the sharing of ideas and experiences ($7 \times S$, $5 \times U$), cultural exchange ($8 \times S$, $6 \times U$) and interacting with other musicians, music educators and researchers ($5 \times S$, $4 \times U$). Three students mentioned networking. The verbs *learn* ($5 \times S$, $1 \times U$) and *share* ($7 \times S$, $4 \times U$) were mentioned often, especially among students.

> Working together from different countries, nationalities and cultures in a way that enriches each other's practices.
>
> (U5)

Personal growth seemed to be an important issue to many respondents. Ten persons out of 27 (37 per cent) answered that this international cooperation had to some extent affected their ways of thinking. In the answers, attendees used descriptions such as 'mind opening' and 'opening doors and a new ideology of music'. The participants noticed having learnt about other cultures and the similarity of people, despite cultural differences (S1) and on the other hand how different people perceive music and how they value it (U14). The importance of sharing was mentioned in connection with personal growth (S6). Teachers found cultural encounters important in students' own growth and development; that they were eye-openers and provided new possibilities (U4); and that they would have an impact on their commitment to studying in the long run (U10).

> It has given me a broader perspective on how different people perceive music and how they value it. Despite the differences in mus.ed. policies, there seems to be a lot of common ground in terms of music and mus. ed.'s importance. NSS has given me wonderful experiences that I will never forget!
>
> (U14)

Pedagogical perspectives were strongly emphasized in international collaboration. In 14 responses (52 per cent of the total), issues of learning, teaching or one's own pedagogical thinking and actions were mentioned. In the answers given by the teachers ($9 \times U$), pedagogical viewpoints were more frequently emphasized than in the answers given by the students ($5 \times S$). Sharing ideas and thoughts was considered as important in developing one's own work, as well as getting concrete working tools from collaboration (U5).

The impact of collaboration and cultural encounters emerged as an important factor also in the employment process and career making. One of the participants (U4) emphasized the fact that events such as the project intensive courses give encouragement and self-confidence to people working in various fields of music education.

> Great inspiration to younger scholars and something to always look forward to.
>
> (U1)

> It was also enriching to realize how much positive energy there is and how many inspiring projects are being done to promote music education.
>
> (U4)

Suggestions for developing the courses

The participants had many suggestions on how to improve the courses. One may argue as well that the large variety of suggestions shows the commitment of the participants. They consider that developing this operational model is worthwhile. The participants were asked two questions on their development ideas: 'What kind of topics or approaches would you have added to this course?'; 'What other suggestions do you have to develop these courses?'

The biggest group of development ideas concerning the topics and approaches ($6 \times S$, $3 \times U$) dealt with issues of practical music making and the desire to put more emphasis on that. The participants wanted more activities on instrumental performance – both African and Western ($2 \times S$, $3 \times U$), voice training ($2 \times S$) and organizing performing groups such as orchestras and choirs ($2 \times S$). One participant had an idea about practical music making that would at the same time have an impact on creating togetherness during the course:

As participants who are multicultural, we must try to form groups and present prepared activities on the last day of the workshop e.g. forming a mass choir, playing instruments. We must have time to practice, given the expertise in the areas.

(S12)

The second-largest group of participants (4 × S, 2 × U) wanted to have more topics related to music education. The educational aspects that were missed were connected to philosophy and didactics of music education (3 × S, 2 × U); 'the easy way of teaching music' (S2); 'how to teach Western instruments in African schools' (S8); and multicultural as well as interdisciplinary teaching and learning approaches (U3). There was also a desire to discuss the role of music in overall social life and its contribution to music education (S7).

Five participants (2 × S, 3 × U) wanted to have more of the kind of approaches that would increase togetherness or utilize the possibilities for co-operation. More co-operation was wanted inside the IP in the form of joint research projects (fieldwork during an IP, U4), performance (forming a mass choir or an orchestra, S12, U1) and discussion (lunchtime debate on a random and well-known topic, S6). On the other hand, one person suggested co-operation with local schools and teachers (U2).

Some people wished to have more topics on African music and preserving the culture (2 × S, 3 × U). They wanted to learn strategies on how to help societies to gather lost musical elements and encourage more people to pre-serve the culture in music (2 × S). 'Notation of Afro-American rhythms' was one suggestion for a topic that would help local teachers to write down their music (U14). Another idea around this area was to add a presentation on 'Indigenous music through modern technology' (U6). One participant sug-gested that people should arrange their traditional music for the purpose of teaching (U5).

Three university teachers wanted to have more on approaches to music research. They wanted to maximize better the privilege of having research specialists assembled. More time could be offered for consultation on research proposals (U13) and joint research projects could be planned (U4). One uni-versity teacher called for more critical theory. He claimed that 'some presen-tations lack critical vigour and are full of unexamined assumptions' (U8).

Other requests for topics or approaches dealt with out of school music activities and community development (S2, U9), music therapy and the healing aspect of music (2 × S), history of music development in the countries present (S6) and study possibilities (MA/PhD) available in each of the sister universities to share with students (U10). Three people (1 × S, 2 × U) had nothing to add to the course: 'I think the number of people now involved in this project guarantees a very good variety of topics and presentations' (U12).

The most mentioned idea for developing the structure of the courses (3 × S, 4 × U) was to increase the time that is available for discussion or rest. The ten-day period was quite packed with a great variety of presentations and workshops, and there was only one free day in the middle of the period. Participants missed for example 'room for thorough discussion' (U3) and 'one or two free afternoons' (U7) and wanted fewer days used for the course because it is difficult to fit ten days into participants' normal workloads (U4).

Three participants thought that the topics of the course should be organized according to themes ($1 \times S$, $2 \times U$), but on the other hand three people said that there should be more variation in presentations ($1 \times S$, $2 \times U$). One underlined that offsetting presentations with other activities would provide a valuable variety of learning experiences (U10); another wanted to alternate western presentations with African ones on the same day (S3); and one thought that there should not be too many presentations by the same person (U4). In addition to these people, two others wanted to have more practical workshops and demonstrations (S13, U14).

Four people wished to have more shared material and networking ($2 \times S$, $2 \times U$). There was a suggestion of making a booklet about the presentations that could be sent to members (S2). On the other hand, sharing could happen using a website for the NSS MECI program (S7). Also shared mentorship between the universities and follow-ups for younger scholars were called for ($2 \times U$).

Six people had ideas/suggestions/opinions on participation. One teacher wished for more participation of students (U9). On the other hand, two students suggested that there should be competitive activities in order to motivate the participants and encourage those who were not fully taking part ($2 \times S$). Two students and one university teacher called for more equally balanced contributions from all partner institutions ($2 \times S$, $1 \times U$). They hoped that everyone could attend actively to the whole course or that there should be a balance in presentation from all the participating universities.

To sum up the survey results, it seemed to be evident that the kind of collaboration practised in the MECI project so far has been rewarding to everyone involved and that collaboration activities have been efficient and beneficial.

Conclusion

As can be noticed from the above, the project activities have played a significant role in the participants' lives. To the general comment already referred to above ('Participating in the NSS programme changed my life in very fundamental, but extremely positive, ways'), one could add many more examples on how both students and teachers have experienced the project activities in the past, and how they have applied what they have learned from the project in their own lives and careers.

Regarding what the project has meant for students, it has made an immense contribution towards expanding their views and perspectives. The MECI intensive course, held in Pretoria during 2012, where all the participating countries joined and shared ideas, was also a very valuable experience to students. Opportunities were created in which they could share in music making, and also where they could take part in critical discussions and seminars with researchers – both experienced experts and young scholars – from Africa and Finland.

The participants joined the course with very different – even opposite – orientations. In the end, everyone had gained something important from the period, so obviously the variety of topics was wide enough. Maybe there was already too much in the programme since many wished for more free conversation or time to rest. In the future, it should be remembered to give sufficient time for networking in both ways: through conversations and music. Informal action promotes the overall aims of the MECI programme as well – collaboration, networking in the areas of research and education as well as deeper understanding and learning. During previous courses, good experiences have been gained for example from centralized accommodation. It should be remembered as well to utilize the possibilities of joint musicking in creating trust, networks and interaction.

MECI intensive courses are valued for increasing equality. For many students and teachers, they provide an opportunity to join an international academic conference in spite of their economic situation. The collaboration has led to many joint articles, and it has been a great inspiration for writing a master's thesis for many. It has also been seen as important for becoming employed.

The fact that collaboration of this kind was experienced as important from the perspective of personal growth by many participants (37 per cent of the total) can be regarded as significant. This can be understood as how when people representing different cultures meet during courses such as this, sustainable development is created – some essential growth in the self takes place and gets new meanings. Since nearly all participants were either (music) teacher educators or (music) education students, all this will be transmitted to generations to come via school education in the participating countries, and hence its importance cannot be overestimated.

To conclude, the authors have experienced the MECI collaboration as a long-enduring developmental project. The continuation of this project is currently not guaranteed; yet we want our experiences to encourage others to take up similar kinds of multicultural collaboration projects in different fields of music and music education. As mentioned in the first section, the main reason for our survey was to collect data from course participants related to their experiences and perceptions of activities (both past and present) within the MECI project, the contents of the course programme and the proposed aims of the MECI project. We found the results most encouraging and live in hope that there will be continuation of our collaborative efforts in future, since it seems that there is a need for music and music education projects such as this.

Note

1 During the North–South phase, collaboration existed only on a bilateral basis (in our case between University of Jyväskylä and University of Pretoria). Since 2007, the overall title of the network has been North–South–South, thus denoting both the importance of getting more partners involved and attempts to strengthen collaboration between partner institutions in South.

Bibliography of texts used in MECI

Bakan, M. B. (2013). *World music: Traditions and transformations*. New York: McGraw-Hill.

Blacking, J. (1973/2000). *How musical is man?* Seattle: University of Washington Press.

Bohlman, P. V. (2002). *World music: A very short introduction*. New York: OUP.

Cook, N. (2000). *Music: A very short introduction*. New York: OUP.

Nettl, B. (2005). *The study of ethnomusicology: Thirty-one issues and concepts*. Urbana, IL: University of Illinois Press.

Patton, M. Q. (1990). *Qualitative evaluation and research methods* (2nd ed.) Newbury Park, CA: Sage.

Schippers, H. (2010). *Facing the music: Shaping music education from a global perspective*. New York: OUP.

9 Towards contextual understanding of gender

Student teachers' views on home economics education and gender in Ghana and Finland

Hille Janhonen-Abruquah, Hanna Posti-Ahokas,
Hannah Benjaba Edjah and
Manasseh Edison Komla Amu

The diversity among students is to be recognised and respected, so gender needs to be taken into consideration (Lahelma, 2011). Through culturally responsive education (Gay, 2013), the contextual and relational aspects of learning can be emphasised, and, thus, gender can be acknowledged. The focus of this chapter is on the contextual understanding of gender in home economics education as it is perceived by university teacher students at the University of Helsinki, Finland, and the University of Cape Coast, Ghana. Finland is characterised by a seemingly gender-neutral approach to home economics education, whereas Ghana has a feminised approach. Following the researchers' commitment as teacher educators to precipitate change and transformation in education, this empirical analysis draws on group discussions with future home economics teachers at two universities in these countries.

Home economics and its multiple content areas (e.g. food and nutrition, consumer issues, family studies, sustainable living) are understood and emphasised in different contexts in various ways (McGregor, 2011; Wahlen, Posti-Ahokas, & Collins, 2009). In the school subject of home economics, gender may be more visible and determinative of pupils' participation and roles than in other subjects. In both Ghana and Finland, home economics has a relatively strong position at different levels of education. In both contexts, gender has been defined as a critical yet overlooked issue in home economics education (Amu & Edjah, forthcoming Anttila, Leskinen, Posti-Ahokas, & Janhonen-Abruquah, 2015). In Ghana, gender inequality is recognised as a critical societal problem and discussed in relation to education policy, including setting targets for equal access and enrolment for male and female students. In addition, demand to meet the Millennium Development Goals focused on eliminating gender discrimination and inequalities in access and achievement at all levels of education requires attention to the subject of home economics, as it is a heavily female-dominated field of study across the educational system. In Finland, education policies and the national curriculum increasingly emphasise the importance of replacing the prevailing gender-neutral rhetoric of current education policies and practices with gender awareness to advance gender equality (FNBE, 2014). Finnish home economics education, particularly at the basic education level, has been widely considered gender neutral (Turkki, 2011). However, the growing gender awareness promoted through research, policy and curricula has resulted in an increasing focus among home economists on gender-related problems within their field (Amu & Edjah, forthcoming; Anttila et al., 2015; Turkki, 2011).

Defined as an academic discipline and curriculum area connected to everyday living in households and wider societal arenas (International Federation for Home Economics (IFHE), 2008), home economics (education) is in a good position to capture, discuss and advance gender-related issues from multiple perspectives and at different levels, from individual perspectives to wider policy frameworks. However, gender is difficult to address as it runs through structures, cultures and subjectivities, and the concept of gender has different meanings for different people (Lahelma, 2011, 2014). Therefore, challenging the normative, dichotomised perspectives on gender is simultaneously one of the most critical tasks and the greatest opportunities for home economists working in different countries (Pipping-Ekström & Hjälmeskog, 2006; Thompson, 1986).

Culturally responsive teaching (Gay, 2010, 2013) can act as the pedagogical practice of gender awareness, as it aims to achieve meaningful learning for all. Learners are addressed in a comprehensive way and are multidimensionally engaged in learning activities. Learning aims for change and freedom and is both transformative and emancipatory (Gay, 2013, p. 52). Attention to gender is needed for teaching to become truly transformative and emancipatory. In home economics education, whether seen as a feminine subject as in Ghana or as a gender-neutral subject as in Finland, gender plays a critical role. Through this chapter, the authors argue for the importance of analysing the various contextual, multi-dimensional understandings of gender and their influence on practices in home economics education and on the image of the profession. Drawing from online and focus group discussions of home economics university students facilitated by the authors in 2013 and 2014, this research analyses home economics student teachers' perceptions of gender in Finland and Ghana. The aim is to deepen understanding of the influence of gender on attitudes, practices and policies in home economics education. This understanding is one of the ways to move towards cultural responsiveness in education, which contributes to more equal and just societies.

Research on students' voices in higher education development (e.g. Seale, 2010) has been reported in home economics education by Turkki (2005), who demonstrates the richness of perspectives provided by home economics student teachers on improving teacher education and the image of the home economics profession. Additionally, McGregor (2011) has emphasised the importance of pre-professional socialisation in the future of home economics. This study is linked to the regular learning activities at two universities, creating a space to co-construct understanding of gender. For teacher educators, this research provides an opportunity to listen to students' voices, which can facilitate responding to the needs and expectations of student teachers. The study is connected to the activities of the North–South–South network: 'Culturally responsive education' and is part of on-going research-based development of home economics teacher education in Ghana (e.g. Amu & Edjah, forthcoming; Edjah & Amu, 2012) and Finland (Janhonen-Abruquah, Posti-Ahokas, Palojoki & Lehtomäki, 2014; Posti-Ahokas, Janhonen-Abruquah, & Johnson Longfor, 2015).

Home economics education and gender equality

Gender has been an integral part of the development of the home economics field throughout its 120-year history. Thompson (1986) contends that home economics, though a female-defined discipline, was never intended to be for women only. She applies a metaphorical model with classical roots to describe the lived space where the public Hermean sphere, named after the Greek god of communication, is visible and masculine, and the Hestian world, named after the Greek goddess of the hearth and home, is private, invisible and feminine (Thompson, 1986). The domains are not mirror images of one another but exist in relation to each other while remaining distinctive. They are complementary and interdependent. According to Thompson (1986), understanding the essence of home economics requires a shift from a male-defined Hermean mind-set to a female-defined Hestian mind-set. This perceptual shift, claims Thompson (1986), brings into focus a holistic reality and raises thinking beyond gender to more complex levels of social and intellectual organisation. Thompson's (1986) metaphor helps understanding of the complementary male and female mind-sets and allows the viewing of the two simultaneously existing spheres as less defined by biological sex, permitting individuals to shift from one world to another in a more flexible manner.

Thompson (1986) demands that home economics be recognised for its potential to contribute to reducing the gender-role stereotyping of necessary everyday tasks. In more recent home economics research, the gender perspective is typically present in investigations of the division of household work and parenting (e.g. Aalto, 2014; Braun, Lewin-Epstein, Stier, & Baumgärtner, 2008; Lewin-Epstein, Stier, & Braun, 2006). However, the underlying structures influencing the division of work and other gender-related phenomena in everyday life have received less research attention.

Some recent research on home economics education has focused on the gender perspective and contributed to the analysis of the influence of gender on education practices. In a study on the home economics teaching profession in Australia, Pendergast (2001) analyses home economics teachers as representatives of a female-dominated profession and the stereotypes attached to them. She argues that the stereotypes do not correspond with teachers' identities, and, thus, it is essential to deconstruct these stereotypical views to revive the profession (Pendergast, 2001). Petterson's study (2007) on Swedish home economics education describes the various imaginative ways students perform gender in home economics classes and thereby re-negotiate their biological sex and change the gender order in various contexts and situations. According to Petterson (2007), home economics classes are characterised by a strong female genderisation combined with striving for gender equality. Anttila et al. (2015) study the performance of gender and agency in Finnish home economics textbook illustrations and conclude that home economics textbook images reflect traditional, heteronormative gender positions and styles. The agency portrayed in home economics settings is strongly gendered and performed within predetermined gender categories: for example, picturing cooking males as chefs and women as housewives.

Research in two African contexts – Tanzania (Stambach, 2000) and Ghana (Amu & Edjah, forthcoming) – analyses students' perceptions of home economics education in secondary-level education and discusses the prevailing attitudes towards home economics as a subject characterised by strong gendered assumptions. These studies depict how home economics operates between traditional gender roles and the ideals of changing contemporary society in which a more flexible performance of gender is allowed and gender equality is enhanced.

In this chapter, gender equality is approached from the perspective of creating equal empowerment and enabling conditions. The importance of practical and art subjects in providing spaces to advance gender equality within and through education is emphasised (Berg et al., 2011; Turkki, 2009).

Current issues related to gender and home economics education in Ghana

In the Ghanaian education system, pupils are introduced to aspects of home economics at the primary level. Home economics is introduced as a course at the basic level in junior high school (ages 12–15). In the first year of junior high school, all students are exposed to a compulsory subject called basic design and technology, which is a combination of home economics, visual arts and pre-technical skills. All students, regardless of gender, are introduced to these three areas and informed before selecting to continue in one of these three areas in their second and final years of junior high school education.

At the senior secondary-school level (ages 16–18) in Ghana, home economics is an elective course. At this level, the course consists of three subjects: food and nutrition, clothing and textiles and management in living. The main aim is to equip students with basic life and employment skills, making the course both useful and gainful. Students of home economics have the option of specialising in either food and nutrition or clothing and textiles. The home economics course is not offered in all senior high schools in

Ghana. Out of 562 senior high schools in Ghana, a total of 67 are single-sex, with 43 for females while the remaining 24 are for males (Ghana Education Service, 2015). Male students in these single-sex schools do not have access to home economics programmes of study. This set-up deprives a large number of male students from acquiring knowledge in home economics that could help them decide whether it is of interest to them. Similarly, in female single-sex schools, technical courses are not offered, depriving female students of access to knowledge in technical programmes at the senior high-school level. These divisions are a subtle way of reinforcing gender-stereotyped roles, which are deeply rooted in Ghanaian culture.

Upon completion of senior high school, students have options for further study in education colleges, nurses' training colleges, polytechnic institutes and universities. Students who wish to further their studies at universities are given the opportunity to continue specialising in either food and nutrition or clothing and textiles, with resource management as a core component. Of the eight public universities in Ghana, four offer home economics education.

In Ghana, home economics as an academic programme is female dominated, with males accounting for less than 5 per cent of enrolment (Neequaye, Darkwa, & Amu, 2014). Home economics programmes in schools at all levels are dominated by female students, and the field is seen in many countries as a professional field for women, as Saleem (1998) points out. The female-dominated nature of home economics in Ghana can be traced to the way and manner in which the programme was introduced into the formal education system. As noted by Amu, Offei-Ansah and Amissah (2015), from the very beginning, the content and scope of home economics in Ghana were limited to traditional feminine roles, and boys were discouraged from performing these perceived female roles. As girls were offered the home economics course, boys took other courses, such as agriculture, and this gendered pattern has persisted in the programme to date. In a study of 290,000 junior high school applicants to senior high schools in Ghana, Ajayi and Buessing (2013) find that 1 of every 4 girls selected home economics as their first choice, compared to 2 of every 100 boys. Ajayi and Buessing (2014) also find that male students are more likely to choose agricultural science, general science, business and subjects which they believe can lead to the traditionally socialised gender-stereotyped roles.

In the Ghanaian context, gender inequality is seen as fuelled by cultural attitudes and values present in the society. Ghanaian society is a clear mirror of most African communities' prescriptions for appropriate male and female roles (Ampofo, 2001). The cultural construction of masculinity and femininity in Ghanaian society is founded on a belief in fundamental biological distinctions between male and female human natures and corresponding behavioural prescriptions typically expressed in societal norms and values (Abu, 1991; Adinkrah, 2012; Nukunya, 2003). Household tasks are often gender stereotyped, which encourages the disparities between gender enrolments in different subjects. In Ghana, distinguishing male and female characteristics are inculcated and absorbed from early childhood (Amoah, 1991; Nukunya, 2003). Akotia and Anum (2012) explain that these differentiated socialisation paths for boys and girls have impacts on their gender role perceptions in adulthood and influence their programme and career choices as they transition from childhood.

Current issues in Finnish home economics education

In Finland, home economics is taught as a compulsory subject for all seventh-grade students (age 13) in basic education. In the eighth and ninth grades (ages 14 and 15), home economics is one of the most popular optional subjects. More recently, home economics has been introduced at the elementary-school level and is taught in some general upper-secondary schools (Venäläinen, 2015). At the secondary-school level, home economics is taught mainly in vocational upper-secondary schools that have home economics-related training programmes in catering, hospitality services and domestic services. In universities, home economics science can be studied as a major at the bachelor's, master's and doctoral levels.

In basic education, the main objective of home economics education is to develop pupils' skills in cooperation, information acquisition and the practical work necessary to manage daily living. Topics taught include family and living together, nutrition and food culture, the consumer and changing society and the home and the environment. The aim of the subject is to teach general life skills for personal growth and development (Finnish National Board of Education, 2004).

Promoting gender equality is one of the goals of home economics education (FNBE, 2004). However, a recent national assessment of home economics learning outcomes (Venäläinen, 2015) identifies significant differences in boys and girls' learning outcomes. Similarly, Anttila et al. (2015) warns of the risk of taking for granted the expected promotion of gender equality by the common home economics education for boys and girls. Given that the general curriculum for basic education (FNBE, 2014) to be implemented in 2016 encourages the enabling of individual learning paths free from predominant gender positions, it is essential to consider how gender is reconstructed and discussed in home economics teacher education.

Gender has been recognised as an overlooked issue in Finnish teacher education that should be given more attention if gender equality is to be taken seriously. To illustrate the controversies in the Finnish debate around gender and education, Lahelma (2011) gives examples of teachers and teacher educators who suggest that gender is not a problem in schools but, in the same breath, express concerns about poor achievement among boys. Therefore, a more gender-aware approach is needed to advance gender equality in seemingly gender-neutral basic education in Finland (Lahelma, 2011, 2014).

Study of Finnish and Ghanaian home economics student teachers' views of gender

This study applies critical, student-centred approaches to education research. Research on students' voices in higher education (Lehtomäki, Moate & Posti-Ahokas, 2015; McLeod, 2011; Seale, 2010) foregrounds students' perspectives to inform development oriented towards transformation and change in education. Connecting this study with the regular practices of home economics teacher education and the development of university degree requirements at both participating universities are strategies supporting the research-based development of home economics education at the university level. Additionally, the study was a shared dialogic learning process across the two countries, benefitting from the North–South–South network and especially the student and staff mobility, which permitted data collection and time for joint writing.

Data were collected from home economics student teachers who will enter the teaching field. Exploring their ideas can prompt deliberation about their practices in their future profession. Home economics student teachers' views of gender in home economics education were captured in students' online and focus group discussions at the University of Helsinki, Finland, and the University of Cape Coast, Ghana. In Finland, data collection was conducted through an optional master's-level course on gender and home economics taught by one of the authors of this chapter in the autumn of 2013. Sixteen students (2 male, 14 female)[1] participated in the course and the data collection of the study. The analysed data were drawn from students' online discussions in the electronic learning platform used in the course. Throughout the course, students were asked to discuss the role of home economics in advancing gender equality, focusing on the following questions:

- Is promotion of gender equality an implicit assumption in home economics education?
- Are traditional gender roles automatically or unconsciously reproduced?
- What is education in gender equality like in the practice of home economics education?

The Finnish data consist of 18 written contributions ranging from 40 to 250 words. Students were free either to start their own discussion or to react to previous contributions. In the end, the on-line discussion had 8 separate chains which each included 1–4 contributions. While some contributions reflected on the course readings, others were reflective of personal experiences and opinions, portraying a variety of perspectives and different levels of theorising.

The encouraging experience and the thought-provoking contents of the online discussion motivated a discussion organised around similar themes at the Ghanaian partner, the University in Cape Coast. Two focus group discussions were carried out in March 2014 with 16 third- and final-year bachelor students, of whom 2 were male and 14 female.[2] These discussions were facilitated by two university lecturers in home economics, and each lasted for approximately 1 hour 30 minutes. The questions presented to the students participating in the discussions were:

- What do you see as the role of home economics education in promoting or advancing gender equality?
- Are there practices that unconsciously reproduce traditional gender roles? In secondary education? At the university level?
- How can home economics teachers and educators advance gender equality? Please give examples of practices of education for gender equality in home economics. In secondary education? At the university level?

The discussions were recorded and transcribed by a research assistant. The analysed data consist of 32 single-spaced pages of transcripts. The Ghanaian data differ from the Finnish dataset as the focus group discussions in Ghana were not part of formal learning activities. This resulted in students discussing the topics based on their own experience and their education in general. Gender is not a distinctive topic in the bachelor's-degree programme in home economics offered at the University of Cape Coast.

At both universities, participating students signed a written consent form agreeing to the use of their written or spoken views for research purposes. In the following results section, students' anonymity is protected by referring to individual students by numbers and their biological sex. The selected direct quotations from the Finnish data used in the article were translated into English from the online discussion conducted in Finnish. The two data sets were subjected separately to qualitative content analysis (Silverman, 2006; Wolff, 2007). Preliminary themes were identified in the data. The four researchers collaboratively performed the steps of content analysis. They discussed the themes, categories and alternative ways of analysing the data, both face to face and in online discussions. The research findings are jointly written.

Findings

Ghana: overcoming structural and cultural constraints on gender equality

It is evident in the discussions of the Ghanaian home economics students that the educational structure itself provides fertile grounds and foundations for gender inequality. In the second year in junior high school (age 13), pupils begin to separate and study in depth the subjects they have been socialised to believe are appropriate for certain genders. For example, boys at the junior high school level are more likely to choose pre-technical skills, and girls are most likely to select home economics, while the visual arts are likely to be chosen by both genders. Psychologically, boys do not believe that they have equal access to home economics, as they have been brought up to believe that the subject involves mostly female-dominated activities. Girls, in contrast, are oriented to engage less in tasks that involve a lot of physical strength. Consequently, they tend to select home economics for the remaining two years of study as it involves the use of little physical strength in most practical activities, such as cooking, laundry and sewing, compared to pre-technical skills. In this way, learners align themselves to the beliefs of society, perpetuating existing inequalities.

The name of the programme was also considered to be inimical to male participation. Participants believed that a name change could bring more men into the programme. This perception is voiced by female student 5:

> the name 'home economics' makes people turn their minds to [the] home.... Since traditionally, Ghanaian men think work in the home is for women, they do not want to be associated with a subject that teaches issues of the home.

This finding is in agreement with that of Firebaugh (1980) in North America.

Regarding the cultural context of education, female student 3 in the first group states that 'our culture is such that, in the house, most of the domestic activities are done by the females, so children grow up with that perception'. In other words, as pupils begin learning lessons that have a direct relationship to the home, the general thinking is that this content (subject) is for females. Consequently, learners make choices corresponding with their mind-set moulded by society. The agents of socialisation ensure that social norms, values and beliefs are inculcated through socialisation and that individuals imbibe them early in childhood. Helgeson (2009) suggests that theories about gender-role socialisation indicate that different people and objects in children's environment provide rewards and models that shape children's behaviour to fit the gender role norms in their particular society. Various agents in children's environment, including parents, peers, teachers and the media, influence children's gender role attitudes. These socialisation agents usually enforce what is gender-appropriate behaviour through the use of rewards, sanctions and punishments (Nukunya, 2003). In the focus group discussions, these agents were identified as behaving in ways that advance gender inequality. Male participant 1 states that: "Most parents, when their children are selecting home economics as a course to read at the secondary level, discourage the males from selecting that course as they believe it's for females."

Teachers, who one might think should push for more equality, also tend to act in ways that reduce the opportunities male learners have to study home economics. Some teachers who male respondents have experienced or come into contact with suggested that home economics is a female-oriented curriculum. The male facilitator of this discussion shared his own experience when, in their first contact, his secondary school teacher said, "'This course is for women'…. Then the teacher sees a guy and remarks 'Oh! What are you doing here?" ' This report indicates a subconscious imprint made in the mind of the male student that, regardless of his interest, he does not have the right to study home economics. Male participants 1 and 2 in the second group both identified with this experience shared by the facilitator and added that it is not always explicitly evident, but even the subtle comments made and attitudes revealed by both teachers and learners regarding males studying home economics lay bare the gender inequalities that exist within the educational environment. Amu and Edjah (forthcoming) suggest that some parents and teachers discourage males from studying home economics and often express displeasure at such attempts by their male children. Sometimes, male students do not have access to certain options even within the home economics programme. These societal perceptions about home economics have made it unattractive to male students and affected the attitudes of male students who enrol in the programme. Male participant 2 shares his experience:

> In the school where I had my internship, there was this guy who wanted to read home economics (food and nutrition option) but was forced to do the clothing and textiles option instead…. He was always out of class during clothing and textiles lessons.

The issue of student achievement tied to various subject areas also came up during the discussion. Participants raised the issue of teachers trying to influence pupils with good general performance to further their studies in any area other than home economics or vocational studies. The entry requirements for home economics programmes at various secondary schools are generally lower than those for other subjects, such as science, business and general arts. This discourages students of both genders who perform well and are interested in home economics, as the impression created by the differences in the entry requirements is that it is a subject for low-performing learners. This also has implications for gender enrolment in home economics in Ghana. Even though both genders are affected, female students are more subtly encouraged to enrol in the programme than males. This is because, in Ghana, high-achieving students are less likely to select gender-stereotyped programmes, such as home economics (Ajayi & Buessing, 2014). Ajayi and Buessing (2014) note that home economics is more popular among girls from deprived areas of Ghana who are more likely to achieve less (academically) than boys from urban areas who are more likely to attain higher academic achievement, especially at the basic level. In Ghana, girls growing up in rural areas with a strong gender bias against females might be discouraged from attending school and consequently have lower academic achievement or tend to select traditionally female-dominated programmes, such as home economics.

Suggested need for content changes

The most frequently highlighted activities of home economics education in Ghana are cooking and sewing. This tendency reinforces the narrow perception that it is a course that deals solely with cooking and sewing:

> I think home economics is seen here in Ghana as a female course. In the past, it was introduced as a course for sewing and cooking, and it was only for women. This has not changed much. It has to be changed; without that, it will still be for only females.
>
> (Female student 7)

> But if you look at the course itself, it is a course that is supposed to be viewed as a life-oriented course for both boys and girls. So if the course is structured like that and made compulsory at the basic level, then the inequality that exists in enrolment may decrease.
>
> (Female student 4)

The students suggested that the three main areas should be organised into one course with major components so that both boys and girls could benefit and develop equal interest in the course. Also, the science background and components within the home economics subject should be emphasised in the basic-level content.

Based on students' views, the cultural values of Ghanaian society should also be re-defined, so people gain an understanding that domestic activities are for both genders, not only females. This view should be consciously emphasised in the socialisation of children so that, as they grow up, they understand that they need home economics knowledge to work in the home as individuals. For this to happen, parents holding traditional concepts of domestic roles as a female domain need some form of re-orientation.

Participants also suggested that teachers should give priority to males in home economics classes and not overtly or covertly discriminate against males through actions or comments. As Agyare-Kwabi (2013) notes, Ghana has recently given much attention to gender parity in school enrolment, an agenda largely driven by the desire to meet the second and third Millennium Development Goals which focus on eliminating gender discrimination and inequalities in educational access and achievement at all levels. Home economics, therefore, stands as an appropriate programme to contribute to the realisation of this goal.

Finland: from gender neutrality to responsive gender awareness

In the online discussion conducted during the course on gender and home economics at the University of Helsinki, student teachers started by discussing the seemingly gender-neutral context of Finnish home-economics education at the basic level. Students reflected on the fact that home economics education is a compulsory subject for both boys and girls. They assumed that, in Finland, gender equality is taken as a given.

> Home economics education has not been divided separately into women and men's chores, but home economics is for everyone.
>
> (Female student 8, male student 2)

> Since home economics education has been a common subject for both boys and girls since the beginning of comprehensive school reform, this must have been taken as a major gesture for gender equality.
>
> (Female student 5)

> Gender equality is a vast and undefined concept. It is difficult to get hold of it as the basic assumption is that in Finland, gender equality exists.
>
> (Female student 6)

Finland is seen as a country in which gender equality has been achieved (Lahelma, 2011). However, 'genderless gender' (Ronkainen, 2001) is created when mute or hidden gendering and sexualisation converge with the gender-neutral rhetoric of the individual self. Gender neutrality has been understood as gender equality and means that talking about gender is avoided; accordingly, the impacts of gender are muted (Lahelma, 2011). For example, students in this study commented that teaching should be the same for all learners:

> In my opinion and based on my own experience, contemporary home economics education promotes gender equality only if the learner her/himself is open to receiving information. Gender equality education is evident in home economics teaching: all of my pupils carry out exactly the same tasks – everyone according to her or his skills.
>
> (Female student 1)

Changes in society have influenced the gender equality discussion over time (Holli, Magnusson, & Rönnblom, 2005). The historical transition from an agricultural society to contemporary society has diminished the importance of dividing household chores based on biological sex:

> I think that young fathers have been exemplary in combining child and household care and performing it together with mothers.
>
> (Female student 1)

> Men are more and more taking part in household activities, and many enjoy food preparation at least as a hobby.
>
> (Female student 1)

Our field has long been a 'women's area'. The world has really changed. Gender has been a bit like a taboo. These things were not questioned or pondered this way before.

(Female student 2)

Even though society has changed, students gave examples of how home economics education still re-creates normative gender roles:

Classes were about cooking. Work division was done equally. Although everyone was cooking, girls were the ones who were setting the table and putting the kitchen in order in the end. It was also obvious on the teacher's part that she required tidying up and cleaning chores more from the girls, whereas boys had more freedom to act as they wished. The teacher's attitude was that boys need to be understood as they are boys, and girls ought to be neat.

(Male student 2)

As in Finland gender equality is seen as a platitude, I believe that, at the same time, it reinforces and re-creates normative gender roles.

(Female student 6)

Gender equality was seen from the female orientation, and home economics was reasoned to be a female-dominated area:

The focus has been on women, and males have not been seen as active agents within the home. Thus, gender has been looked at from the female point of view.

(Male student 1)

Lahelma (2011) confirms student teachers' beliefs, stating that the theoretical and empirical results of recent gender research in education have not been included in mainstream teacher education. Lahelma (2011) further claims that it is possible for student teachers to graduate without learning about the requirements set by the Act on Equality Between Women and Men (1986/2005) or what these requirements mean in the processes and practices of schools. Gender has been – and still seems to be – the blind spot in teacher education (Lahelma, 2011).

Suggestions for increasing gender awareness

Students' online discussion generated valuable ideas on how to move from gender neutrality towards home economics education that is increasingly gender aware and advances gender equality in a responsive way. Student teachers suggested that the teaching of home economics should be diversified based on learners' individual interests:

> Gender equality in home economics classes means that different person-
> alities and individuals are taken into consideration. Everyone should be
> given a chance and stimulus to work with and take part in class activities.
>
> (Female student 2)

> I observed a seventh-grade home economics class. The teacher supported
> her pupils individually no matter their sex. One boy was good at
> cooking. His interest was in food, colours and food-related themes. The
> teacher recognised the boy's interest and enabled his creative work. She
> gave him more hints to work with, showed him books for extra reading
> and discussed with and encouraged the boy to create a table setting that
> pleased him. This type of teaching is needed more: arousing one's interest
> and making use of it in teaching.
>
> (Female student 3)

Student teachers recognised the need to change the content of home economics teaching to promote gender equality:

> One of my supervisors in teaching practise criticised my choice of a dish
> for being too girlish even though the learners were men. Since then I've
> been wondering whether recipes are gendered as well. I think this is
> about individual preferences and not about differences defined by gender.
> Someone likes detailed decorations; another, rougher baking.
>
> (Female student 4)

> It is important to understand home economics as something else other
> than cooking and cleaning. Individuals' roles in society have to be
> emphasised as well. Then home economics can be seen to promote
> gender equality as then, the field is not restricted only to the domestic
> sphere. This does not mean that the everyday life in the home is not
> important, to the contrary.
>
> (Male student 1)

Some students found it difficult to define the concept of equality and argued
that gender is not always thought of as a factor contributing to inequality:

> The concept of equality is a disturbingly vast concept. To my under-
> standing, it has been connected lately with immigrants and pupils with
> different cultural backgrounds.
>
> (Female student 5)

This difficulty in recognising the importance of gender may be due to the
gender-neutral rhetoric within the education system at all levels. The
forthcoming basic education curriculum for home economics education in
Finland (FNBE, 2014) calls for gender equality but does not define it clearly.

Therefore, the authors strongly call for conducting more content-related studies on gender equality in teacher education to increase future teachers' understanding of issues related to gender. Lahelma (2011, p. 11) argues that making visible the gendered inequalities built into teaching and learning practices helps student teachers see the same patterns in society, including in their own lives and partnerships. Therefore, gender awareness is not a personal characteristic that a teacher either has or does not have; rather, through theoretical knowledge, it can be learned and then applied to identify and understand gender and (in)equality. This goal should be part of pedagogical training (Lahelma, 2011).

Discussing experiences of introducing gender into Finnish teacher education since the 1980s, Lahelma (2011) and Vidén and Naskali (2010) describe their feelings of happiness when students' awareness of gender is awakened. After the courses, the general feeling has been that this knowledge should be obligatory for every teacher (Lahelma, 2011; Vidén & Naskali, 2010). Similarly, a student participating in the course in which the online discussion took place states that 'this course has surely opened my eyes in many ways!' (female student 9). Several students recognised deficiencies in the current content of Finnish home economics teacher education:

> The perspective of gender does not even come to mind as it has not been included in our studies.
>
> (Female student 8)

> The gender theme is kind of artificially kept in the courses, like 'You know, boys should not be allowed to act any more wildly than girls'.
>
> (Female student F2)

> Our education does not give tools to tackle gender equality.
>
> (Female student 7)

The authors' own experiences in teaching the course on gender and home economics have been very encouraging, and the teaching has inspired new research on gender and home economics, including the present study. Gender will be mainstreamed in the forthcoming degree requirements to provide home-economics student teachers with more opportunities to engage with gender-related issues in their field.

Discussion and conclusion

The gender positions present in the home and society at large influence the practices of home economics education in school. In Ghana, the gendered division of labour is still prevalent in many communities. The domestic work of cooking, cleaning and childcare is normally considered women's work, a perception which feeds into the culture of schools. Various agents of socialisation usually enforce what is gender-appropriate behaviour through the use of rewards, sanctions and punishments (Nukunya, 2003). These appropriate behaviours do not necessarily advance gender equality but, rather, societal norms. In Ghana, the socialisation process fosters gender-stereotyped roles in the minds of children from infancy. This process is reflected in their education and programme choices at the junior high school level. Participants were of the view that the structure of the Ghanaian educational system at the junior high school level appears to entrench the status quo (see also Akotia & Anum, 2012). Male students select programmes that help portray masculine gender roles, and female students those that help in playing feminine roles. At higher levels of the education system, students continue to select programmes that reflect this gendered-stereotyped mind-set about the division of labour implanted by society. This mind-set is further reinforced later in life by parents, teachers, peers and others in society, causing men to shy away from home economics as they see it as a programme related to female gender roles. This process has resulted in the unequal representation of male and female students in home economics programmes in Ghana. Participants suggested that the cultural values of Ghanaian society should be re-defined, so people could gain the understanding that domestic activities are essential components of healthy living and well-being for all individuals, society and the world at large.

In Finland, gender is a less defining factor in socialisation and education choices. The socialisation of children is done in such a manner that both males and females accept the idea of gender equality. Gender parity in home economics is attributable to the changing gender roles in the Finnish home. In home economics education, the compulsory course in seventh grade provides both boys and girls opportunities to learn about home economics and consider it as a future profession. Teachers in home economics programmes can support these opportunities by ensuring that boys and girls are given equal attention and tasks during home economics lessons. Therefore, (at least most) programmes of study are seen as available to all. The findings from the Finnish student teachers' online discussion reflects the gender-neutral rhetoric that remains heavily present in the equality discourse. However, increased gender awareness emerged in student teachers as the discussion continued throughout the course. Students started to recognise problems in education practices and began to question practices that maintain and reinforce normative gender roles. For future changes, both pre-service and in-service teacher education have crucial roles to play in shifting towards gender awareness.

Even though the societal contexts within which this research was conducted are very different, the findings point to similarities and common challenges. First, the female dominance of the field is not an ideal situation, and collective effort is needed to ensure equal access and participation in home economics subjects, courses and programmes of study. Second, student teachers have relevant suggestions and valuable perspectives to share and should be listened to. This study also points to the immediate need to include more gender-related content in the home economics curriculum at the universities in both countries.

Throughout history, significant legislative steps towards gender equality have been taken, including women's right to vote and participation in the labour market and the development of child care facilities outside the home, to mention only a few. These efforts to promote gender equality have mostly taken place in the public, Hermian, mind-set (see Thompson, 1986). In the Hestian mind-set, such equality measures have not been seen to the same extent. In the private space, there is still room for both Hestian and Hermian mind-sets to complement each other (Thompson, 1986).

Home economics education is, and should be, closely linked to pupils' home culture (Venäläinen, 2010) and able to respond to present societal needs and challenges (Janhonen-Abruquah & Palojoki, 2015). This analysis points to the variety of gender-related interconnections between home economics education and changing societal contexts. Based on this analysis, gender provides a useful lens for culturally responsive education by pointing out the various connections influencing the way we see the world and by making 'culture' more tangible, being represented in everyday practices as well as larger structures. Paying more attention to these interconnections can make unequal structures and cultural practices visible to learners and open up avenues to discuss gender in a contextually relevant and culturally responsive manner. Culturally responsive education calls for knowing learners, so their voices were heard in this study, focusing on home economics student teachers' perceptions. Through this study, the authors aimed not only to hear university students' voices but also to implement a gender awareness approach into current and forthcoming teaching modules at universities. Listening to student teachers' voices on gender can open up opportunities to enhance the cultural responsiveness of teacher education. By acknowledging student teachers' prevalent values and attitudes, together with newly emerging ideas, teacher educators can support the development of the gender responsiveness of future teachers. For the students, this course and the study process served as eye-openers and positioned them to implement more gender-aware approaches in their future careers as teachers and educators.

Notes

1 This ratio reflects the current gender division in enrolment in home economics teacher education at the University of Helsinki.
2 This ratio is equal to that of participants from the University of Helsinki and reflects the gender division in enrolment in the home economics programmes at the University of Cape Coast.

References

Aalto, K. (2014). Arjen rytmit perhe-elämän muutoskohdissa 1979–2009 [Rhythm of everyday life in family transitions 1979–2009]. In P. Korvela, & T. Tuomi-Gröhn (Eds), *Arjen rakentuminen ja rytmit perhe-elämän käännekohdissa*. Helsinki: Kuluttajat-utkimuskeskus, 46–75.

Abu-Lughod, L. (1991). Writing against culture. In R. G. Fox (Ed.), *Recapturing anthropology: Working in the present*. Santa Fe: School of American Research Press, 137–154.

Adinkrah, M. (2012). Better dead than dishonored: Masculinity and male suicidal behavior in contemporary Ghana. *Social Science & Medicine, 74*(4), 474–481.

Agyare-Kwabi, P. (2013). Gender, social inclusion (GESI) and education in Ghana. *Policy Brief.* UKAID, USAID and DANIDA.

Ajayi, K., & Buessing, M. (2013). *Gender parity and schooling choices.* 22nd International Association for Feminist Economics (IAFFE) Annual Conference. Stanford University 12–14 July, 2013, Palo Alto, CA.

Akotia, C. S., & Anum, A. (2012). The moderating effects of age and education on gender differences on gender role perceptions. *Gender and Behaviour, 10*(2), 5022–5043.

Ampofo, A. A. (2001). "When men speak women listen": Gender socialisation and young adolescents' attitudes to sexual and reproductive issues. *African Journal of Reproductive Health*, 196–212.

Amu, M. E. K., & Edjah, H. B. *(forthcoming).* Males in female dominated fields: Home economics case in Ghana.

Amu, M. E. K., Offei-Ansah, C., & Amissah, A. A. (2015). *Teaching home economics: A practical approach to teachers and student teachers.* Ghana Universities Press.

Anttila, S., Leskinen, J., Posti-Ahokas, H., & Janhonen-Abruquah, H. (2015). Performing gender and agency in home economics text book images. In K. Hahl, P-M. & Niemi, R. Johnson Longfor (Eds), *Diversities and interculturality in textbooks: Finland as an example.* Newcastle upon Tyne: Cambridge Scholars, 61–84.

Berg, P., Guttorm, H., Kankkunen, T., Kokko, S., Kuoppamäki, A., Lepistö, J., Turkki, K., Väyrynen, L., & Lehtonen, J. (2011). Tytöille tyttömäistä ja pojille poikamaista – yksilöllisten valintojen viidakossa?: Sukupuolitietoisuus taito- ja taideaineiden opetuksessa ja tutkimuksessa. [Feminine for girls and masculine for boys – in the jungle of individual choices. Gender awareness in practical and art subjects and research] In J. Lehtonen (Ed.), *Sukupuolinäkökulmia tutkimusperustaiseen opettajankoulutukseen.* Helsinki, Finland: Helsingin yliopisto, Käyttäytymistieteiden laitos, 91–116.

Braun, M., Lewin-Epstein, N., Stier, H., & Baumgärtner, M. (2008). Perceived equity in the gendered division of household labor. *Journal of Marriage and Family, 70*, 1145–1156.

Edjah, H. B., & Amu E. K. M. (2012). Correlation of tutor characteristics with student performance in home economics at colleges of education in Ghana. *56th Year Book on Teacher Education.* ICET.

Finnish National Board of Education (FNBE). (2004). *National core curriculum for basic education 2004: National core curriculum for basic education intended for pupils in compulsory education.* Retrieved from www.oph.fi/english/curricula_and_qualifications/basic_education.

FNBE. (2014). Perusopetuksen opetussuunnitelman perusteiden luonnos [Draft core curriculum for basic education]. Retrieved from www.oph.fi/ops2016/peruste-luonnokset/perusopetus.

Firebaugh, F. M. (1980). Home economics in higher education in the United States: Current trends. *Journal of Consumer Studies and Home Economics, 4,* 159–165.

Gay, G. (2010). *Culturally responsive teaching: Theory, research, and practice.* Multicultural education series. Teachers College Columbia University.

Gay, G. (2013). Teaching to and through cultural diversity. *Curriculum Inquiry, 43*(1), 48–70.

Ghana Education Service. (2015). *Register of programmes and courses for public and private senior high schools, technical and vocational institutes.* Retrieved from www.ghanawaec. org/Portals/0/PDF/SCHOOL%20REGISTER%202015%20FINAL_prog.pdf.

Helgeson, V. S. (2009). *The psychology of gender.* Upper Saddle River, NJ: Pearson.

Holli, A. M., Magnusson, E., & Rönnblom, M. (2005). Critical studies of Nordic discourses on gender and gender equality. *Nordic Journal of Women's Studies, 13*(3), 148–152.

IFHE (International Federation for Home Economics). (2008). *IFHE position statement: Home economics in the 21st century.* Retrieved from: www.ifhe.org.

Janhonen-Abruquah, H., & Palojoki, P. (Eds). (2015). *Creative and responsible home economics education: Luova ja vastuullinen kotitalousopetus.* Kotitalous- ja käsityötieteiden julkaisuja 38. Helsinki: Unigrafia.

Janhonen-Abruquah, H., Posti-Ahokas, H., Palojoki, P., & Lehtomäki, E. (2014). Developing learning games for culturally responsive home economics learning. *International Journal of Home Economics, 7*(2), 2–16.

Lahelma, E. (2011). Gender awareness in Finnish teacher education: An impossible mission? *Education Inquiry, 2*(2), 263–276.

Lahelma, E. (2014). Troubling discourses on gender and education. *Educational Research, 56*(2), 171–183.

Lehtomäki, E., Moate, J., & Posti-Ahokas, H. (2015). Global connectedness in higher education: Student voices on the value of cross-cultural learning dialogue. *Studies in Higher Education.* doi: 10.1080/03075079.2015.1007943.

Lewin-Epstein, N., Stier, H., & Braun, M. (2006). The division of household labour in Germany and Israel. *Journal of Marriage and Family, 68,* 1147–1164.

McGregor, S. L. T. (2011). Home economics in higher education: Pre-professional socialization. *International Journal of Consumer Studies, 35,* 560–568.

McLeod, J. (2011). Student voice and the politics of listening in higher education. *Critical Studies in Education, 52*(2), 179–189.

Neequaye, N. K., Darkwa, S., & Amu, M. E. K. (2014). Students' perspectives of the food and nutrition program at the University of Cape Coast Home Economics department and its implication on curriculum change. *Science, 2*(1), 4–11.

Nukynua G. K. (2003). *Tradition and change in Ghana.* Accra, Ghana: University Press.

Pendergast, D. (2001). *Virginal mothers, groovy chicks and blokey blokes: Re-thinking home economics (and) teaching bodies.* Brisbane: Australian Academic Press.

Pettersson, M. (2007). *Att genuszappa på säker eller minerad mark: hem- och konsumentkunskap ur ett könsperspektiv.* [Gender zapping on safe or mined ground: Home economics and consumer studies from a gender perspective] Doctoral Dissertation, Gothenburg University.

Pipping Ekström, M., & Hjälmeskog, K. (2006). 150 år av 'outsourcing' av hemarbete. [150 years of outsourcing domestic work]. In K. Hjälmeskog (Ed.), *Lärarprofession i förändring: från "skolkök" till hem- och konsumentkunskap.* Uppsala, Sweden: Föreningen för Svensk Undervisningshistoria, 171–191.

Posti-Ahokas, H., Janhonen-Abruquah, H., & Longfor, R. (2015). Urban spaces for intercultural encounters: Cultural plunges for future teachers. *World Studies in Education, 16*(2), 45–55.

Ronkainen, S. (2001). Gendered violence and genderless gender: A Finnish perspective. *Kvinder, Kön och Forskning, 2/*2001, 45–57.

Saleem, N. (1998). *Development of home economics extension programme for socio-economic uplift of the underprivileged.* Doctoral Thesis. University of Punjab, Lahore.

Seale, J. (2010). Doing student voice work in higher education: An exploration of the value of participatory methods. *British Educational Research Journal, 36*(6), 995–1015.

Silverman, D. (2006). *Interpreting qualitative data.* London: Sage.

Stambach, A. 2000. *Lessons from Mount Kilimanjaro: Schooling, community, and gender in East Africa.* New York: Routledge.

Thompson, P. J. (1986). Beyond gender: Equity issues for home economics education. *Theory into Practice, 25*(4), 276–283.

Turkki, K. (2005). Pre-professionals' perceptions of home economics in Finland. *International Journal of Consumer Studies, 29*, 273–282.

Turkki, K. (2009). Koti ja kotitalous – elinikäistä oppimista ja kasvamista vastuullisuuteen [Home and home economics – Life-long learning and growing towards responsible living]. In J. Lampinen & M. Melén-Paaso (Eds), *Tulevaisuus meissä: Kasvaminen maailmanlaajuiseen vastuuseen.* Opetusministeriön julkaisuja 40. Helsinki: Yliopistopaino, 101–107.

Turkki, K. (2011). Kotitalouskasvatuksella tasa-arvoa. [Equality through home economics education] In Lehtonen, J. (Ed.) (2011). *Sukupuolinäkökulmia tutkimusperustaiseen opettajankoulutukseen.* TASUKO-hanke, Käyttäytymistieteiden laitos, Helsingin yliopisto, 103–106.

Venäläinen,S. (2010). *Interaction in the multicultural classroom: Towards culturally sensitive home economics education.* Home Economics and Craft Studies Research Reports. Helsinki, Finland: University Print.

Venäläinen, S. (2015). *Arjen tiedot ja taidot hyvinvoinnin perustana. Kotitalouden oppimistulokset perusopetuksen päättövaiheessa 2014.* [National Home Economics learning assessment]. Kansallinen koulutuksen arviointikeskus. Tampere. Juvenes Print – Suomen Yliopistopaino.

Vidén, S., & Naskali, P. (2010). *Sukupuolitietoisuus Lapin yliopiston opettajankoulutuksessa* [Gender awareness in teacher education at the University of Lapland]. Lapin yliopiston kasvatustieteellisiä julkaisuja 22. Rovaniemi.

Wahlen, S., Posti-Ahokas, H., & Collins, E. (2009). Linking the loop: Voicing dimensions of home economics. *International Journal of Home Economics, 2*(2), 32–47.

Wolff, K. (2007). Content analysis. In G. Ritzer (Ed.), *Blackwell encyclopaedia of sociology.* Oxford: Blackwell Publishing.

10 Dialogues on culture(s) of inclusion between African and Finnish educators

William Nketsia, Said K. Juma,
Abebe Yehualawork Malle, Raija Pirttimaa
and Elina Lehtomäki

Introduction

"What is the difference between culturally responsive education and inclusive education?" asked one of the participating students during a seminar where we were having dialogue during two ongoing North–South–South cooperation projects. In this chapter, our aims are to respond to this important question by analysing dialogues on inclusive education from different cultures, and to discuss how inclusion is and could be embedded in culturally responsive education.

The dialogues analysed here were conducted during the project *African–Finnish network for inclusive teacher education* (AFNITE) in 2013–2015. The project was funded by the Government of Finland as a part of the North–South–South programme, with the aim of enhancing human capacity in participating countries and higher education institutions through mobility, interaction, and training. The programme was designed to contribute to the globally set Millennium Development Goals and also to the implementation of the Finnish development cooperation policies, thus emphasizing the capacity development in institutions in the official development cooperation partner countries in the Global South (CIMO, 2015).

The AFNITE project has focused on reduction of inequality in lifelong learning and promoted 'inclusive education' as defined by UNESCO (1994, 2010) in the broad sense, referring to all but also recognizing the existing marginalization on the basis of learners' characteristics, such as gender, ethnicity and language, socio-economic status, living conditions, special educational needs, and disability. In developing countries, Croft (2010) has argued for more focus on disabled children to improve their meaningful learning because such a broad approach to inclusive education has the tendency to neglect disabled children. The partners of the AFNITE project have been Addis Ababa University, Ethiopia; University of Dar es Salaam (UDSM), Tanzania; Dilla University (DU), Ethiopia; Sebastian Kolowa Memorial University (SEKOMU), Tanzania; and JAMK University of Applied Sciences (JAMK), Finland. The coordinator has been the University of Jyvaskyla in Finland. For all partners, this type of thematic network on inclusive teacher education with the focus on activities in both North and South has been new. Yet all the university teachers and students involved in the AFNITE project activities have had previous experience in inclusive education, either through work or studies, were aware of the challenges of implementing inclusion, and were interested in learning through collaboration.

The objectives of the AFNITE network and collaboration were to: (1) define criteria for good inclusive practices in post-primary education and life-long learning; (2) identify good inclusive practices in post-primary education and lifelong learning in the participating countries by exchange activities including learning and teaching tasks and study visits; (3) share information and experiences during exchange activities; (4) deepen understanding of educational inclusion through intensive courses; and (5) disseminate information in the participating higher education institutions and among their stakeholders. The project activities included student and staff exchange, two one-week-long intensive courses, school visits, seminars, meetings, and regular correspondence. These activities were planned in collaboration among the partners and organized by the host university. During the intensive courses and seminars, individuals from organizations of people with disabilities and local schools were invited to contribute and participate. Both African and Finnish doctoral students conducting research on inclusive education were invited to contribute during the intensive courses and seminars.

A critical issue in the implementation of AFNITE, as a project with officially set objectives and plans, approved by the participating institutions as well as by the programme management (CIMO) and funding agency (the Finnish Government), is whether we succeeded in reaching beyond cooperation and collaborate to the real meaning. Collaboration requires reciprocity and synergy between the partners (Bedwell et al., 2012) and respect for national policies on issues such as special needs education (UNESCO, 1994). The ethical ethos of AFNITE was based on sharing and understanding, while acknowledging that different societies have various cultural values that influence the ways diversities are defined and addressed. Thus, the aim was collaboration and development of a 'community of learning' (Wenger, 1998; Wenger, McDermott, & Snyder, 2002) comprising collaboration in knowledge transmissions, dialogues on meanings and values, learning from each other, and, as a community, creating new knowledge and enhancing inclusive practices. Indeed, the foundation of a community of learning with an emphasis on social justice and human dignity, and aiming for social change, is close to the core idea of inclusion (Lawthom, 2011).

Studies on cross-cultural collaboration related to inclusive education are rare, though inclusive education has been on the global education development agenda since 1994. There is, however, research on international cooperation and its effects. The first models for inclusive education policies and practices were designed in western countries and applied in developing countries. However, an internationally accepted practice is not necessarily appropriate in certain development contexts (Le Fanu, 2010, p. 3). The implementation of these practices without analysing the socially and culturally constructed meanings of inclusion in various contexts, and without sufficient support to practice level implementation, has been critiqued as external influence or even manipulation at the policy level (Armstrong, Armstrong & Spandagou, 2011; Carrington & Duke, 2014; DuToit & Forlin, 2009). Armstrong, Armstrong and Spandagou (2010) argue that inclusion means different things to people, and the way inclusion is conceptualized and practised may differ in national educational contexts because of local social, cultural, and historical differences.

Conditions in developing countries are different from those of the developed countries where the concept of inclusion was originally developed and applied. Therefore, Education For All (UNESCO, 2014) has to be examined and understood in terms of the historical, social, cultural, financial, and political contexts within each specific country (Armstrong et al., 2010). Other, more critical perspectives, as well as collaboration for more culturally responsive approaches to inclusive education, have been suggested. Le Fanu (2010, 2013) has argued that any effort on the part of international organizations to promote inclusive education in developing countries should adopt more responsive and participatory approaches.

In this chapter, we explore the cross-cultural collaboration and implementation of inclusive education through the culturally responsive education lens. This means, according to Gay (2013), that we not only acknowledge the cultural differences, but teach to and through them. Thus, taking into consideration the broader historical, social, cultural, and political contexts of the countries where the AFNITE project participants work or study has required reflections on perceptions, interpretations, and practices. It is the participants' reflections that have contributed to the dialogues and created the spaces for sharing meanings.

In the Sub-Saharan partner countries of the AFNITE project, the education systems fail; regardless of national commitments to international policies, the education systems fail. This is due to rapid increases in enrolments, limited resources, shortage of qualified teachers, poor working conditions, weak management, financial and human resource constraints, and large classes (Charema, 2010; Croft, 2010; Nketsia & Saloviita, 2013). Some have argued that developing countries have been caught in a wave of change towards inclusive education while educational institutions were still working to improve integration. Regular schools in developing countries are unprepared, and the actual implementation of inclusive education will require having the right attitudes, values, beliefs, and political will (Charema, 2010). In these highly challenging contexts, engaging in professional development and learning communities may be difficult or even risky. In this chapter, we analyse the dialogues of teachers and students from five African and two Finnish universities. Previous research indicates that, in partnership work between two (or more) professional communities, learning and identities develop amid tensions, power dynamics, and diverse sets of values (Alasuutari, 2015; Waitoller & Kozleski, 2013). What happened in our collaboration and dialogues?

Dialogues: material analysed

The qualitative material analysed for this chapter comprises dialogues conducted throughout the project activities, including meetings; discussions during the intensive courses and seminars; interviews (face-to-face and via e-mail) concerning the topics, results, and quality of project reports produced while by visiting students and teachers; feedback sessions with exchange students; and responses to an open questionnaire during the last intensive course in 2015. The main material we utilize here was collected in 2015 during the final intensive course. Participants from five countries answered the questionnaire, which consists of open-ended questions. There were a total of 5,800 words in this material. The additional material used was compiled after each student exchange period by group interviews, and by the end of the AFNITE project, the key people from each country were either interviewed or asked by email to evaluate the project.

The analysis was qualitative in nature, with emphasis on exploring how knowledge was shared and how collaboration was experienced by the participants during the project. The quotes selected for this text depict the key messages of the project participants concerning their experiences in learning together about inclusive education across diverse contexts. The next section focuses on the highlights evident across the different materials.

Highlights

Platform and interaction

Reflecting on the project, one participant stated that "[AFNITE] created a good platform for us to share our experiences as regards best practices in inclusive teacher education. The professional interaction among partners was very beneficial to us as teachers and students who participated". The intensive courses were organized in the South, creating opportunities for students and teachers to build networks, share experiences, and compare the state of the art of inclusive education in different Sub-Saharan African countries. Intensive courses encouraged participants to share their ideas and experiences, and during study visits they were able to explore the local situation of education and transitions from school to vocational education and training or employment.

Interaction between representatives from different cultures and societies was a fruitful and worthwhile experience. Participants noticed differences in the social, cultural, and political contexts of the participating countries, but found that it is possible to discuss the concept of inclusion together. One cannot speak about inclusion without sharing information about one's own culture, educational system, and society broadly.

> We have a lot of the same ideas and practices but our societies and regulations are quite different; we are at different stages in inclusion.

Sharing experiences is always important. I think we also learned a lot about our cultures, traditions and so on.

[the sharing] contributed to scale up my knowledge about the human diversity which is the source of beauty of our world.

Most of us have the same problem in the implementation of inclusive education despite coming from different countries.

Different cultures form a different base for different solutions to organize education.

Thus we can assume that inclusion means some kind of common understanding, an assumption supported by the Salamanca Statement (UNESCO, 1994) and human rights declarations (United Nations, 2006). But these declarations are not enough to build good understanding of the concept. As Engsig and Johnstone (2014) state, inclusion has many definitions, which depend on policy- and culture-driven interpretations. A study in Uganda found that teachers lack understanding of the distinction between integration and inclusive education, and the former seems to be the dominant practice in schools (Arbeiter & Hartley, 2002). In educational research in Tanzania, the concept of inclusive education has been increasingly used, though there seems to be little shared understanding about its meaning (Lehtomäki, Tuomi, & Matonya, 2014). Therefore, in the AFNITE project, these concepts and interpretations were the starting point for discussions and the participants agreed that such dialogues need to be continued.

I would like to learn more about the demarcation between mainstreaming, integration, and inclusion. I would like to study and make clearer the concept of inclusion and to develop new practices.

It is quite a challenging phenomenon to define. It is a process.

Conceptual discussions during exchange and intensive courses between students and staff offered opportunities for deepening the understanding of the conceptualization of inclusive education. Furthermore, they encouraged students to start research concerning inclusion.

Those who participated in intensive courses especially the graduate students ended up identifying their research topics on inclusive education.

Thomas (2013) connects the concept of inclusion with such terms as social capital, social connections, and communities of learning. In addition to the policy-level interaction between nations, governments, and policy makers, the possibility of intense discussion between professionals and education students from different countries and universities has the potential to broaden views over the national or school-level perspective.

South–South collaboration: a variety of contexts

The participants valued the opportunities to learn and share ideas in an open and interactive way, especially with colleagues in the South. For students, the South–South collaboration meant immense opportunity to gain information and knowledge about the contents of the educational and training policies and legal frameworks of other countries. Intensive courses were designed to be interactive, enabling students through intimacy and contact to expose one another to their different professional qualifications, experiences, and abilities. During the interactions, the participants also had the opportunity to collect valuable data for research and promote their future academic careers.

The combination of experienced partner universities in capitals and new emerging universities in regions outside the capitals broadened the participants' understanding of how inclusive education has been realized differently in a variety of country contexts, though with similar aims. The responsibility for providing inclusive education was discussed among the participants and ideas for improvements were shared, particularly during intensive courses involving school visits and analysis of teacher development initiatives.

All were aware that there is still work to be done for inclusive education: participants expressed a wish to develop their own skills in inclusive pedagogies and engage in the process of implementing inclusive education. They also stressed that organizing teacher education and educational structures is important. There is also a need for information and learning materials. Some have argued that it is important that inclusion is seen as a process and not a goal to be achieved. It is about identifying and overcoming barriers to participation (Ainscow 1999; Booth, 2000), collaborating with those targeted by inclusive education policies, i.e. children, students, families, and parents, and finding ways to listen to the experiences of learners, including children and youth with disabilities (Lehtomäki & Hukkanen, 2015). In line with this argument, Croft (2010) admonished that every stakeholder in a developing country must be made to understand that inclusive education is a journey. The AFNITE project participants wanted to share their experiences in home universities and schools.

> What contribution are we making in the world? As an ambassador for inclusive education, I would like them [my colleagues] to be part of the process for ensuring the success of inclusive education in my home country.

Professional identity and value of work

The university teachers, most of whom work as teacher educators, highlighted how collaboration has strengthened their professional identities and given value to their work among students (with learning difficulties or disabilities) who are often neglected in schools and society. To develop something new means that teachers must be lifelong learners; they must be flexible and able to work in close cooperation with other professionals. Today, rebuilding professional identity is a continuous challenge. Discussions on this issue were possible in groups where the participants came from different backgrounds. Research has suggested that teachers' collaboration, such as co-teaching, supports their professional identities and improves practices (Rytivaara & Kershner, 2012).

Community of professionals

In the project, participants' words, belonging to a community of professionals interested in their work and promoting inclusive education, were invaluable. The AFNITE project emphasized gender equality and equity and encouraged participation of students and teachers with disabilities. Realizing inclusion in practice instead of talking about theories and principles of inclusive education was new to some participants, while to others the participation of people with disabilities as teachers and students was their everyday university life. The role of participants with disabilities, use of assistants, and Sign Language interpreters was an eye-opening and powerful experience for many participants. Networking opportunities, for instance, supported one participant with a visual handicap to conduct his research in other countries. He found voluntary support from his intensive course mates to assist him in travelling and contacting key persons to collect his data.

> One of the AFNITE's strengths is the close connection to real life and practical inclusive education.

Discussion

Usually equity, equality, and human rights are approached as so-called 'cross-cutting' issues in educational development and, we claim, too often it is assumed that they are realized. The AFNITE project, as the project title states, has focused on inclusive teacher education. Each country and university has implemented inclusive education in their own way depending on resources and priorities, and consequently, situations differ. Therefore, the most important issue in AFNITE has been the possibility for partners in the South to share their experiences, knowledge, good practices, and views. The dialogues show the need for continuation of sharing and building a common understanding with respect to the variety in resources and realization.

Inclusive education with an emphasis on the right to education and child rights requires further collaboration, particularly between African countries. All the AFNITE partners and participants would like to continue cooperating and networking, and extend to new forms of collaborating. Sustainability depends now on Finland's readiness to realize the value of this type of collaboration, and on funding decisions.

Building trust takes time: how ethical and sustainable is short-term funding? A short-term project has little influence on capacity development. Zeelen (2012) has argued that African universities are dysfunctional, in terms of wasted human capacity and financial resources, while they have the responsibilities for producing relevant new knowledge, fostering critical thinking, preparing students with the knowledge and skills required in the labour market, and contributing to the development of communities. Yet the dialogues conducted during the AFNITE project resonate with the findings in previous research on learning communities related to inclusive education, which have highlighted the importance of collaboration, despite differences in defining, understanding, and implementing inclusive education (Brandon & Charlton, 2011; Lawthom, 2011; Waitoller & Kozleski, 2013). In this case, the community of professionals created opportunities for sharing, critical thinking, and producing new knowledge. In future, networks and collaboration could be used for planning and conducting joint research projects in inclusive education.

The participation of both men and women, students and teachers, and people with and without disabilities offered the learning community the experience of inclusion in practice, in addition to knowledge sharing. Project participants appreciated the project's accessible learning and collaboration environments, such as ICT and open information, research literature, and databases. These are the essential aspects of universal design and ensuring inclusive education.

This served to emphasize that the network partners implemented what they talked about, which is similar to the proven powerful transformations, when those targeted by education policies are involved in negotiations concerning their education and participation (e.g. Kiragu, Swartz, Chikovore, Lukalo, and Oduro, 2011). From the Finnish development policy perspective, promoting a human–rights–based approach, all stakeholders and especially those marginalized in education should not only be ensured a voice but also opportunities for participation on equal terms (Katsui et al., 2014, Katsui, Lehtomäki, Malle, & Chalklen, 2016).

In future the AFNITE project participants hope for better use of online opportunities in addition to, not replacing, face-to-face meetings and sharing. New topic suggestions include guidance and counselling students with disabilities before or during transitions; learning and learning processes in inclusive settings; and tutoring towards employment and strategies towards inclusion. Many participants wanted to discuss the existing negative attitudinal barriers and traditions in society and how to overcome them and speak about inclusion in the community and in the whole world. According to a recent joint report from the UNESCO Institute for Statistics and UNICEF (UNESCO-UIS, 2015), 30 million children who are out of school in Sub-Saharan Africa might never go to school at all. The report identifies social stigma, institutional barriers, and environmental barriers linked with disability as some of the things that keep children out of school.

How to sustain the collaboration is the question we need to find a solution for – this may depend on information and communication technology (powerful fibre cables, new social media channels?), availability of electricity (solar panels at our partner institutions in the South?), and many practical matters, but most importantly, on the motivated colleagues, university teachers, and staff at all partner institutions. The participants from the five African universities valued especially the dialogues with their African colleagues and, therefore, an African network of inclusive education is needed to provide opportunities for regular South–South collaboration and cooperation. Finland should be one of the engaged partners facilitating the development of this learning community for inclusion. One of the visiting students from the African partner universities to Finland suggested that boundary crossing and learning across cultures need to be reciprocal.

It is my advice that students from Finnish universities go to study in Africa [...] particularly for the purpose of learning cultural differences and proving actual world realities in developing nations.

References

Ainscow, M. (1999). *Understanding the development of inclusive schools*. London: Falmer Press.

Alasuutari, H. (2015). *Towards more ethical engagements in North–South education sector partnerships*. Doctoral dissertation, Acta Universitatis Ouluensis, E, 160. Oulu: University of Oulu.

Arbeiter, S., & Hartley, S. (2002). Teachers' and pupils' experiences of integrated education in Uganda, *International Journal of Disability, Development and Education*, *49*(1), 61–78.

Armstrong, A. C., Armstrong, D., & Spandagou, I. (2010). *Inclusive education: International policy and practice*. London: Sage.

Armstrong, D., Armstrong, A. C., & Spandagou, I. (2011). Inclusion: By choice or by chance? *International Journal of Inclusive Education*, *15*(1), 29–39.

Bedwell, W. L., Wildman, J. L., DiazGranados, D., Salazar, M., Kramer, W. S., & Salas, E. (2012). Collaboration at work: An integrative multilevel conceptualization, *Human Resource Management Review*, *22*(2), 128–145.

Booth, T. (2000). *Progress in inclusive education, executive summary EFA 2000 Assessment*. Retrieved from www.unesco.org/education/efa/efa_2000_assess/studies/inclusion_summary.

Brandon, T., & Charlton, J. (2011). The lessons learned from developing an inclusive learning and teaching community of practice, *International Journal of Inclusive Education*, *15*(1), 165–178.

Carrington, S., & Duke, J. (2014). Learning about inclusion from developing countries: Using the index for inclusion. In C. Forlin, & T. Loreman (Eds), Measuring inclusive education, *International Perspectives on Inclusive Education, Vol. 3* (189–203). Bingley, UK: Emerald Group Publishing.

Charema, J. (2010). Inclusive education in developing countries in the Sub-Saharan Africa: From theory to practice, *International Journal of Special Education*, *25*(1), 87–93.

Croft, A. (2010). *Including disabled children in learning: Challenges in developing countries. Research monograph no. 36.* Falmer: Create, University of Sussex.

CIMO, Center for International Mobility (Finland). (2015). *North–South–South Higher Education Institution Network Programme.* Retrieved from http://cimo.fi/programmes/north-south-south.

DuToit, P., & Forlin, C. (2009). Cultural transformation for inclusion: What is needed? A South African perspective, *School Psychology International, 30*(6), 644–666.

Engsig, T., & Johnstone, J. (2014). Is there something rotten in the State of Denmark? The paradoxical policies of inclusive education – lesson from Denmark, *International Journal of Inclusive Education, 19*(5), 1–18.

Gay, G. (2013). Teaching to and through cultural diversity, *Curriculum Inquiry, 43*(1), 48–70.

Katsui, H., Lehtomäki, E., Malle, A. Y., & Chalklen, S. (2016). Questioning human rights: The case of education for children and youth with disabilities in Ethiopia. In S. Grech, & K. Soldatic (Eds), *Disability in the Global South: The critical handbook.* Amsterdam, NL: Springer.

Katsui, H., Ranta, E. M., Yeshanew, S. A., Musila, G. M., Mustaniemi-Laakso, M., & Sarelin, A. (2014). *Reducing inequalities: A human rights-based approach in Finland's development cooperation with special focus on gender and disability.* Turku: Institute for Human Rights.

Kiragu, S., Swartz, C., Chikovore, J., Lukalo, F., Oduro, G. Y. (2011). Agency, access, silence and ethics: How young people's voices from Africa can contribute to social and educational change in adult-dominated societies. In C. Day (Ed.), *International handbook of teacher and school development* (254–263). London: Routledge.

Lawthom, R. (2011). Developing learning communities: Using communities of practice within community psychology, *International Journal of Inclusive Education, 15*(1), 153–164.

Le Fanu, G. (2010). *Promoting inclusive education in Papua New Guinea (PNG).* EdQual policy brief no. 7. Bristol: EdQual.

Le Fanu, G. (2013). The inclusion of inclusive education in international development: Lessons from Papua New Guinea, *International Journal of Educational Development, 33*(2), 139–148.

Lehtomäki, E. & Hukkanen, S. (2015). Girls and women with [dis]abilities in Tanzania claim their right to education. In F. Kiuppis, & R. Sarromaa Hausstätter (Eds), *Inclusive education twenty years with Salamanca* (231–249). New York: Peter Lang.

Lehtomäki, E., Tuomi, M. T., & Matonya, M. (2014). Educational research from Tanzania 1998–2008 concerning persons with disabilities: What can we learn? *International Journal of Educational Research, 64*, 32–39.

Nketsia, W., & Saloviita, T. (2013). Pre-service teachers' views on inclusive education in Ghana, *Journal of Education for Teaching, 39*(4), 429–441.

Rytivaara, A., & Kershner, R. (2012). Co-teaching as a context for teachers' professional learning and joint knowledge construction, *Teaching and teacher education, 28*(7), 999–1008.

Thomas, G. (2013). A review of thinking and research about inclusive education policy, with suggestions for a new kind of inclusive thinking, *British Educational Research Journal, 39*(3), 473–490.

UNESCO. (1994). *The Salamanca statement and framework for action on special needs education.* Paris: UNESCO.

UNESCO. (2010). Reaching the marginalized. *Education for All Global Monitoring Report 2010.* Paris: UNESCO.

UNESCO (2014). Teaching and learning: Achieving quality for all. *Education for All Global Monitoring Report 2013/14.* Paris: UNESCO.

UNESCO Institute for Statistics (UIS) and UNICEF, (2015). *Fixing the broken promise of Education for All: Findings from the global initiative on out-of-school children.* Montreal: UIS. Retrieved from http://dx.doi.org/10.15220/978-92-9189-162-7-en.

United Nations (2006). Convention on the rights of persons with disabilities. Geneva, United Nations.

Waitoller, F. R., & Kozleski, E. B. (2013). Working in boundary practices: Identity development and learning in partnerships for inclusive education, *Teaching and Teacher Education, 31,* 35–45.

Wenger, E. (1998). *Communities of practice: Learning, meaning and identity.* New York: Cambridge University Press.

Wenger, E., McDermott, R., & Snyder, W. M. (2002). *Cultivating communities of practice: A guide to managing knowledge.* Boston: Harvard Business School.

Zeelen, J. (2012). Universities in Africa: Working on excellence for whom? Reflections on teaching, research, and outreach activities at African universities, *International Journal of Higher Education, 1*(2), 157–165.

11 Motives and motivations for mature women's participation in higher education in Ghana

Christine Adu-Yeboah

Introduction

Reports on global education strongly argue that every human being is entitled to a decent education, which has been recognised as highly important for the development of individuals and the nation-state (United Nations Education, Scientific and Cultural Organisation – UNESCO 2007, 2009a). In some middle and low-income countries with low levels of enrolment and completion of primary education, it has been noted that the reading and numeracy skills acquired through basic education are relevant for learning skills in technical and vocational education, and ensure the trainability of youth for employment (Yuki & Kameyama, 2013). Participation in higher education is also recognised to bring private and public returns through higher earnings, improved individual social and economic status, and reduced poverty, income and social inequality (Morley, 2007; World Bank, 2002). However, in both high and low-income countries, certain socio-cultural values and practices and socio-economic conditions have been reported to act as barriers to females' education and, in some situations, to prevent their successful completion of school (Morley & Lussier, 2009; UNESCO, 2009a).

In many African countries, including Ghana, there is a strong division of labour supported by prevailing beliefs among men and women that women should cook meals and generally make sure that the home is clean and well kept (Manuh, 2004). Men should be the heads of households and breadwinners who provide for all household members, including their wives. The assumption is that, to discharge these responsibilities, men need higher income, which education makes possible (Bortey & Dodoo, 2005), but women do not require formal education to perform their roles. In Ghana, there is even a fear that a girl's marriage prospects will be diminished if she obtains education equal to or surpassing men's (Manuh, 2004). Females often internalise these beliefs so that they think that a little education, ending at the secondary or vocational level, is sufficient for them (Boohene, Kotey, & Folker, 2005).

Higher education (HE) facilities in Ghana began as hugely elitist and male-dominated institutions (Daniel, 1996; Dei, 2005), a situation partly explained by patriarchal culture. In the early 1980s, for example, women made up only 18 per cent of students enrolled at the country's three oldest public universities (NCTE, 2000). However, advocates for change gained more serious policy attention after the Fourth United Nations World Conference on Women in Beijing in 1995 (United Nations, 1995) and the African governments' preparatory meeting for the UNESCO World Conference on Higher Education in 1997 (UNESCO, 1997). This change arose from awareness that women can play a major role in the development of the African region, and, therefore, measures to increase their participation in HE are needed. The most recent figures available indicate that, in Ghana, female enrolment stands at 35 per cent in public universities and 41 per cent in private universities, while national policy targets 50 per cent parity (UNESCO, 2009b).

The strategies employed in Ghana to make HE accessible to more non-traditional students, including women, are affirmative action and alternative part-time routes, such as distance education, evening classes and mature-student programmes. Usually, full-time residential HE programmes are characterised by high enrolment of younger students without career or family commitments. This route still seems to be the preferred choice of many, although the available statistics show that mature women in full-time residential programmes have a higher withdrawal rate than their counterparts in other programmes and lower academic achievement than those who access HE through direct entry (Morley et al., 2010). Students with direct entry are those who enter higher education directly after secondary education. Therefore, the objective of this study was to examine what external and internal drives and rationales triggered a group of mature women to return to study in full-time residential HE programmes.

Next, the conceptualisation of the study is discussed, followed by the methodological framework, including the research design and data collection procedure. The discussion then turns to examining the motivations and motives to which participants attributed their return to study. Finally, the conclusions drawn from the findings are presented.

Conceptualising the study

Throughout the development discourse, education has been primarily perceived as the gateway to employment (Morley, 2007; World Bank, 2009). Robeyns (2006) interprets this as the instrumental role of education, which is the core focus of the human-capital approach to education. This approach aims to enable people to obtain knowledge and skills that make an investment in their productivity and allow them to earn higher wages and improve their living standards. In this sense, education plays a range of personal and collective economic and non-economic instrumental roles.

The non-economic role of education is to open students' minds and make information accessible to them. Consequently, they are positioned to critically engage with, challenge and change taken-for-granted socio-cultural assumptions and norms and potentially to expand opportunities for all members of society. Education also has an intrinsic role, as one's pursuit of knowledge might or might not be relevant (instrumental) to one's life in the future (Robeyns, 2006).

This chapter combines Robeyns' (2006) instrumental/intrinsic rationales for HE and Scanlon's (2008) conceptualisation of motive, which is derived from Schutz (1972) and Hewitt's (1997) interpretive framework. In this framework, Schutz (1972) and Hewitt (1997) distinguish between the origin of motives as oriented towards the past or the future: in-order-to and because-of motives. Based on Hewitt's (1997) definition of motive as what people say about what they do, Scanlon (2008) interprets the notion as the choices individuals make among alternative acts after carefully considering their various anticipated consequences and the actions necessary to achieve them. Schutz (1972) and Hewitt (1997) argue that the present in which motives are formed encompasses both the future and the past. In-order-to motives, in which an already existent project is the reason for an action, focus on a future goal, while because-of motives have a past focus, and an event that happened in the past supplies the present motivation for action. In this study on mature women's return to HE, motivation is used to identify the factors that facilitated women's return to HE, while their motives for doing so are interpreted as personal reasons resulting from either a past condition or a future project.

Mature women's motives and motivations for HE participation

Instrumental and career-related motives drawn from human capital theory and intrinsic personal development (Robeyns, 2006) are prominent themes in the literature on mature students in general (Edwards, 1993; Reay, 2003; Scanlon, 2008; Hinton-Smith, 2012). However, research shows that, in this heterogeneous group, mature students' motives for HE are 'as numerous as there are members of a specific course' (Boshier, 2006, p. 89). Consequently, mature women's motives for returning to study in HE have been explained differently depending on the context.

In some high-income countries, such as the United Kingdom, single mothers without HE are perceived as welfare recipients (Hinton-Smith, 2012). In this status and in the broader socio-cultural context, lone mature women reportedly tend to be vilified as lazy and feckless, a drain on public resources and unfit role models for their children (Hinton-Smith, 2012). For these women, HE may be essential to improve their job prospects and earning capacity and gain financial stability.

Research in high-income countries shows that there are complex, inter-woven intrinsic and instrumental goals for women's participation in HE, which are not exclusively instrumental motives, such as improving their personal circumstances, providing for their dependents, setting a positive example for their children, doing something for themselves, developing self-esteem, escaping the house and meeting new people (Edwards, 1993; Reay, 2003; Scanlon, 2008; Hinton-Smith, 2012). In the literature, it is also noted that, in many cases, the decision to return to HE has been an individually nurtured desire or triggered by life incidents, such as moving to a new area, job loss, a new relationship, divorce, loss of a partner or other traumatic experience (Crossan, Field, Gallacher, & Merrill, 2003; Jones, 2006; Scanlon, 2008; Hinton-Smith, 2012).

The complexities surrounding women's education in developing countries where welfare systems are non-existent are recognised in the development discourse. In these contexts, women's education, especially at the HE level, tends to be explained relationally in terms of the economic returns and contributions to social development, such as decreased infant mortality, a higher probability that children will get a good education and, most importantly, women's potential as income generators to increase the family's economic power-base (Forum for African Women Educationalists (FAWE), 2001; Hannum & Buchmann, 2004). This discourse seems to assume that the rationales for women's education are only expressed in terms of its instrumental role in socio-cultural and economic development and not in terms of women's own rights.

In Ghana and Tanzania, for example, conventional-aged students cite multiple motives and motivations for entering HE, ranging from determination to create alternative futures to a desire to provide overall benefits for the family and society at large (that is, for local and national development), to build capacity, to escape poverty and to serve self-interests, including adding value to oneself (Morley & Lussier, 2009; Posti-Ahokas & Okkolin, 2015). However, research on Ghanaian mature women's rationales for participating in HE is not available. It was this gap that this study was aimed at filling, by examining a group of mature women's motives and motivations for returning to study in HE. In this context, the question that guided the study was: What are Ghanaian mature women's motives and motivations for returning to study in HE, and what facilitates this action?

Method

In this study, my goal was to act as a mediator for mature female students to reflect on their motivations and motives for returning to HE. With this intent, I found the interpretive qualitative approach to be the most relevant philosophical option, as the social reality under investigation is subjective and resides with the individual participants in the study. The life history narrative method, as a retrospective account of an individual's thoughts, intentions and hidden or silenced life (Goodson & Sikes, 2008), was also considered the most appropriate for this study. This method is known to be effective at providing insights into complex, contextualised experiences (Benson, Hewitt, Heagney, Devos, & Crosling, 2010). It must be noted that this chapter is part of a larger study on which my doctoral study was based. This chapter reports only on participants' background characteristics, the factors that facilitated their return to HE and their rationales for returning.

Flick's (2002) episodic–narrative method was adopted instead of a single, overall narrative which would produce large volumes of irrelevant data. The chosen method is a narrative interview approach, whose core feature is the periodic invitation for the interviewee to present narratives of relevant, meaningful experiences and concrete situations in order to obtain the most pertinent information. Also, use of this method, whose object is episodes, allowed the eliciting of relevant concrete situations and life experiences through the use of key questions (research and interview guide questions) concerning the situations to be recounted, instead of the entire narrative of participants' life histories. The key areas of the participants' lives considered relevant to the study included their personal lives from childhood and particular incidents that might have influenced their HE participation.

Research context and participants

A public university in southern Ghana was chosen as the site for this study due to its expanded participation strategies, which provide a number of access routes, including a programme for mature students. All 65 mature undergraduate women in their first and final years of study in the Department of Basic Education and Sociology were targeted. These two departments were chosen as they are where mature female students are known to cluster. There were 50 such students in the Department of Basic Education and 15 in the Department of Sociology.

Eight women (Table 11.1) older than 25 at year of entry were purposively selected (Merriam, 1998) to ensure that the group had a socio-economically

Table 11.1 Profile of participants

Name	Age	Prog./year	Location (rural/urban)	Socio-economic status	
				Father's job	Mother's job
1 Maimuna	34	Ed. Yr 1	Urban	Retired teacher	Ward assistant
2 Fafa	43	Ed. Yr 1	Urban	Agriculturalist	Seamstress
3 Maame	35	Ed. Yr 4	Rural	Farmer	Farmer
4 Koutuma	42	Ed. Yr 4	Rural	Farmer	Farmer
5 Krambaa	46	Soc. Yr 1	Urban	Prison officer	Trader
6 Adjoa Kom	42	Soc. Yr 1	Rural	Postmaster	Trader
7 Naana	30	Soc. Yr 4	Urban	University lecturer	Petty trader
8 Akua	40	Soc. Yr 4	Rural	Miner	Seamstress

Key to abbreviations:
Prog.   Programme
Ed.   Education
Yr.   Year
Soc.   Social Science

and culturally diverse background. To do so, participants' biographical data were obtained through a questionnaire on which they indicated their age, cultural and socio-economic backgrounds (ethnicity and parental socio-economic status), and their willing consent to participate. Participants' ages ranged from 30 to 46. Five were married with children, two were single parents, and one was single and did not have children. In the Department of Sociology, two participants were police officers, one a secretary, and one a teacher. All the participants in the Department of Basic Education were teachers. Their fathers had had more education than their mothers, as commonly found in the literature (Shabaya & Konadu-Agyemang, 2004). Moreover, the spouses of all five married participants had a university education. All the participants were first-generation HE students.

Participants were contacted and appointments made for individual interviews at a time and venue convenient for them in May 2009. At the interviews, it was agreed that pseudonyms would be used to ensure anonymity and confidentiality. The interviews were then transcribed, analysed for themes, compared across cases and grouped according to common and isolated themes (Creswell, 2003). To avoid distancing myself from the transcripts through the use of computer-assisted programmes, which objectifies research participants (Humphreys, 2005), I personally transcribed all the interviews, printed the transcripts, and read and re-read them thoroughly. I then applied my intuition to systematically analyse them by assigning codes to common and isolated ideas or phrases suggestive of common themes.

The analysis began with a narrative description of some individual stories. I followed this with the thematic analysis and comparison of cases and then the identification and grouping of participants according to common or isolated themes (Creswell, 2003). Merriam (1998) refers to this process as within-case and cross-case analysis, which helps identify processes and outcomes which occur across individual cases and eventually enables the building of abstractions across cases.

Results and discussion

Motivations for returning to study

Only two of the eight participants in this study revealed that they were self-motivated to enter HE to fulfil a latent (childhood) desire to acquire knowledge. Interestingly, they nurtured this desire in childhood even when they lived in remote rural areas. Later in their lives, various factors enabled them to achieve this long-held desire. These factors included parental and family signals, partners' encouragement, childcare arrangements, geographical relocation and social networks.

Parents' motivation

The findings from this study show that parents influence their children's educational attainment through the signals they send about the level of education they want their children to attain. As noted, participants' fathers had more education than their mothers, and, although the fathers' attitudes towards females' HE differed, some gave signals which made their daughters consider acquiring HE. Koutuma, for example, states that her illiterate father:

> was the first to send his daughter to school in the village as he worked in the mines [in the south], and he used to admire those [female staff] at the offices.
>
> (Koutuma, age 42)

He gave Koutuma motivational support, saying: "if you are highly educated, you'll be better in your marital home than if you're not". According to her, that made her focus on her education. Her story was similar to Fafa's, whose father had a master's degree:

> I was working with some factory sewing singlets, so my father said that's not where he wanted me to be. So he was not happy with what I am doing. He said marriage should be after you've completed higher education and working, so I used to think about that.
>
> (Fafa, age 43)

Both Fafa and Adjoa Kom's fathers, who had a master's degree and secondary education, respectively, advocated female HE. Adjoa Kom's father demonstrated his attitude towards her education through his constant interest in her examination results and reassurance that he would give everything to send her to the university. These stories resonate with earlier research findings that, once people experience education themselves, they encourage others around them to do the same (Morley et al., 2006) and that parents' education influences their attitude and support for female education (Mulugeta, 2004; Reay, David, & Ball, 2005).

In four cases in this study, both parents of participants were willing and committed to send their daughters to HE, while in four cases, the mothers were more proactive. Maimuna, for example, stated that, although her father was a trained teacher, he did not care about her education. Her mother, a middle school leaver, supported and motivated her through her schooling. This story aligns with Mulugeta's (2004) finding that mothers' understanding of educational issues is crucial to the support they give their daughters' education, as they may spare their daughters from household activities that conflict with their education.

Sometimes, other relatives and acquaintances were the driving force behind women's participation in HE. Maame's uncle, for example, was a university lecturer and cultivated her interest in HE. In Naana's story, a family acquaintance used the promise of employment to entice her into HE.

> A family friend, I used to tell him that he should look for a job for me, but he told me I had to get a degree first.
>
> (Naana, age 30)

In all these stories, participants' parents or family members could not educate them at HE level but sent signals that contributed to their interest and later entry into HE. These parental and family signals are suggestive of instrumental motives as they indicated that daughters could obtain white-collar jobs through HE.

Partners' encouragement, socio-economic status and childcare arrangements

All the married women stated that their partners, who were also university graduates, encouraged them to obtain HE. Although their reasons were not explicitly stated, this action seems to confirm earlier studies conducted elsewhere in Ghana, which found that educated men in urban areas desired educated wives who could match their urbanised lifestyle (Ardayfio-Schandorf, 1994). While Koutuma described her husband as a 'book-long man' who wants people around him to acquire knowledge, Maimuna stated that her husband had 'always been asking me [about HE], so when the [application] forms finally came, he bought it for me'. Fafa, Maame and Adjoa Kom also shared similar experiences of their husbands' desire for their HE.

It is important to note that all the women were receiving salaries while in HE, and their husbands' support for their education was indicative of their socio-economic status and ability to support their children and spouses' education. For example, Koutuma, who had four children, aged 4, 6, 9 and 14, described her family's social status through her husband's position as the head of procurement at the National Revenue Office with its associated privileges and through external indicators of wealth, such as a house and a car. Maimuna, with three children, aged 4, 6 and 9, and Maame, with two children, aged 2 and 4, had husbands who lived in the country's capital city, were average income earners and owned cars. Similarly, Adjoa Kom and Fafa, who each had two teenage children, also had husbands of average socio-economic status.

Parents' and husbands' support for women's HE can be viewed as a process of de-traditionalisation (Morley et al., 2006) and rejection of community, cultural and social beliefs about girls' education, although devotion to gender-assigned roles remains. This is quite different from the description of de-traditionalisation given by Morley et al. (2006), which asserts that changes in gender roles in wider civil society and in attitudes and educational opportunities allow women to move out of the traditionally prescribed roles of wives and mothers. In this study, it is changes in men's attitudes towards female education that lead them to encourage and support women to obtain HE.

The benefits that women obtain from participating in HE, particularly increased earnings and improved life chances, are highlighted earlier in this chapter. Although it is not culturally desirable in Ghana for wives to have more education than their husbands, this study found that the husbands' push for their wives' enrolment in HE confirmed the relational aspect of women's education: women should be highly educated to enhance their husbands' social status, as if women are not entitled to HE in their own right.

The single women with children also saw themselves as socio-economically advantaged, as they had fulltime employment and other income-generating activities that made it possible for them to make childcare arrangements. For example, Akua (two children, aged 9 and 11) described her advantaged socio-economic status in her position as an international police detective and engagement in other income-generating activities, which enabled her to provide for her children's schooling and her HE. The stories in this study, therefore, suggest that participants' socio-economic status contributed to the childcare arrangements made and women's motivation to enrol in full-time university study.

Geographical relocation and social networks

In Ghana, widespread migration, which has resulted in increased urbanisation, is driven primarily by employment, better job prospects or for marital reasons. In this study, women saw relocation as an opportunity to acquire HE through more available institutions. Earlier studies have found that parents from rural areas send their daughters to live in cities with relatives for the purpose of education (Quarcoopome & Ahadjie, 1981; see also Mulugeta's (2004) study in Ethiopia) as rural areas tend to lack HE institutions, role models and ambitions to which to aspire. In the case of the mature women in this study, not education but employment and marriage supplied the initial purpose for relocation. However, for some women, relocation provided them with social capital that made HE possible.

Three participants indicated that they had not considered HE as an option, but secondary schoolmates and, in some instances, work colleagues persuaded them to go to university. Maame, for example, recounted:

> In secondary school, I had about five friends, four boys and a girl. Right from the secondary school, they went to university. They motivated me more to come to university.
>
> (Maame, age 35)

In the cases of Krambaa and Akua, social acquaintances and work colleagues made their HE participation possible:

I had been meeting people, and they also inspired me. They would ask me some questions, and when I answered, then they would say, "You have to pursue higher education". Some even offered to pay my school fees if I should go. And when we went for peace-keeping, there was in-service training. I excelled, and an officer said I should go to school.

(Krambaa, age 46)

Some of my friends even had their second degree. It was actually a friend who motivated me to come to HE. He would say, "This particular person, you are even better than her. She has had university education. You are still here". He bought the [application] form for me. He just dragged me. Had it not been for him, I might not have gone.

(Akua, age 40)

Similar to other studies on resources that make HE accessible to poor students in developing countries, these narratives suggest that mature women who have access to social and cultural capital can participate in fulltime HE more easily than those without it. These resources are paternal and maternal capital, marital support, financial ability, social networks and relationships. These findings seem to confirm Morley and Lussier's (2009) conclusion that, in developing countries, "participation in higher education is not just about individuals, but is about positional advantage and the relations and spaces between social groups" (p. 82).

Motives for entering HE

In addition to the motivations for HE study mentioned, participants also had personal reasons for their action. In this section, I discuss their motives for entering HE as the result of either a past condition or a future project (Scanlon, 2008; Schutz, 1972). Three motives were identified in the narratives: breaking the cycle of poverty, personal development and obtaining HE status.

Higher education as a tool for breaking the cycle of poverty

Some women had had unpleasant childhood experiences, which seemed to live with them in the present and serve as the impetus for their desire to build a better future through HE. Their stories revealed differences in their social classes which influenced their motives for participating in HE. Whereas some enjoyed the privileges associated with their parents' social status and wealth, others recalled the deprivation they experienced in childhood. For them, HE was the gateway to employment, which would yield higher earnings for better social and economic status (Morley, 2007; World Bank, 2002).

Maame, for example, experienced poverty in a typical rural village with no electricity, pipe-borne water, medical facilities or good roads. Her parents were uneducated subsistence farmers who could not afford to feed her before she made the daily 3 km journey to and from the nearest school. She reported that her family's disadvantaged socio-economic status would have made her secondary-school education impossible but for her uncle's timely intervention. Although a trained teacher, she sought better social standing through HE as teaching is poorly paid. For her, HE was the route to a better life, probably abroad:

> I want to travel. I want to do my masters. I can't do it here. The stress is too much for me here. I don't like teaching. In my family, those who went abroad – almost everybody is okay. They have money; they are living in their big houses, driving their cars.
>
> (Maame, age 35)

Naana had slightly better socio-economic status as a child than Maame but has an unfulfilling, low-income job as an administrative assistant in a private elementary school. In her childhood, she also experienced and witnessed the financial hardship that her mother suffered. Although her father was a university lecturer, Naana had to help her mother make sales as petty trader to provide for the family.

> Wherever I went, I looked at where I came from. My mother was really suffering. She was trying her best to take care of us. Even though my father was supporting her, you could see that it wasn't enough. I think it's because my mother didn't go to school.
>
> (Naana, age 30)

Other women who had relatively better life circumstances in childhood and later life also perceived HE as the route to a better social life. Krambaa, for example, was a police officer who also had other business ventures that gave her average social status. However, when her businesses collapsed, she resorted to HE:

> I was doing business. I had two shops, left them and travelled on peace-keeping. When everything collapsed, then I felt it was the time to find my way to education. I have seen that now, if you are not highly educated, you can't make it.
>
> (Krambaa, age 46)

One wonders whether Krambaa would have considered HE if her business had not collapsed. In Ghana, many businesspeople are financially better off than highly educated public servants, so HE sometimes does not seem to be the key to wealth and social prestige. As a public servant, Krambaa resorted to HE due to her collapsed businesses, knowing that her higher academic qualifications would earn her promotions in the police service and increase her earning capacity.

For Maame and Naana, HE was the means to escape the poverty prevalent in their childhood homes and communities, which they attributed to a lack of education. For them, HE was the key to opening the doors to better employment that would be personally gratifying and financially rewarding. Their instrumental economic reasons are similar to the findings reported in studies from high-income countries that financial need framed the lives of welfare recipients striving to be self-sufficient (Hinton-Smith, 2012). These stories also resonate with the adult students' because-of and in-order-to rationales for obtaining HE recorded by Scanlon (2008).

Personal development

Another motive for mature women's entry into HE was to expand their knowledge and aid their personal development. The women in Hinton-Smith's (2012) study described this as broadening their horizons. In the present study, all participants had a post-secondary education and full-time employment, and sought to obtain greater knowledge. For some, self-development and broadening knowledge meant expanding their job-related knowledge, while for others, it meant changing careers and obtaining better jobs. Two of the eight participants (both teachers) indicated their desire to change jobs. For example, Adjoa Kom said that she wanted "to divert to get a broader scope of knowledge" and appeared to want to fulfil her long-held dream to be a banker:

> I said to myself I will be a banker, where I would walk on high heels.
>
> (Adjoa Kom, age 42)

Similarly, Maame, who explicitly declared "I don't like teaching", sought HE to provide herself with more opportunities and make herself more market-able. In addition, it would give her higher academic and professional quali-fications, which could help her earn job promotions and increased earnings.

"Everybody was going, so I wanted to go"

The current trends of the knowledge explosion and HE massification have created demand for HE in both high- and low-income countries. This devel-opment was succinctly described by two participants:

> With how the world is changing now, we also need to be abreast of the changing times.
>
> (Koutuma, age 42)

> The way I look at certain things, things will change, so education will make you a better person.
>
> (Maimuna, age 34)

In Ghana, it has become so fashionable to have a degree that, in many public service institutions, people who once missed the opportunity have accessed HE through the many available routes. This trend was illustrated in the words of one participant:

> I actually wanted to go just because my friends were going. I didn't see any need as I was working and getting something and providing for myself, so I didn't see the need. But somewhere along the line, everybody was going, so I wanted to go.
>
> (Akua, age 40)

Considering the private and public returns of HE for the individual and the nation, the demand for HE can be interpreted as a good sign for Ghanaian social and economic development and for the agenda to increase female enrolment in HE.

Conclusions

A combination of factors influenced women's return to HE and exerted different effects at various points in their lives. For example, the observable changes wrought by HE made close family members and friends, both educated and uneducated, in rural and urban areas encourage their female acquaintances to obtain HE. The situation in which husbands pushed their partners to obtain HE is contrary to what is known about the Ghanaian culture of male dominance and female subordination and relegation to the private sphere.

Previously, men chose as wives women with little education who they could presumably control. In this study, however, educated men urged their wives to obtain HE, likely to match their modernised, urbanised lifestyle (Ardayfio-Schandorf, 1994). The change in attitudes towards female education expressed by men as both fathers and husbands marks a process of de-traditionalisation (Morley et al., 2006), which may indicate a motive of neglect of the past and a new focus on the present.

It is also evident that previously held notions about women's underrepresentation and participation in education in general and in HE in particular as a result of female subordination might not be applicable to some contexts in Ghanaian society. This change is likely due to the present economic decline in Ghana, which makes it difficult for men's income alone to support families. For this reason, there has also been a change in men's attitudes towards women's HE, allowing women to earn more money to supplement the family income.

Mature women's socio-economic status is also highly instrumental in their completion of HE. Especially for women with school-age children, family income is a major determining factor in their participation in HE. Nevertheless, women's financial ability to pursue HE does not only depend on their marital status, as this study shows.

Similar to findings from some high-income countries (Morley & Lussier, 2009; Hinton-Smith, 2012), there are complex, interwoven, intrinsic and predominantly instrumental motives for Ghanaian mature women's pursuit of HE. While difficult past experiences drive because-of motives, in-order-to motives further impel participation in HE to gain better social status. Intrinsic rationales for obtaining HE are explained as broadening job-related knowledge and developing oneself, but HE also provides a means to obtain better jobs. It is evident that many people, both young and old, men and women, seek university degrees for the sake of prestige and social status.

Acknowledgements

This chapter draws on my doctoral research on mature women students in Ghana, conducted as part of the research project *Widening participation in higher education in Ghana and Tanzania: Developing an equity scorecard* funded by the Economic and Social Research Council (ESRC) and Department for International Development (DFID). I thank the ESRC and DFID for supporting the doctoral research from which this article has been developed. Special thanks are also due to Professor Louise Morley for supervising this study and to the anonymous reviewers for their useful comments, which helped improve this chapter.

References

Ardayfio-Schandorf, E. (1994). *Family and development in Ghana*. Accra: Ghana Universities Press.

Benson, R., Hewitt, L., Heagney, M., Devos, A., & Crosling, G. (2010). Diverse pathways into higher education: Using students' stories to identify transformative experiences. *Australian Journal of Adult Learning, 50*, 26–53.

Boohene, R. A., Kotey, B., & Folker, C. A. (2005). *Explaining gender differences in performance among small and medium enterprise owners in Ghana*. Paper presented at the World Conference of the International Council of Small Business, June, Washington DC, USA.

Bortey, C. A., & Dodoo, F. (n.d.). *Adolescent attitudes regarding gender roles in Ghana*. Retrieved from www.forms.gradsch.psu.edu/equity/sroppapers/204/BorteyChristiana A.pdf.

Boshier, P. (2006). *Perspectives of quality in adult learning*. London: Continuum.

Creswell, J. W. (2003). *Research design* (2nd Ed.). Thousand Oaks, CA: Sage Publications.

Crossan, B., Field, J., Gallacher, J., & Merrill, B. (2003). Understanding participation in learning for non-traditional adult learners: Learning careers and the construction of learning identities. *British Journal of Sociology of Education, 24*(1), 55–67.

Daniel, G. F. (1996). The universities in Ghana. *The Commonwealth Universities Year Book 1997–1998, 1,* 649–656.

Dei, G. J. S. (2005). Social difference and the politics of schooling in Africa: A Ghanaian case study. *Compare: A Journal of Comparative Education, 35*(3), 227–245.

Edwards, R. (1993). *Mature women students: Separating or connecting family and education*. London: Taylor and Francis.

Flick, U. (2002). *An introduction to qualitative research.* London: Sage.

Forum for African Women Educationalists (FAWE). (2001). *Girls' education and poverty eradication: FAWE's response.* Paper presented at the Third United Nations Conference on the Least Developed Countries, 10–20 May 2001, Brussels, Belgium.

Goodson, I., & Sikes, P. (2008). *Life history research in educational settings.* Maidenhead: Open University Press.

Hannum, E., & Buchmann, C. (2004). Global educational expansion and socio-economic development: An assessment of findings from the social sciences. *World Development, 33*(3), 333–354.

Hewitt, J. P. (1997). *Self and society: A symbolic interactionist social psychology.* Boston: Allyn & Bacon.

Hinton-Smith, T. (2012). Lone parent students' motivations for and hopes of higher education engagement. In T. Hinton-Smith (Ed.), *Widening participation in higher education: Casting the net wide?* (108–126). Basingstoke, UK: Palgrave Macmillan.

Humphreys, S. (2005). *Schooling and identity: Gender relations and classroom discourse in selected junior secondary schools in Botswana,* a DPhil thesis submitted to the University of Sussex, UK.

Jones, K. (2006). Valuing diversity and widening participation: The experiences of access to social work students in further and higher education. *Social Work Education: The International Journal, 25*(5), 485–500.

Manuh, T. (2004). Gender and contemporary challenges in Ghana. *Ghana Association of Arts and Sciences Proceedings 2004 on Gender: Evolving roles and perceptions* (109–137). Accra: Black Mast.

Merriam, S. B. (1998). *Qualitative research and case study applications in education.* San Francisco: Jossey-Bass.

Morley, L. (2007). The X factor: Employability, elitism and equity in graduate recruitment in the 21st century society. *Journal of the Academy of Social Sciences, 2*(2), 191–207.

Morley, L., & Lussier, K. (2009). Intersecting poverty and participation in higher education in Ghana and Tanzania. *International Studies in Sociology of Education, 19*(2), 71—85.

Morley, L., Gunawardena, C., Kwesiga, J., Lihamba, A., Odejide, A., Shackleton, L., & Sorhaindo, A. (2006). *Gender equity in Commonwealth higher education: An examination of sustainable interventions in selected Commonwealth universities.* London: DFID.

Morley, L., Leach, F., Lussier, K., Lihamba, A., Mwaipopo, R., Forde, L., & Egbenya, G. (2010). *Widening participation in higher education in Ghana and Tanzania: Developing an equity scorecard.* An ESRC/DFID Poverty Reduction Programme Research Project, Draft Research Report.

Mulugeta, E. (2004). Swimming against the tide: Educational problems and coping strategies of rural female students in Ethiopia. *EASSRR XX(2),* 71–97.

National Council for Tertiary Education (NCTE) (2000). *Statistics on tertiary education in Ghana.* Accra: Ministry of Education.

Posti-Ahokas, H., & Okkolin, M. A. (2015). Enabling and constraining family: Young women building their educational paths in Tanzania. *International Journal of Community, Work and Family,* 1–18. Retrieved from www.tandfonline.com/loi/ccwf20, http://dx.doi.org/10.1080/13668803.2015.1047737.

Quarcoopome, A., & Ahadzie, W. (1981). *Girls' and women's access to education in rural areas.* Accra: NCWD.

Reay, D. (2003). A risky business? Mature working-class women students and access to higher education. *Gender and Education, 15*(3), 301–317.

Reay, D., David, M. E., & Ball, S. J. (2005). *Degrees of choice: Class, race and gender.* Stoke-on-Trent: Trentham Books.

Robeyns, I. (2006). Three models of education: Rights, capabilities and human capital. *Theory and Research in Education, 4*(1), 69–84.

Scanlon, L. (2008). Adults' motives for returning to study: The role of self-authoring. *Studies in Continuing Education, 30*(1), 17–32.

Schutz, A. (1972). *The phenomenology of the social world.* London: Heinemann.

Shabaya, J., & Konadu-Agyemang, K. (2004). Unequal access, unequal participation: Some spatial and socio-economic dimensions of the gender gap in education in Africa with special reference to Ghana, Zimbabwe and Kenya. *Compare, 34*(4), 395–424.

UNESCO (1997). *Declaration and action plan on higher education in Africa: African regional consultation preparatory to the world conference on higher education.* Dakar: UNESCO.

UNESCO (2007). *Education for all by 2015: Will we make it? Summary.* Paris: UNESCO.

UNESCO (2009a). *World conference on higher education: The new dynamics of higher education and research for societal change and development.* Paris: UNESCO.

UNESCO (2009b). *Global education digest 2009: Comparing education statistics across the world.* Montreal: UNESCO Institute of Statistics. Retrieved from www.unesco.org/fileadmin/MULTIMEDIA/HQ/ED/ED/pdf/WCHE_2009/FINAL%20COMMUNIQUE%20WCHE%202009.pdf.

United Nations (1995). *Fourth world conference on women: Action for equality, development and peace.* 4–15 September 1995, Beijing, China. Retrieved from www.un.org/womenwatch/daw/beijing.

World Bank (2002). *Constructing knowledge societies.* Washington, DC: World Bank.

World Bank (2009). *Accelerating catch-up: Tertiary education and growth in Sub-Saharan Africa.* Washington, DC: World Bank.

Yuki, T., & Kameyama, Y. (2013). Improving the quality of basic education for the future youth of Yemen post Arab Spring. *Global Economy & Development Working Paper* 59.

Concluding remarks

12 Epilogue

Reflections on cultural responsiveness

Päivi Palojoki

This anthology is based on the pedagogical dialogue started during the Culturally Responsive Education (CRE) project from 2012 to 2015. The various network activities gave opportunities for students, teachers and teacher educators to exchange ideas and peer review good practices in partner universities. This anthology serves the purpose of distributing the gained experiences and findings and bringing these back to the learning communities of the participants.

Our cooperation was inspired by the global changes that affect school systems and educational structures all over the world. We were all in our respective countries meeting diversity in its various forms, which challenges contemporary education. This diversity requires teachers to be more and more culturally aware and responsive, to know about various cultural orientations and to act meaningfully within a culturally heterogeneous group of learners. Contemporary and future teachers need the knowledge and skills not only to understand the cultural heterogeneity that exists in classrooms but also to act meaningfully in classroom situations and in cooperation with parents. This places new demands on the development of teacher education and the organisation and contents of in-service teacher education as well as on the pedagogical leadership in various countries.

This anthology and our CRE project have been inspired by the seminal work of Geneva Gay (2000). In her book (Gay, 2000) about the theory, research and practice of culturally responsive teaching, she claims the following:

> The knowledge that teachers need to have about cultural diversity goes beyond mere awareness of, respect for, and general recognition of the fact that ethnic groups have different values or express similar values in various ways. Thus, the second requirement for developing a knowledge base for culturally responsive teaching is acquiring detailed factual information about the cultural particularities of specific ethnic groups. This is needed to make schooling more interesting and stimulating for, representative of, and responsive to ethnically diverse students. There is a place for cultural diversity in every subject taught in schools.

However, diversity is not only due to ethnic variety, and therefore her term 'cultural diversity' reflects our thoughts better than ethnicity in this anthology. At this point, there is also a need to reflect on our understanding of globalisation. Teaching and learning practices in different countries have been shaped throughout history by the experience of globalisation (Lavia & Sikes, 2010). In this anthology, several articles stem from countries which have a colonial history. The independence and aspirations to develop intellectually free school environments need critical discussion on issues such as historicity, reflexivity, relationality, positionality and criticality. This leads to operationalised questions which are critical in every country: who has the right to access education (Posti-Ahokas, 2014)? Who is missing and why? Whose voices get the right to provide the dominant discourses (Lehtomäki et al., 2014)? How are the students experiencing globalisation in their personal and professional lives?

The effects of globalisation are also discussed in this anthology in the light of politics. The personal and professional aspects of education have become political, and researchers and teachers should be aware of these premises. Increasingly more relevant questions need to be reflected upon. Whose aspirations are to be realised while developing schools and teacher education? Whose contexts and living conditions are to be prioritised (Posti-Ahokas & Palojoki, 2013)? These haunting thoughts do not leave even researchers in peace. In whose service do academics and researchers work?

These issues have been discussed and reflected upon in the various personal and group meetings of the CRE project. The experiences gained during exchange study visits and joint research projects are more valuable than ever. The possibility of fathoming one's own profession practised in another cultural context allows us to learn more about ourselves and the teaching profession and thus develop both further. In the following, I use Gay's (2013) definition of the "Five dimensions of culturally responsive education" in order to give examples of how her perspectives are visible in the chapters of this anthology.

The need to ensure that basic education is accessible, understandable and compulsory for all is discussed in many of the articles. These articles confirm that education is a vital tool in the war against poverty. As Komba states in her article, in all of the educational policies and programmes, education is cited as a means of combatting the three national archenemies: poverty, ignorance and disease. Yet the education sector is still experiencing a number of challenges, including truancy, dropout and poor learning outcomes as well as unequal gender policies, whereby many children complete primary schooling without acquiring basic literacy and numeracy skills.

Komba discusses the reasons for dropping out in South African schools and concludes that the majority of children who are dropping out of school may be from economically disadvantaged families. Hence, it may be assumed that children from economically disadvantaged families are more likely to remain trapped in the cycle of poverty. Adding the notions of Ghartey Ampiah et al., the picture might be more complex, as it is also related to the language used in the classroom. Using English as a shared language for all requires understanding from parents. They should encourage their children's schooling and advise them to read and work hard at school.

As stated earlier in Posti-Ahokas's (2014) dissertation, parents' reluctance to support their children could be explained by their ignorance regarding the future benefits of education for their children and the community. This is especially true for girls, who need support for carrying on with their schooling. Interestingly, in Western countries such as Finland, gender issues might actually disfavour boys. As Janhonen-Abruquah et al. discuss, here schools may design learning environments disfavouring boys and discouraging their achievement. Gender issues should be more openly discussed both ways: shedding light on undiscussed gender roles and dismantling the existing barriers.

Many chapters in this anthology emphasise the importance of collaboration between educational leaders, teachers and families in improving the quality, cultural responsiveness and, thus, the overall relevance of schooling. As Komba argues, families should not be taken as an empty vacuum to be fed with policy-makers' knowledge. Involving families contributes much to the provision of culturally responsive education.

Adu-Yeboah reminds readers that, in many African countries, there is a strong division of labour backed by prevailing attitudes, which nurture in males and females the belief that "it is the woman who cooks the meals and generally sees to it that the house is clean and well kept". Men, on the other hand, are supposed to be heads of households and breadwinners and cater for all household members, including their wives. The assumption is that, whereas men need higher income to discharge these responsibilities, which is possible by obtaining education, women's role does not require formal education to perform. However, this issue also arises in high-income countries, too: both men and women without higher education are perceived to be dependent on welfare services. In this status, and in the broader socio-cultural context, they are in danger of being stamped as lazy and feckless, a drain on public resources and not exemplary for their children. As Adu-Yeboah reminds us, for these people, higher education may be essential to enhance their job prospects and earning capacity and make them financially stable.

The curriculum, the school system and the qualifications of teacher education are powerful tools through which the politicians can use their power to favour their own interests. There are many examples of countries which have struggled for their freedom from past oppressive political systems. For example, in Europe, the Baltic countries got their freedom from Soviet rule in the 1990s, and, in these countries, teacher education has faced different periods and authorities that have altered it in accordance with the political and social landscape (Taar, 2015; Paas, 2015). Changes in the teaching profession and teacher education require time, as changes do not happen overnight, and the results of such changes often became evident only after the graduates

Table 12.1 Examples of how the dimensions of culturally responsive education (Gay, 2000) are reflected in this anthology

Culturally responsive teaching	Definition by Gay (2000)	Example of chapter in this anthology	Key notions of the chapter
Validating	Using the cultural knowledge, prior experiences, and performance styles of diverse students to make learning more appropriate and effective for them.	Janhonen–Abruquah et al., Towards contextual understanding of gender: Student teachers' views on home economics education and gender in Ghana and Finland.	Gender inequality is recognised as a critical societal problem and therefore discussed in relation to education policy, including setting targets for equal access and enrolment for males and females.
Comprehensive	Teaching the whole child, culturally responsive teachers realize not only the importance of academic achievement, but also the maintaining of cultural identity and heritage.	Ghartey Ampiah et al., Implementing the language of instruction policy in a complex linguistic context in Ghana.	The use of the mother tongue makes the curriculum more relevant by connecting the learning to the pupil's experience, environment and culture. The linguistic heterogeneity of the many school contexts discussed in this anthology is great. It is important to know how educators manage to tackle this challenge.
Multi-dimensional	Applies versatile curriculum content, learning context, classroom climate, student–teacher relationships, instructional techniques, and performance assessments.	Kahangwa, Cultural strategy for developing a knowledge-based economy in the Global South: the case of Tanzanian higher education.	Hegemonic cultures are not necessarily appropriate especially for countries in the Global South, which are still challenged to make their education systems stable, strengthen their economies and make a significant contribution in an increasingly multicultural global society.

Empowering	Emphasizing critical–democratic pedagogy for self and social change; students must believe they can succeed in learning tasks and have motivation to persevere.	Komba, Relevance of schooling in Tanzania: educational leaders' perspectives on economically disadvantaged families.	Families should not be taken as an empty vessel to be filled with policy-makers' knowledge. Arguably, involving families may contribute much to the provision of culturally responsive education.
Transformative	Helping students to develop the knowledge, skills, and values needed to become social critics who can make reflective decisions and implement their decisions in effective personal, social, political, and economic action.	Adu-Yeboah, Motives and motivations for mature women's participation in higher education in Ghana.	The old view of men choosing women with little education in order to 'control' them needs to be challenged. However, educated men here urged their wives to obtain HE probably so as to match up to their modernised, urbanised lifestyle. Both as fathers and husbands, the change in the men's attitude about female education is a process of de-traditionalisation.
Emancipatory	Guiding students in understanding that no single version of 'truth' is total and permanent; acceptance of knowledge as something to be continuously shared, critiqued, revised, and renewed.	Mohlakwana & Aluko, Teacher professional development through open distance learning: introducing a new learning culture.	If educators are to meet the demands of the society in the twenty-first century, there is a need to unlearn old skills and learn new ones in all levels of the school system.

apply their skills and knowledge in practice. In this anthology, Mohlakwana and Aluko present a similar story put into the historical context of South Africa. According to them, it would take centuries to train teachers solely through the conventional mode of education. Therefore the education of in-service teachers and the tools provided by open-distance learning have become valuable. They have noticed a very general phenomenon, applicable to all educational systems: if teachers are to meet the demands of society in the twenty-first century, there is a need to unlearn old skills and learn new ones. In this context, the inner motivation of teachers and student teachers is essential. They formulate the new culture of learning as comprising two elements: the ability to learn alone and the motivation to learn from others; and imagination and play as fuel sustaining learning. School can catalyse the changes in the society wherever there are working teachers' positive attitudes and their desire to make a difference (Paas, 2015).

Political desires are also linked to the rules of the language/s used in schools. In this anthology, Ghartey Ampiah et al. conclude that many teachers in Ghana have communication challenges with the children due to factors such as children or teachers not understanding the language of the community, a lack of textbooks to facilitate learning in the local language and classes being multilingual, leading to the marginalisation of some children. The practice of adopting the dominant language of the community is not culturally sensitive to the language of some of the children, especially when there are children who do not speak or understand the dominant language.

Adhiambo Puhakka states in her article that a multilingual society can also have positive effects and be seen as having value in and of itself. Multilingualism at a personal level always implies some degree of fluency in more than one variety. Her example of a multilingual country in Sub-Saharan Africa is Kenya. She notes that conflicts from diversity can be productive when people strive to understand one another, opening up new business opportunities and markets, by widening the customer base and by being able to better address specific consumers' needs in the multicultural society. She has purposefully avoided using the term 'challenges' in her chapter with regard to culture and language diversity, because she sees this multilingual diversity as a rich resource that should be preserved and understood. If adapted wisely into the school system, multilingualism acts as a rich resource in providing meaningful comparative learning in any society and across the globe.

However, the use of language is always related to ways new knowledge is created: if the distance between 'academic language/s' and 'everyday language/s' is too large, the country loses part of its developmental potential. In his chapter, Kahangwa takes the idea of culturally responsive education to argue that the consideration of the cultural environment/context (internal and external) that surrounds higher education in a certain country well suits its efforts to develop a knowledge-based economy (KBE). According to him, hegemonic cultures are not necessarily appropriate, especially for countries in the Global South, which are still challenged to make their education systems stable, strengthen their economies and make a significant contribution in an increasingly multicultural global society. Neoliberalism has brought aspects of marketisation and/or commercialisation into the academic world. Ideas of entrepreneurial universities and academic capitalism have greatly influenced higher education in many European countries and in the USA. Based on Tanzanian experiences, Kahangwa reminds us that, in the Global South, the commercialisation of university research has been taken up in educational policies and practices that support the development of KBE. A shift can be seen from considering research results (knowledge) as a public good to a private one, bearing a commercial value. He wisely warns that if countries in the Global South continue to take a neoliberal approach to developing a knowledge-based economy, they will be adopting a Western culture. It is now seen in European countries, and in Finland as well, that highly skilled countries can be brain-drained, as is manifested in the exodus numbers versus incoming 'brains' in different countries. The innovative and intellectual use of knowledge is a supportive factor of production in all economic sectors and is a base in some sectors which are not engaged in the extraction and process-ing of natural resources and production of consumer goods but rather in the provision of services, the processing of information, the search for further knowledge and the distribution of the same. If universities forget this basic rule, the neoliberal and capitalist values will take the helm instead of human capacity building: for the successful development of KBE in a country, being mindful of the cultural context is extremely significant.

This anthology also includes chapters addressing issues related to research methodology. The aim of these chapters is to inspire the pedagogical thinking of researchers, lecturers and teachers and lead to educational innovations, which, in turn, will equip future schools to respond to the challenges of a changing society and culture. Holm and Lehtomäki remind readers that the issues of understanding and including diverse voices and views in educational development are more important than ever before, due to the pertaining inequity, insecurity and unequal power structures in many countries. They emphasise that, in education, culture is always present and embedded in con-tents, activities and communication styles. However, researchers should become better aware and understand their own standpoint as well as how to approach and be close to the culture of those people they work with or study. They often face unequal power relations, which can be local and/or global. They draw examples from the context of Sub-Saharan Africa, where, espe-cially in rural areas, younger people are to respect older persons, and girls are expected to be silent and obedient. It is a challenge for researchers to capture the experiences and views of those traditionally 'silenced' in the patriarchal culture, where boys and their education are more valued.

Alsudis and Pillay reach personal levels of narration in their chapter exploring how culturally situated narrative writing serves as a methodological tool for meaning making across cultures. They demand that readers be involved in their own acts of cultural construction and meaning making while reading of the experiences of the supervisor–doctoral student relationship. Even though the sample size (four) is small, the in-depth conversations conducted draw an interesting picture of various cross-cultural barriers and stories of how to overcome them.

Salminen et al. describe music education students' experiences from the MECI network (Music, education and cultural identity), coordinated by the Department of Music of the University of Jyväskylä. Opportunities were created where the participants could share in music making and also where they could take part in critical discussions and seminars with researchers – both experienced experts and young scholars – from Africa and Finland. Their conclusions emphasise the same experiences shared from other North–South–South projects, too: the project activities have played a significant role in the participants' lives and the participants have been able to create long-lasting personal relationships with the others. Music is a shared language, and the possibilities of cultural encounters are limitless.

Nketsia et al. discuss in their chapter how dialogues on inclusive education from different cultures could be embedded in culturally responsive education. Inclusive education with an emphasis on the right to education and child rights for every child is not self-evident. Much needs to be done in order to make equity, equality and human rights realised at every level of the educational system. There needs to be more dialogue showing the need for culturally sensitive inclusion. Through this, a common understanding could be created with respect to the variety in resources and educational values. Ensuring the participation of both men and women, students and teachers, persons with and without disabilities offered the learning community the experience of inclusion in practice, in addition to the sharing of knowledge. Accessible learning and collaboration environments, such as ICT and open information, research literature and databases, were appreciated by the project participants. These are the essential aspects of universal design and ensuring inclusive education.

In summary, this anthology brings together some of the important issues discussed during the various activities accomplished in our North–South–South network. And, as stated previously in the introduction to this anthology: "Culturally responsive education is not only a phenomenon under study but also a part of the authors' daily work". The international cooperation involved in exchange study visits and joint research projects is today more valuable than ever. Our stories told here confirm that culturally responsive teaching is emancipatory and can, as Gay (2000) has stated, lead to improved achievements, including clear and insightful thinking; more caring, concerned and humane interpersonal skills; better understanding of interconnections among individual, local, national, ethnic, global and human identities; and acceptance of knowledge as something to be continuously shared, critiqued, revised and renewed.

References

Gay, G. (2000). *Culturally responsive teaching: Theory, research, and practice.* New York: Teachers College Press.

Gay, G. (2013). Teaching to and through cultural diversity. *Curriculum Inquiry, 43*(1), 48–70.

Lavia, L., & Sikes, P. (2010). 'What part of me do I leave out?': In pursuit of decolonising practice. *Power and Education, 2,* 1.

Lehtomäki, E., Janhonen-Abruquah, H. T., Tuomi, M., Okkolin, M-A., Posti-Ahokas, H., & Palojoki, P. (2014). Research to engage voices on the ground in educational development. *International Journal of Educational Development, 35,* 37–43.

Paas, K. (2015). Overview of Estonian home economics teacher education. In Janhonen-Abruquah, H., & Palojoki, P. (Eds), *Luova ja vastuullinen kotitalousopetus – Creative and responsible home economics education.* Kotitalous- ja käsityötieteiden julkaisuja; 38, 150–163. Helsinki: Unigrafia. http://hdl.handle.net/10138/157591.

Posti-Ahokas, H. (2014). *Tanzanian female students' perspectives on the relevance of secondary education.* Kotitalous- ja käsityötieteiden julkaisuja, 37. Helsinki: Unigrafia. Doctoral dissertation. https://helda.helsinki.fi/handle/10138/45346.

Posti-Ahokas, H., & Palojoki, P. (2013). Navigating transitions to adulthood through secondary education: Aspirations and value of education for Tanzanian girls. *Journal of Youth Studies.* doi: 10.1080/13676261.2013.853871.

Taar, J. (2015). From Kodumajandus into Kodundus: Home economics curricula in Estonia. In Janhonen-Abruquah, H., & Palojoki, P. (Eds), *Luova ja vastuullinen kotitalousopetus – Creative and responsible home economics education.* Kotitalous- ja käsityötieteiden julkaisuja; Nro 38, 164–177. Helsinki: Unigrafia. http://hdl.handle.net/10138/157591.

Index

Page numbers in *italics* denote tables, those in **bold** denote figures.